PENGUIN BOOKS

Truth

[handwritten note] read for more outside my subject

Simon Blackburn is Professor of Philosophy at the University of Cambridge and one of the most widely respected philosophers of our time, renowned for making his subject relevant to everyday life and accessible to a wide audience. He is the author of many influential books, including the bestselling *Oxford Dictionary of Philosophy*, and the popular titles *Think* and *Being Good: A Short Introduction to Ethics*. Blackburn edited the philosophy journal *Mind* from 1984 to 1990, is a Fellow of the British Academy, as well as a frequent contributor to *New Republic* and to discussion programmes on Radio 4 in the UK, and reviews for the *Independent* and the *Sunday Times*. He is also a popular public lecturer.

SIMON BLACKBURN

Truth

A Guide for the Perplexed

PENGUIN BOOKS

PENGUIN BOOKS

Published by the Penguin Group
Penguin Books Ltd, 80 Strand, London WC2R ORL, England
Penguin Group (USA) Inc., 375 Hudson Street, New York, New York 10014, USA
Penguin Group (Canada), 90 Eglinton Avenue East, Suite 700, Toronto, Ontario, Canada M4P 2Y3
(a division of Pearson Penguin Canada Inc.)
Penguin Ireland, 25 St Stephen's Green, Dublin 2, Ireland
(a division of Penguin Books Ltd)
Penguin Group (Australia), 250 Camberwell Road,
Camberwell, Victoria 3124, Australia (a division of Pearson Australia Group Pty Ltd)
Penguin Books India Pvt Ltd, 11 Community Centre,
Panchsheel Park, New Delhi – 110 017, India
Penguin Group (NZ), cnr Airborne and Rosedale Roads, Albany,
Auckland 1310, New Zealand (a division of Pearson New Zealand Ltd)
Penguin Books (South Africa) (Pty) Ltd, 24 Sturdee Avenue,
Rosebank, Johannesburg 2196, South Africa

Penguin Books Ltd, Registered Offices: 80 Strand, London WC2R ORL, England

www.penguin.com

First published by Allen Lane 2005
Published in Penguin Books 2006

1

Set in 9.25/12.5 pt Linotype Sabon
Typeset by Palimpsest Book Production Limited, Polmont, Stirlingshire
Printed in England by Clays Ltd, St Ives plc

ISBN-13: 978-0-141-01425-8
ISBN-10: 0-141-01425-3

Contents

CHAPTER 4

Nietzsche: the Arch Debunker

CHAPTER 5

The Possibility of Philosophy

CHAPTER 6

Observation and Truth: from Locke to Rorty

CHAPTER 7

Realism as Science; Realism about Science

CHAPTER 8

Historians and Others

Preface

It is easy to feel frightened at the beginning of the twenty-first century. And among the most frightening things are the minds of other people. The beliefs and faiths that move people to behave as they do are opaque to others; as we read or watch the news, lunacy together with mutual suspicion and contempt seem to be the order of the day.

If only people would be sensible. If only they would submit to the order of reason. This has been the lament of philosophers for millennia, and in times like these it becomes the lament of more than mere philosophers. But it is to the philosophical tradition that we have to look if we want to know what is required to be sensible, or what the order of reason might be.

Unfortunately, when we do look to the tradition, the picture is confused and convoluted, and it may not give us much help. This is particularly true if we look to the recent picture. Many of the philosophers I talk about in this book have been suspicious of the whole project of epistemology – of saying which intellectual habits deserve respect, and which ones do not. Words like 'relativism' and 'post-modernism' signal a resulting culture in which 'anything goes', and although this itself is an object of suspicion to innocent outsiders, they are unlikely to understand them well enough to oppose them effectively. This book tries to help us to do better. It is therefore something of a guide for the perplexed.

In writing it I have many sources to acknowledge. The material was presented as a set of eight Gifford lectures at the University of Glasgow in the spring of 2004, and my first debt is to the Trustees of that excellent fund, and to the questioning audience. Lord Gifford's will is a shining example of a kind of liberalism that is often sneered at, and seldom equalled. A theist himself, he made it very clear that the lectures he founded were not for theists only, but for any serious thinkers to explore serious questions about the place of humanity in the world. I do not believe that the gods of human beings do much credit to their inventors and interpreters, but I hope my lectures qualified as serious. A second class of debts arise because the material here draws upon or overlaps a number of published papers of mine. Chapters 2 and 3 follow in some parts the Voltaire Lecture that I gave to the British Humanists Association in 2002. I am grateful to the University of Aarhus for the invitation to give the first Justin Hartnack Lecture in 2004, which was a predecessor of part of chapter 3. Chapter 4, on Nietzsche, owes much to a conference at Urbana-Champaign in the autumn of 2003, to which, although I am no Nietzsche scholar, I was kindly invited by Richard Schacht and Michael Moore. I profited a great deal from the presence of Maudemarie Clark, Lanier Anderson and Nadeem Hussain. Chapter 5.7, on some features of Wittgenstein, closely follows my 'Wittgenstein's Irrealism', in *Wittgenstein: Towards a Re-Evaluation*, ed. Rudolph Haller and Johannes Brandl, Vienna: Verlag Hölder-Adler-Tempsky, 1990, pp. 13–26. Chapter 6 includes material that originally appeared in *Prospect*, in a survey article on the philosophy of Richard Rorty, as well as thoughts occurring in my review of Robert Brandom's collection *Reading Rorty*, in *The New Republic*. Chapter 7 draws heavily on my 'Realism: Deconstructing the Debate', *Ratio*, vol. 15, June 2002, 111–34, while aspects of my discussion of Davidson in chapter 8 also appeared in 'Relativism and the Abolition of the Other', in *International Journal of Philosophical Studies*, vol. 12(3), 245–58. I am grateful to editors and publishers for their generosity in enabling me to revisit this work. Finally, chapter 8 also contains material on Hume and Collingwood given to a historical seminar run by John Marenbon in Trinity College, Cambridge, shortly after I arrived in 2001, and has benefited from the discussion the paper received on that occasion.

In 2001 an Erskine Fellowship at the University of Canterbury, in Christchurch, New Zealand, enabled me to try out many of these ideas, and I owe thanks to the Trustees of the fund, and particularly to Cindy and Graham Macdonald for the invitation. I am also grateful to the City University of New York graduate school which invited me to give joint seminars with Paul Horwich in autumn 2003, and to Paul himself for his insights and criticisms on those occasions.

Finally, like all writers, I owe a frighteningly large debt to those immediately around me: college and faculty, editors, colleagues and students. As always I had the unceasing support of my wife Angela, who had to put up with it all.

Simon Blackburn
Cambridge, 2004

Introduction

There are real standards. We must fight soggy nihilism, scepticism and cynicism. We must not believe that anything goes. We must not believe that all opinion is ideology, that reason is only power, that there is no truth to prevail. Without defences against postmodern irony and cynicism, multiculturalism and relativism, we will all go to hell in a handbasket.

So thunders the conservative half of us – of each of us. But perhaps the thunder and conviction betray an anxiety. We may fear that there is another side to it, that our confidence is dogma, that our bluff may be called. There are people who are not impressed by our conviction, or by our pride and our stately deportment. They hear only attempts to impose just one opinion. They hear nothing but the machinations of power and attempts at suppression of alternatives. They hear bluster, the usual disguise for insecurity. The citadel of conservativism is prey to the whispers of doubt. This is a book about this confusing conflict; a book about a war of ideas and attitudes.

The sides in this conflict have various names: absolutists versus relativists, traditionalists versus postmodernists, realists versus idealists, objectivists versus subjectivists, rationalists versus social constructivists, universalists versus contextualists, Platonists versus pragmatists. These do not all mean the same, and some people who stand on one side or the other would be choosy about allowing them to apply to themselves. So for the moment they simply act as pointers.

Put like this, it may sound as if only special kinds of people, philosophers and theorists, would sign up as warriors in this fracas. It would sound easy to be a non-combatant. But I think this is wrong.

For first, the conflict is not only between different people, but grumbles within the breast of each individual, as we find voices within ourselves pulling us to one side or the other. And second, the conflict is about our conception of ourselves and our world, about the meaning of our sayings, and indeed the meaning of our activities and of our lives. It is about ideas that make up the 'spirit of the age', and that determine the atmosphere we breathe. If the ideas are inadequate or dangerous, then we need an immune system to protect us from them, and the only immunity would have to be conferred by better ideas.

Today, the stakes in this war are enormous. Relativism in the ancient world typically issued in scepticism, whose main result was to be the suspension of all judgement. The sceptic, having recognized all that is to be said on both sides of any question, found that they balanced evenly, and therefore suspended belief, resigning himself to a state of *epoche* or lack of opinion. So doing, he stopped bothering, and enjoyed all the benefits of tranquillity of mind, *ataraxia*. Today this is not the way it goes. Today's relativists, persuading themselves that all opinions enjoy the same standing in the light of reason, take it as a green light to believe what they like with as much conviction and force as they like. So while ancient scepticism was the sworn opponent of dogmatism, today dogmatisms feed and flourish on the desecrated corpse of reason. Astrology, prophecy, homeopathy, Feng shui, conspiracy theories, flying saucers, voodoo, crystal balls, miracle-working, angel visits, alien abductions, management nostrums and a thousand other cults dominate people's minds, often with official backing. 'Faith education' is encouraged by the British Prime Minister, while Biblical fundamentalism, creationism and astrology alike stalk the White House. We might be reminded of G. K. Chesterton's remark that the problem with people who lose belief in God is not that they end up believing nothing, but that they will believe in anything.

The urbane eighteenth-century Scottish philosopher David Hume seldom put a foot wrong, but he did say that while mistakes in religion are dangerous, generally speaking mistakes in philosophy are merely ridiculous. I believe he was mistaken about this, as does anyone who supposes that there is something diabolical in the region of relativism, multiculturalism or postmodernism, something which corrupts and corrodes the universities and the public culture, that sweeps away moral standards, lays waste young people's minds, and rots our precious civilization from within. For the issue is a philosophical one. It is about the sources of reason, and the control of belief by fact. It is an epistemological issue (from the Greek *episteme*, meaning knowledge), an issue about which methods of inquiry and which claims to authority and knowledge we should endorse. It is no coincidence that theorists attracted to relativism first take aim at epistemology, hoping to destroy the pedestals that elevate some beliefs above others.

The implications of relativism, and the flashpoints that concern us today, may be new, but the war between those who locate themselves as something like 'relativists' and those who sound more like 'absolutists' is not. We know that it raged a long time ago, when Socrates confronted the sophists in the Athens of the fifth century BC. It was probably old by then, but that encounter will form one point of entry.

What, then, is the conflict about? When we are absolutists we stand on truth. We like plain, unvarnished objective fact, and we like it open, transparent, and unfiltered. We may not like it everywhere, so we may feel like confining truth to some area: scientific truth, or perhaps common sense and scientific truth, but not aesthetic truth or moral truth, for example. But somewhere the absolute truth can be found. And as well as truth, absolutists cherish its handmaidens: reason, which enables us to find it or certify it, and objectivity, which is the cardinal virtue of reasoning.

Relativists mock these ideals. They see nothing anywhere that is plain, unvarnished, objective, open, transparent or unfiltered. They debunk and deny. They see everywhere what the philosopher William James called the trail of the human serpent. They insist upon the universal presence of happenstance, brute contingencies of nature or culture or language or experience, that shape the way we see things. Nietzsche said 'There are no facts, only interpretations'. That will do as a relativist slogan, and in many people's eyes Nietzsche is a high priest of relativism (we explore whether this is right in chapter 4).

The talkative royal butler Paul Burrell claimed that the Queen said to him, speaking of the death of Princess Diana, 'there are dark forces at work, of which we know nothing'. I do not have much confidence that the Queen said any such thing, but if she did, she was unconsciously following the way the relativists see things. The dark forces of language, culture, power, gender, class, economic status, ideology and desire are always assailing us, but their works remain dangerously hidden in our blindspots, waiting only to be revealed by future generations, who will have other blindspots of their own.

Of course, if correctly reported, the Queen was skating on thin ice, since if we know nothing of these dark forces we cannot even know that they are at work. The relativist must concede that we know enough to be sure in general terms that they are present, but not much more. For if we do know much more, we can take steps to make ourselves safe. We can guard against bias once we can recognize it.

The issue is not centrally about the virtues of truth-telling: sincerity and accuracy, as Bernard Williams has them.[1] These provoke many issues, but it is not, or should not be, people's integrity that is being doubted. When people worry about a 'crisis of truth', for instance in the humanities, they are not primarily worrying about the sincerity and anxious care for accuracy of those in the field. They are worrying that however sincere and careful we are, we are trapped in partial or perspectival or outright illusory and fictional views, with little or no chance of realizing our plight. But ideals of sincerity and accuracy do become collateral damage of the wars about the nature of truth. The idea that our stories about the world and ourselves are just transient constructions, that our perspective is just one among many, or that illusion and fiction are pervasive, undermines the seriousness with which we can regard defects of sincerity and accuracy. If truth is thought of as a goal that can never be attained, those who rather conspicuously do not care much about it will seem that much less villainous than they are.

We may be apt to associate relativism with a soggy, tolerant, happy-clappy attitude to things. The two relativist mantras are: 'Who is to say?' (who is to say which opinion is better?) and 'That's just your opinion' (my opinion is on all fours with yours); the implication is that there are only different views, each true 'for' those who hold them. This attitude sounds spineless, and this spinelessness is one of the things that haunts the conservative commentators' minds when they lecture their readers on the evils of postmodernism and pluralism. Hilaire Belloc put it memorably in 'Lines to a Don'. Placing the conflict within the ancient universities, he condemned the modern university teacher, the 'ineffectual don':

> Don different from those regal dons
> With hearts of gold and lungs of bronze
> Who shout and bang and roar and bawl
> The absolute across the hall.

Here it is the absolutists who shout and bang, and that sounds tough: the kind of toughness that would appeal to those conservative commentators. However, William James famously called the relativist 'tough-minded', and he had an important point.[2] Typically, the relativist takes himself to have unmasked or seen through the dogmatism of the absolutist. The absolutist is tender to himself, happy in his own convictions, probably not caring to sympathize with those of others. Absolutism gives us security and self-assurance; the relativist sees dangerous unthinking innocence and complacency.

James describes the absolutist as having a religious temperament, whether the object of his religion is some traditional text or deity, or a new one, such as the Market, or Democracy, or Science. This may also seem surprising, since religious lives can be full of doubt and worry and dark nights of the soul, and as we have already seen, in the modern world it is the relativists as much as the absolutists who belong to the cults. But James may be right to see the absolutist as suffering from something very like a religious ambition. He seeks something 'haughty, refined, remote, august, exalted'.[3] He wants communion with a higher authority, a provider of guarantees that, acting and thinking as he does, he is at the same time acting and thinking *rightly*. Victorians described whatever was needed to make absolutism true as 'The Absolute', a term which, for better or worse, has largely been lost. And William James rightly describes the Absolute of Victorian philosophers as the giver of moral holidays – the aspect of reality that reassures us that just exactly what we are doing is *absolutely right*.

The relativist revolts from this conviction, and with the relativist frame of mind can come a generally good thing, toleration. But it is important to distinguish them. In the intellectual world, toleration is the disposition to fight opinion only with opinion; in other words, to protect freedom of speech, and to confront divergence of opinion with open critical reflection rather than suppression or force. Toleration therefore gives us only the dictum attributed to Voltaire, that I disapprove of what you say but I will defend to the death your right to say it. Relativism, by contrast, chips away at our right to disapprove of what anybody says. Its central message is that there are no asymmetries of reason and knowledge, objectivity and truth. Relativism thus goes beyond counselling that we must try to understand those whose opinions are different. It is not only that we must try to understand them, but also that we must accept a complete symmetry of standing. Their opinions 'deserve the same respect' as our own.

So, at the limit, we may have Western values, but they have others; we have a Western view of the universe, they have theirs; we have Western science, they have traditional 'science'; and so on. And then, once the symmetry of standing takes possession of the relativist, other things may come to fill his head, and they need not involve toleration at all. The dogmatic faith in homeopathy quickly leads to intolerant rejection of double-blind tests for the efficacy of treatments, or intolerant campaigns for diversion of funds from medicine that works to medicine that does not. The dogmatic faith in the market requires destroying any faith in the kind of mixed economy that actually created and still sustains western Europe and the United States. The faith that wisdom and the recipe for living are written in one text or another rapidly brings cries of death to the infidel.

Although relativism can have a soggy appearance, at least in his own view the relativist is tough-minded, because faith and zeal strike him as untroubled and innocent, but for that very reason incapable of standing up to the tough knocks and blows of what we understand about the real world. The absolutist may talk his talk, celebrating his cosy relationship with truth, reason and objectivity, but perhaps he is just whistling to keep his spirits up, deliberately but self-deceivingly in denial about the dark forces that create his blindspot. The relativist has confronted the uncomfortable truth that it is just whistling, and that there is a blindspot.

This tough relativist is apt to associate with those other tough-minded philosophers: cynics, sceptics and nihilists. There are differences, however, and sometimes they matter. For instance, a sceptic properly believes that there is truth, somewhere, only it is not to be had by us. Perhaps truth would be precious, could we get it, but our tragedy is that we cannot. This scepticism about *possession* of truth actually conforms well with absolutism about the *nature* of truth. For to the sceptical mind, one implication of the absolute and demanding nature of truth may well be that we are always at risk when we claim it. A relativist by contrast can be more cavalier about his convictions, since he holds that truth is too cheap to care about: his truth, your truth, my truth.

Both the relativist and the absolutist temperaments have an illustrious intellectual ancestry. The absolutist descends from Plato through almost all religious philosophers, through Descartes to G. E. Moore, and in modern times to writers such as Iris Murdoch or Thomas Nagel. The relativist temperament descends from the Greek sophists such as Gorgias and Protagoras, through Hobbes to Darwin (whom we shall discover as an honorary or co-opted member), to Nietzsche and William James, and in our own generation to writers such as Michel Foucault or Richard Rorty. Wittgenstein, we shall find, can be claimed by both sides, or he may, as I shall argue, stand somewhere else again.

One moral I bring out in this book is that there are ways in which the two sides tend to talk past each other – as classical philosophers liked to say, you can give something with the right hand but it may be taken by the left. The absolutist trumpets his plain vision; the relativist sees only someone who is unaware of his own spectacles. The absolutist parades his good solid grounding in observation, reason, objectivity, truth and fact; the relativist sees only fetishes. The absolutist takes himself to speak to the ages, with the tongue of angels, but the relativist hears only one version among others, the subjectivity of the here and now. The absolutist takes himself to read nature in her very own language, but the relativist insists that nature does not speak, and we hear only what we have elected to hear. The absolutist lays down the law, but the relativist hears only roaring and bawling. Or, when the relativist voice, as it is heard from philosophers such as Nietzsche or James, itself starts to grate and sounds shrill, as it often does, and when the relativist then offers concessions, the absolutist hears only insincerity. The war of words can often turn into a dialogue of the deaf, and this too is part of its power to arouse outrage and fury.

In this book I want to uncover some of the thinking necessary to do justice to each tendency. For the ground is complicated, strewn with abandoned fortresses and trenches, fought over by shifting alliances. The plot will be that first we talk a little more of the reign of reason. We then confront some of the characteristic theses of relativism, and attempts to unseat them. These attempts are not futile, although they turn out to be less impressive than many philosophers have supposed. We then consider the gale unleashed by the arch debunker, Friedrich Nietzsche. We look at various philosophical options when we consider the status of a discourse – any discourse. We consider the infirmities suffered by notions such as observation, reason and representation, and the impact of all this on the philosophy of the natural sciences. Finally, we think of the prospects for interpretation of ourselves in the human sciences.

In the course of this we find some weaponry for dismantling the debate. But who takes the spoils after the debate has been dismantled? It may turn out that each side can claim a kind of victory, depending on the temperament they brought with them – and that is not a good recipe for putting conflict finally to rest. But it is, I hope, a good recipe for finding the entire issue exciting and engaging: arguably the most exciting and engaging issue in the whole of philosophy.

To describe my book, I like a metaphor William James also uses, crediting his young Italian disciple Giovanni Papini.[4] Papini described James's own philosophy of pragmatism not as a fixed body of doctrine, but as a hotel corridor, off which branch many different rooms (Papini's own corridor took him in and out of many different rooms; he became at various times a nihilist, a futurist and a Catholic). Inside some of the rooms technicians are doing the most detailed and obscure things; we shall not be investigating all of them. But we can peer in, to learn what is bothering them and what they hope to do.

I try to write with the creed that we need to think and to reflect, if we are to be in control of our words and ideas rather than be controlled by them. In this case that means that we should not be slaves of simplistic relativisms, or of equally simplistic absolutisms. And whichever way our temperaments pull us, we should at least know where we are, and what there is to be said on the other side.

And thus a word of warning. I have said that this is a war in which emotions run high. If you have a relativist temperament, you will find some of the arguments on behalf of absolutism unduly conservative. If you have an absolutist temperament, you will find some of the arguments on behalf of relativism equally repugnant. You might fear that understanding your enemies is half-way to sympathizing with them, or a quarter-way to joining them, and if you insist that the dispute is one that has to be polarized, compromise will seem like treason. You fear that if anything at all is said on behalf of the other side the boat will capsize; perhaps you forget that you have your own weight as ballast, with which you can learn to maintain the balance. I suppose I could say: that's just your problem. But in a more positive spirit, I hope that it will be less your problem – less our problem – when the landscape is viewed as it should be.

It would be pleasant if this could be a work of exorcism, and I shall indeed urge that any crude opposition should end, and that, intellectually, the enemies will prove to have been no more than phantoms of our own conjuring. But we should not forget that in the world of ideas, even phantoms can make havoc.

I

Faith, Belief and Reason

The human understanding is not composed of dry light, but is subject to influence from the will and the emotions, a fact that creates fanciful knowledge; man prefers to believe what he wants to be true.

Francis Bacon, *The New Organon*, XLIX, p. 44[1]

1. Clifford's Duties

In the Introduction I mentioned that for classical sceptics, a dearth of arguments, or a clash of countervailing arguments, led to peaceful suspension of belief, whereas in our own times it is seen more as a licence for people to believe what they like. Perhaps this is a consequence of our general appetite for freedom and licence. And there is a general impression that 'scepticism', like 'atheism', is a bad thing. Not having convictions is often bad form, unsociable or unpatriotic. 'Faith' is a word with a positive ring to it, although of course it rings really positively only when it means 'faith like ours' rather than the conflicting faiths of others.

Insincerity still bothers us: even a politician should not be caught saying what he does not believe. But as for what a person *does* believe, well that, we tend to think, is much more his or her own business. It is a morally important fault, we suppose, if politicians claim that some country has weapons of mass destruction when they know that it does not, or if NASA says that a shuttle is safe when it knows it is far from it. But it is not a morally important fault if they believe the same thing although all the evidence points against it. How we weigh evidence, like religion, tends to be regarded as a private affair. Perhaps it does not matter if a thousand flowers bloom, or if we are none too good at distinguishing weeds from flowers. Perhaps our situation is like that of Rome as described by Gibbon: 'The various modes of worship, which prevailed in the Roman world, were all considered by the people, as equally true; by the philosopher, as equally

3

false; and by the magistrate as equally useful.'[2] But is it really the cranky, oversensitive philosopher who spoils the party?

William Clifford was a nineteenth-century Cambridge mathematician and polymath, who partly anticipated Einstein by claiming that mass and energy are each perturbations in space-time. He also has an algebra named after him. He is remembered in philosophy mainly for one classic essay, 'The Ethics of Belief', and that in turn is famous because of the reply to it given by the American philosopher William James.[3] Their dispute may appear to have a dated air about it, defining as it does the state of late-Victorian anxiety specifically about religious faith. But philosophically the issues it raises go deeper than that. They concern not only the *right* to belief, but also the *nature* of belief, and my aim is not so much to judge the debate about anyone's right to conviction, as to follow it into those deeper waters. The philosophy of religion is here only an introductory taster, or a laboratory example, of a wider perplexity.

In his essay Clifford argues that there is a duty to believe carefully, in the light of reason alone. He begins with a story nicely designed to induce a sense of outrage:

A shipowner was about to send to sea an emigrant-ship. He knew that she was old, and not overwell built at the first; that she had seen many seas and climes, and often had needed repairs. Doubts had been suggested to him that possibly she was not seaworthy. These doubts preyed upon his mind, and made him unhappy; he thought that perhaps he ought to have her thoroughly overhauled and refitted, even though this should put him at great expense. Before the ship sailed, however, he succeeded in overcoming these melancholy reflections. He said to himself that she had gone safely through so many voyages and weathered so many storms that it was idle to suppose she would not come safely home from this trip also. He would put his trust in Providence, which could hardly fail to protect all these unhappy families that were leaving their fatherland to seek for better times elsewhere. He would dismiss from his mind all ungenerous suspicions about the honesty of builders and contractors. In such ways he acquired a sincere and comfortable conviction that his vessel was thoroughly safe and seaworthy; he watched her departure with a light heart, and benevolent wishes for the success of the exiles in their strange new home that was to be; and he got his insurance-money when she went down in mid-ocean and told no tales.

Clifford is surely right that we censure the negligent shipowner. We would find his 'faith' in his ship discreditable, even though Clifford is careful to tell us that it is sincere. About this Clifford comments that:

The sincerity of his conviction can in no wise help him; because *he had no right to believe on such evidence as was before him*. He had acquired his belief not by honestly earning it in patient investigation, but by stifling his doubts.

In a marvellous passage Clifford enlarges on the danger of ignoring our duty to reason:

He who truly believes that which prompts him to an action has looked upon the action to lust after it; he has committed it already in his heart. If a belief is not realized immediately in open deeds, it is stored up for the guidance of the future. It goes to make a part of that aggregate of beliefs which is the link between sensation and action at every moment of all our lives, and which is so organized and compacted together that no part of it can be isolated from the rest, but every new addition modifies the structure of the whole. No real belief, however trifling and fragmentary it may seem, is ever truly insignificant; it prepares us to receive more of its like, confirms those which resembled it before, and weakens others; and so gradually it lays a stealthy train in our inmost thoughts, which may someday explode into overt action.

A train, here, is a train of explosive leading from a detonator to a mine. And of course, Clifford is right. Someone sitting on a completely unreasonable belief is sitting on a time bomb. The apparently harmless, idiosyncratic belief of the Catholic Church that one thing may have the substance of another, although it displays absolutely none of its empirical qualities, prepares people for the view that some people are agents of Satan in disguise, which in turn makes it reasonable to destroy them. Clifford also emphasizes our social duty. Our beliefs help to create the world in which our descendants will live. Making ourselves gullible or credulous, we lose the habit of testing things and inquiring into them, and that means 'sinking back into savagery'.

Clifford is admirably stern about the position of the untroubled, unclouded innocent who just believes what he has been told:

If a man, holding a belief which he was taught in childhood or persuaded of afterwards, keeps down and pushes away any doubts which arise about it in his mind, purposely avoids the reading of books and the company of men that call into question or discuss it, and regards as impious those questions which cannot easily be asked without disturbing it – the life of that man is one long sin against mankind.

Thus apologists for religious identity politics sometimes describe themselves as having been born one thing or another: born a Muslim, or a Hindu, or a Jew. According to Clifford this is false consciousness. People are born human beings, but nothing else. They may have been taught to regard themselves as one thing or another, and they may have been taught as well the doctrines and attitudes of particular traditions. But if they choose to go on refusing to question what they have been told, and if, as is so commonly the case, what they have been told is incredible or pernicious, then their continued adherence is, in Clifford's eyes, a sin against mankind.

That's all very well, but what then is the mark of reason? How are we to tell whether particular convictions escape Clifford's rather strenuous call to doubt and query? Are we, like the Greek sceptics, to regard all questions as open questions? That way (as Clifford acknowledges) lies paralysis. Even to conduct the inquiries that Clifford demands, we will have to stand somewhere. To try to unearth historical or metaphysical or other error, we will need to establish contrary truth, and to do that we will need to take many things for granted.

Clifford sees the problem, and answers it in terms of *method* rather than in terms of *results*:

In regard, then, to the sacred tradition of humanity, we learn that it consists, not in propositions or statements which are to be accepted and believed on the authority of the tradition, but in questions rightly asked, in conceptions which enable us to ask further questions, and in methods of answering questions. The value of all these things depends on their being tested day by day.

2. *Will and Passion in James*

Clifford's moral broadside attracted a radical answer, the essay 'The Will to Believe' by William James, and it is some of the insights and confusions of that essay that now define our landscape.

James sees belief in terms of a choice between options. At a particular moment something that we may be asked to believe in may strike us as a 'live' hypothesis, meaning that we think it has some chance of being true. Our choice between believing it and avoiding belief in it is a 'forced' option, for there is no third alternative. And the choice may be momentous, in that important consequences hang on it. When this is all true, James calls the option of belief a 'genuine' option. He thinks there are then the same risks either way:

Our passional nature not only lawfully may, but must, decide an option between propositions, whenever it is a genuine option that cannot by its nature be decided on intellectual grounds; for to say, under such circumstances, 'Do not decide, but leave the question open,' is itself a passional decision, – just like deciding yes or no, – and is attended with the same risk of losing the truth.

There are several things to notice here, all of which, from Clifford's point of view, serve to confuse the discussion. First, we should not be blind to the forces that lead to issues becoming 'live'. James himself recognizes the cultural background to such a view. Perhaps for me the question of whether Jupiter prefers oxen to sheep as a sacrifice, or whether Mohammed took a night flight to Jerusalem, are about as dead as can be. Neither is of any interest at all. If for someone else one or the other or both these questions matter a great deal, we already have a kind of clash. By having a mind prepared to take such an issue seriously, you are already half-way to perdition. Everyone is dead to innumerable actual and possible objects of conviction, from tooth fairies to Santa Claus, so from Clifford's perspective, resurrecting some arbitrarily favoured few from the dead is already to be a victim of unknown dark forces, silently betraying the rule of reason.

Second, we should not be so sure in advance that an issue cannot be 'decided on intellectual grounds'. Many things which have appeared to some people as articles of faith are to others intellectually sufficiently improbable as to be, in effect, decidable: astrology, homeopathy, the transmigration of souls or the belief that the world is the product of an all-good, all-powerful, all-knowing intelligence, for example.

Third, we should certainly not accept that whenever something is not decidable, its probability is evens (so that the risk of believing it and the risk of avoiding belief are the same). It may not now be decidable whether the roulette wheel will show 34 on its next spin, but it is very unwise to be convinced that it will, and very unwise to bet at evens that it will. Where we have a whole slew of possibilities (which is always so since the realm of the supernatural, or in other words the realm of human imagination, has many inhabitants: our gods and other objects of conviction can come in all shapes and sizes) then in the absence of 'intellectual grounds' the probability of any one being true is vanishingly small.

Finally, we may suspect the role of 'passion' in these matters. James is probably not asserting that we have the right to believe whatever we like, or whatever would be pleasant for us to believe, although he comes quite close to it.[4] He does allow our wishes to close the gaps or uncertainties that reason leaves open. And this interplay between what we would like to believe and what we end up believing is deeply disturbing. It is as if James is *objectifying* belief. He treats it as one might treat an ornament, for which the only questions would be: does this suit me; is it a good thing to wear to the social party? And then taking the ornament (conviction) or leaving it behind (avoiding it) are options that may be quite evenly balanced.

Now this is not the ordinary way of thinking about beliefs. Beliefs, we usually suppose, answer to a different set of values: those of truth and falsity. Fairly obviously, there are things it may be expedient (even in the widest sense) for me to believe (for instance, that I am the most popular person in the class) but which are not true, and there are things that may be true which it may be deeply uncomfortable and threatening to believe. Truth has rights and privileges of its own, and they are not just the same as those of utility.

A related charge is that James is *privatizing* belief, concentrating not upon the social trust that is at the forefront of Clifford's discussion, but upon the private satisfactions that follow upon settling a matter in one's own mind. And it is this privatization of belief that leads to relativism: my belief ceases to exist in a public space, up for acceptance or rejection by all who pay attention. It starts to be a matter of 'my truth' or 'your truth', like my ornaments or your ornaments, which serve fine if they are to my taste or yours, and about which we can be indifferent to the taste of others.

This is not how we need to think of beliefs. In philosophers' jargon, a belief is a state with a 'content'. We believe propositions, and when an issue arises, it is some proposition and its truth and falsity upon which our attention turns. If the issue is an historical one, then our attention will be turned to the historical period and the sources that help to establish what occurred. If it is a scientific one, our attention will be turned to whatever experiments or theories are most likely to establish a verdict. The issue determines its own epistemology. The satisfactions of people who hold one or other conviction are not to the point, unless the issue itself is one about those very satisfactions.

This suggests that we simply cannot, self-consciously, bring our passions and desires into the matter as James suggests (although he is also aware of the objection). However vividly we present to ourselves the happiness of believing something (that our children are uniquely brilliant, that our partners are immune to temptation) it will not by itself make us believe it. At best it may dispose us to be seduced into believing it, making us likely to seize upon confirming evidence and to ignore any which fits badly. Our happiness can give us a biased disposition to pay attention to some evidence and to ignore other evidence, but it does not independently give us belief. Indeed, any feeling that it had done so would undermine belief: we would recognize ourselves as defective instruments for registering how things stand. To say that someone is a victim of wishful thinking is to criticize them, and to think that we ourselves may be the victims of wishful thinking is to doubt our own judgement.

Similarly, the conversational move of expressing a belief is not, one hopes, a ploy of pursuing the advantage of having the hearer believe something. It is, or should be, a matter of cooperation rather than manipulation. I may want you to become like-minded with me about some issue, but this should be because that is the *truth* about the issue in my eyes. It should not be because it would be expedient to me for you to be so minded. It is sometimes said that one of the casualties of the general suspicion and mistrust that permeated the old Soviet Union was that the distinction between truth and other motivations to believe tended to break down. Upon hearing a purported piece of information, the reaction was not 'Is this true?' but 'Why is this person saying this? – What machinations or manipulations are going on here?' The question of truth did not, as it were, have the social space in which it could breathe. This is a generalization of the attitude behind the question the trenchant British television interviewer Jeremy Paxman is supposed to ask himself on talking to a politician: 'Why is this lying bastard lying to me?'

Sadly, it may indeed be wise to ask this question, especially in a political culture of mistrust, rhetoric and spin. There are plenty of people of whom Paxman's question is the one to ask, but this is because they are manipulative villains, not because the issue of truth and the issue of utility come to the same thing.

There are other rhetorical devices at James's disposal:

We may regard the chase for truth as paramount, and the avoidance of error as secondary; or we may, on the other hand, treat the avoidance of error as more imperative, and let truth take its chance. Clifford . . . exhorts us to the latter course. Believe nothing, he tells us, keep your mind in suspense forever, rather than by closing it on insufficient evidence incur the awful risk of believing lies. You, on the other hand, may think that the risk of being in error is a very small matter when compared with the blessings of real knowledge, and be ready to be duped many times in your investigation rather than postpone indefinitely the chance of guessing true. I myself find it impossible to go with Clifford. We must remember that these feelings of our duty about either truth or error are in any case only expressions of our passional life.

Here the device is to suppose that the leap of faith (when, we must remember, an issue cannot be decided by other means) gives us 'the blessings of real knowledge'. How can this be so? Suppose, for instance, it occurs to you that the oak tree in your garden might contain the spirit of Napoleon. You find this a momentous thing, and manage to convince yourself that it is so. Now how does 'real knowledge' get into the picture? Even supposing that we waive the difficulties with this notion of 'spirit', the likelihood of you being right must be next to nothing. Even if it makes metaphysical sense to suppose that you *are* right, which most philosophers would deny, your guess is overwhelmingly improbable. (Why your oak tree? Why Napoleon?) And even if you are, against all the odds, right, having guessed so luckily still scarcely brings you the title of knowing anything.

And always, against the alleged blessing of your conviction, we have to lay Clifford's train of social and practical disasters, ready to explode. If the oak tree contains the spirit of Napoleon, perhaps the child contains the spirit of the devil, and the people next door are all creatures of Satan, and need dealing with accordingly.

James also casts doubt on Clifford's attachment to scientific and empirical method:

Objective evidence and certitude are doubtless very fine ideals to play with, but where on this moonlit and dream-visited planet are they found?

But immediately following he protests that he is not after all offering an indiscriminate defence of any kind of irrationality, dogma or bigotry:

I am, therefore, myself a complete empiricist so far as my theory of human knowledge goes. I live, to be sure, by the practical faith that we must go on experiencing and thinking over our experience, for only thus can our opinions grow more true; but to hold any one of them – I absolutely do not care which – as if it never could be reinterpretable or corrigible, I believe to be a tremendously mistaken attitude, and I think that the whole history of philosophy will bear me out.

This sounds close enough to Clifford's 'fallibilism' or open-minded attention to evidence and experience, which he in turn was opposing to dogma and unearned conviction.

James's final strategy is to seize Clifford's ground, surprisingly turning Clifford's own agnosticism into the dogmatic villain. It is, after all, Clifford who is 'vetoing' James's right to whatever faith he chooses, and James rebels:

Better risk loss of truth than chance of error, – that is your faith-vetoer's exact position. He is actively playing his stake as much as the believer is; he is backing the field against the religious hypothesis, just as the believer is backing the religious hypothesis against the field. To preach scepticism to us as a duty until 'sufficient evidence' for religion be found, is tantamount therefore to telling us, when in presence of the religious hypothesis, that to yield to our fear of its being error is wiser and better than to yield to our hope that it may be true. It is not intellect against all passions, then; it is only intellect with one passion laying down its law. And by what, forsooth, is the supreme wisdom of this passion warranted? Dupery for dupery, what proof is there that dupery through hope is so much worse than dupery through fear?

This is the familiar charge that suspension of belief is itself a kind of faith. It is also making the issue into a practical rather than theoretical one – a transformation perhaps encouraged by Clifford's moralizing of the issue. That is, the battle of conviction versus doubt is played as if it were a question of the costs and benefits of each. Whereas we would ideally like a pure, independent ideal of proportioning belief to evidence *regardless* of cost or benefit. We would like truth to have a life of its own.

Even on its own terms, however, James's rhetoric is more impressive than his argument. Once more there is the privatization (as if our own hopes or fears were the only costs or benefits in the case). There is silence about what Clifford sees as the dire consequences of the social habit of irrational conviction. There is the implication that the probabilities are about equal ('dupery for dupery . . .'). And there is the silent assumption that only one religious hypothesis is in question, having some antecedent right to get taken seriously when its innumerable possible, and equally probable, competitors do not.

And James is wrong. Refusal to believe something is not a kind of faith. You may believe that Feng shui really works. I refuse to believe it. I do not necessarily believe that it does not work, I may refuse to come down either way. I may not think it is worth thinking about. I may express myself just by saying that 'it might not', or 'it's not very convincing'. My practical expression of my state of mind would be just not being prepared to risk anything on it, not even crossing the road to look into the shop. Whereas you are prepared for all sorts of practical tests: the more dogmatic and convinced you are, the more you are happy to risk.

The more such faiths you absorb, the more your risks fail to pay off. You make an expensive partner, but is it any worse than that? Clifford, of course, tells us that it is. Your habit is dangerous. Your disrespect for caution, for evidence, for plausibility may lead anywhere. 'Those who can make you believe absurdities,' said Voltaire, 'can make you commit atrocities.' By contrast, my caution cannot do any such thing.

3. Fiction and Myth

This splendid row in the philosophy of religion – which is only a small fraction of our concerns – introduces a deeper problem of truth. For there is a problem of how we interpret religious activities, which arises whether we go in for them, or only observe them from the outside. James can be seen as opening this question. In his reply to Clifford, we found him objectifying and privatizing belief, downplaying its connection with representation and truth, and stressing instead its personal function. We may wonder whether this leaves anything recognizable as belief at all.

So here is a surprising question: is there any such thing as religious belief? Before you say (perhaps with outrage) that there obviously is, or (perhaps with cynicism) that there obviously is not, I need to explain that the question is not intended to be one about the hypocrisy or the sincerity of religious sayings, although that question may often need asking. It is rather about the state of mind that is, or perhaps should be, expressed by those sayings.

Describing how things stand is one of the things we do with language, and the one for which the question of truth directly arises. But there are many other things we also do. Suppose we accept as a datum a spectrum of religious activities, including such things as ritual, penance, prayer, music and finally sayings. What might practitioners be doing? This is the question of how religious activity or the religious 'language game' is to be thought of. What are people about when they perform these activities? Here are some suggestions:

> They are describing events in what they take to be a distant region of space or time, in which people may one day find them.

> They are describing events in what they take to be a distinct and disconnected region of space or time, in which souls and spirits exist.

These two see religion as a question of fact, truth and belief, albeit about special regions of the world. But here are others:

> They are telling stories: satisfying fictions, which help to do various things.

> They are finding metaphors through which to gain some understanding of the human condition.

> They are insisting upon or expressing certain emotional reactions to the human condition: hope, desire, consolation, rebellion, acceptance and guilt.

> They are performing, analogously to performing dances and songs, or reciting poetry.

They are promoting the old human favourites: self-interest, self-importance, the will to power, the illusion of control over events.

They are affirming identities, and cementing local loyalties, or separating themselves from others.

They are giving themselves the illusion of a foundation for their morals and their social practices, in the will of a supernatural agent.

Many of these suggestions can be held together. Unlike the first two on the list, they do not interpret religious activity as essentially a matter of describing a hidden part of reality, either connected with ours, although remote, or altogether distinct. These interpretations avoid the idea of describing or representing a part of reality at all. They substitute other activities, and it is not at all clear that these other activities express beliefs. They have nothing much to do with representing how the world stands. They have more to do with practical reactions to it or attempts to cope with it. Some of them provide the reason the Roman magistrates did not care, but liberally bestowed the freedom of the city on all the gods of mankind.

The idea that some of these capture the essence of religion is not the property of cynical philosophers and atheists; on the contrary, it is more or less orthodox in much theology. In some circles the idea that religion is an attempt to describe what exists (what has an 'ontological' status, or status as part of the world) is regarded as terribly naive and old-hat: 'onto-theology'.[5] The contrasting interpretation is to stress exactly the activities of ritual, prayer and the rest, which we have mentioned, to the exclusion of any ambition to describe exactly how things stand in a 'supernatural' part of the cosmos.

Of course, whether the everyday practitioner would like this re-interpretation of his or her doings is another matter. Perhaps contempt for onto-theology is a 'Government House attitude', fine for the elite, but to be kept hidden from the ordinary man or woman in the pew. Many of those react by calling such theologians atheists in disguise. It can also be argued that without the 'ontological' part, the bit that is supposed to describe the way things are, the attitude part could not be quite what it is. We might say 'God gave us the land' as a kind of amplified way of demanding the land. But the amplifier works only if we suppose we are doing more than voicing the demand – we are making a claim of title and right.

We should however remember a long tradition in philosophy of calling things 'fictions' without disrespect. Matter, force, energy, causes, laws of nature, space, time, possibilities, numbers, infinity, selves, freedom of the will, the will itself, desires, beliefs, identity, things, properties, society, language, money – in fact, everything you can think of, has at some time or another been declared to be a fiction by philosophers bent on keeping a firm check on reality. The German philosopher Hans Vaihinger celebrated 'the philosophy of as-if' in a 1911 book of that title, detailing the useful fictions of science, mathematics, politics, jurisprudence and metaphysics, let alone everyday life and religion, and demoting everything except the stream of sensation to the category of fiction. Fictions are the scaffolding with which we erect ways of dealing with that stream. Vaihinger declares Kant a great exponent of the idea of a fiction, and we meet similar tendencies in Nietzsche, whom Vaihinger much admired, in chapter 4.[6] On the other hand, in the English tradition there is much less sympathy with the idea. Jeremy Bentham's slanging attack on the English common law and its expositors derives largely from his perception that it is shot through with falsehood, corrupted by 'the pestilential breath of fiction'. Yet even Bentham grudgingly granted some fictions (such as rights or duties) a kind of 'verbal reality'.[7]

We may be inclined to grumble that if religious practitioners are not even in the business of representing the world truly, it is a pity that they chose a story told so like a recital of plain truth, in an apparently descriptive, factual language, in order to do whatever it is that they are doing instead. But this grumble may be misplaced. It seems entirely possible that there should be no *better* kind of language to use to do whatever it is that the religious practitioner is doing. This is suggested at one point by Wittgenstein, a prime mover of this kind of attitude to religion: 'It says what it says. Why should you be able to substitute anything else?'[8] We might even mount a Darwinian argument: if there were better ways of doing it, it is surprising that they should not have emerged during the centuries of writing and wrestling that religious people have put into the task. So, for example, suppose the religious person finds 'I know that I shall see my redeemer' a profoundly satisfactory and important thing to say. It seems presumptuous to suppose both that we know just what the satisfaction and importance are, and that we also know of a better way of achieving them.

We might test the non-representational account against the people's own explanations of their doings, but the answers may be disappointing, not just here, but in general. For people can seldom do much better than stay within their chosen sphere. They tend to suppose that they say whatever it is, because . . . – and fill out the dots by repeating whatever it is. We think there is a chair over there because there is a chair over there. We believe the earth to be some 4 billion years old because that is how old it is. A mathematician's explanation of why it is right to think that if five of us set out and we now number only three, two have got lost, is probably going to be that five is two greater than three. Similarly a lawyer's explanation of the foundations of law in terms of a (fictitious) social contract is good, in his eyes, because social contracts do lie at the foundations of law, and a man of God's explanation of why it is right to tell the story of heaven and hell that way, is predictably just to repeat the story of heaven and hell. Why is it right, we might ask the poetry-lover, to be gripped by the thought that 'Life, like a dome of many-coloured glass, stains the white radiance of eternity'?[9] And back comes the reply that it is because this is what life does.

At this point reason totters, and we may be apt to feel a strong sense of outrage. Wittgensteinian theology sounds shifty, as if it is trying to maintain all the benefits of belief without any of the costs. Its implications are serious, but it is protected as only a fiction. It skips away from Clifford's critique too easily. Furthermore, an abyss of 'anything goes' relativism opens up. For these interpretations offer the sayings of religious storytellers a general-purpose immunity to any kind of criticism or evaluation. And then the all-important barrier between fantasy and fact is being dismantled on their behalf.

This is indeed a threat. But at least the Wittgensteinian interpretation does not exempt the religious language from *ethical* criticism. We might know enough of what the satisfaction is to wish that religious people would not go in for it. We might gesture at some of the things that go into the mix, and if we find them distasteful we may campaign against the persistence of the sayings and doings. The storytelling might leave people who go in for it much worse than they would otherwise have been. Or it may be that we can connect their sayings with nothing at all. Wittgenstein says he comes close to this, when he considers the sayings of spiritualists. God is indeed dead, and those who go on being gripped by the stories become incomprehensible.

Bertrand Russell followed Clifford by comparing religious belief with straightforwardly factual kinds of belief, which were as improbable, scientifically, as anything could be: the belief that there is a china teapot in its own orbit around the sun, for example. It is fair to say that this identifies religion with mere superstition and foolishness. Now imagine, however, that this teapot undergoes a sea change. Suppose it becomes an authority (out of its spout come forth important commands and promises). Suppose it becomes a source of comfort, as earthly teapots are, but more so. Suppose it becomes the focus of national identities: it is especially one of our teapots, not theirs. And so on: it answers prayers, adopts babies, consecrates marriages and closes grief. The teapot was cracked, but rose again and is now whole. It has achieved mythical, legendary, even religious status. It becomes crass to ask how big it is, how its orbit is shaped, what china it is made of. These questions demean and belittle the teapot, and probably suggest sacrilegious intent on the part of those who insist upon them. Above all, it becomes a sin and shame to deny the existence of the teapot, whereas it is not usually a sin to deny the existence of anything.

When we imagine a people recounting the now-biblical stories of the teapot, it also belittles them to imagine them as simply pretending or play-acting; recounting what for them are *mere* stories. For them, the stories very probably *require* telling as they have been told (perhaps in the very words in which they have always been told, as children often require of their stories). Perhaps deviation especially angers them, like heresy.

Suppose we say, neutrally, that the practitioners are *animated* by these stories, once they matter to them in the way I have suggested (the idea recurs in chapter 7, in the austere surroundings of the philosophy of science). Is there a difference between animation and belief? Is there really space for theology without onto-theology, and if so, how does one tell the difference?

4. Kinds of Animation

Clifford gives us a clue, when he says that he who 'truly believes that which prompts him to an action has looked upon the action to lust after it; he has committed it already in his heart'. Beliefs are functional states. They are preparations for action. This is their biological function, or what they are for. So perhaps true believers should be distinguished from those who are animated by stories, poems or metaphors precisely by the nature of this preparation.

People who knowingly throw themselves into a story may be very like people who take the story for truth, for a time, but we expect that the difference will come out somewhere. The party finishes, the children go to bed, and Daddy is not a wolf any more. Similarly a diagnostic that people do not really believe what they say they do about, for instance, an afterlife, would be the grief that they feel at the death of a loved one. Voltaire's character Dr Pangloss says that all is for the best in the best of all possible worlds, and in the story is presented as believing it.[10] But he is also presented as wholly unnatural – most people who like to say such a thing would show well enough that they do not really believe it, either by raging at the way of the world, or by trying to improve it.

A similar phenomenon is the way in which what seem to be straightforward contradictions between different religious traditions are often smoothed away and glided over by practitioners. Whereas the belief that there are miracles owing to the divinity of Christ is simply incompatible with the view that there are miracles owing to the divine relations of the Prophet, the attitudes and emotions that gain expression in either story may be quite compatible, and we may expect to find adherents of either story ('people of the book') joining hands in opposing sceptics about each. Whereas in more mundane contexts we notice the contradiction between our own beliefs and those of others quickly enough.

David Hume gives a subtle, and typically humorous, example of this diagnostic. The context is one in which he has posed to himself the problem of how certain words come to have the effects they do. If I say the words 'I promise . . .' or 'I hereby transfer ownership . . .' a whole host of civil and moral consequences follow. I come to be under an obligation to you, and at risk of serious loss of credit if I renege, or you come to own a thing that a minute before you could have gone to prison for stealing. How can this be so? How do words ('mere breath') come to have such extraordinary powers? Hume's answer cites the utility of such public actions. For promises and contracts, it is the public performance that determines social and legal consequences. And he points out that for the actions to have this utility the 'secret direction' of a person's intention is not crucial. I can promise without intending to keep my promise, or transfer property without intending to release it. In each case I will still be bound by my public performance. The fact that I had mental reservations does not nullify my public act, but this contrasts with Church doctrine:

It is a doctrine of the Church of Rome, that the priest, by a secret direction of his intention, can invalidate any sacrament. This position is derived from a strict and regular prosecution of the obvious truth, that empty words alone, without any meaning or intention in the speaker, can never be attended with any effect. If the same conclusion be not admitted in reasonings concerning civil contracts, where the affair is allowed to be of so much less consequence than the eternal salvation of thousands, it proceeds entirely from men's sense of the danger and inconvenience of the doctrine in the former case: And we may thence observe, that however positive, arrogant, and dogmatical any superstition may appear, it never can convey any thorough persuasion of the reality of its objects, or put them, in any degree, on a balance with the common incidents of life, which we learn from daily observation and experimental reasoning.[11]

The 'danger and inconvenience' of making the validity of promises and contracts hinge upon what the parties privately intend is quite obvious in day-to-day living. But in connection with the supernatural, which (Hume dryly remarks) is supposed to be of so much more importance, we do not really care, and thus allow 'theories' that would not survive a moment when we have our feet planted firmly on the ground of observation and experimental reasoning. And this suggests again that 'beliefs' in such a matter are not real beliefs at all.

This connects with the point at the end of the last section, that intensity of conviction is measured by the risk you are prepared to take. And then the problem with supernatural beliefs is that there are no gambles that can as a matter of worldly experience be agreed to succeed if they are true, but not if they are false. If there were, they would have been abandoned long ago, for after all people do not get what they pray for, and it rains alike on the just and the unjust.

We will be apt to talk of animation rather than belief when we have our own explanation of people's attachments to their sayings. The absorbed poetry lover just repeats his Shelley, but the critic (who may love the poetry just as much) can do much better, talking of the context, the point of the metaphor, the direction of Shelley's thought and so on. The moralist may think he believes in human rights because human rights exist, and he is sensitive to them. But from the sidelines the critic (who may love human rights just as much) may give a very different story, whereby the attitude to human life that gets expression in this kind of saying is given a different and more satisfying explanation. It is not, for instance, that we receive information about rights just like we receive information about trees and buses, but instead that we attempt to construct and insist upon boundaries to conduct, and this is the language in which we do it. This gives us an alternative to thinking of rights as fictional, arguably nearer to Bentham's 'verbal realities'. We have constructed a mode of talking and thinking that meets certain needs. We do not have to explain those needs in the language of rights, but can explain the language of rights in terms of its function in meeting those needs.

On the other hand, as we shall find out in later chapters, there may be sayings where there is nowhere for the critic to stand: there may be no sidelines that take us away from absorption in the sayings of common sense and established science. In these areas perhaps there is no (habitable) space between being animated by the words and believing what they say. Perhaps there is no plausible fictionalist or Wittgensteinian reinterpretation of our activities around chairs and tables, viruses and galaxies. And we will find that this in turn explains the sense that truth and its allies get a solid foothold in these areas that they have to struggle to find in others.

Before we return to explanation and its place in these issues, we turn to a different skirmish. This is between those who assert relativism, and those who think it easy to refute it.

2

Man the Measure

The idols of the tribe are founded in human nature itself and in the very tribe or race of mankind. The assertion that the human senses are the measure of things is false; to the contrary, all perceptions, both of sense and mind, are relative to man, not to the universe. The human understanding is like an uneven mirror receiving rays from things and merging its own nature with the nature of things, which thus distorts and corrupts it.

Francis Bacon, *The New Organon*, XLI, p. 41

1. *Turning the Tables: the Recoil Argument*

Some time just before 400 BC Socrates met some followers of the philosopher Protagoras in the market place in Athens. The meeting is described in Plato's dialogue the *Theaetetus*. Protagoras had apparently written a volume called *The Truth*, which is now lost. He was notorious for the saying that man is the measure of all things, 'of those that are, that they are, of those that are not, that they are not'. We shall find that it is not easy to locate the meaning of this dark saying. But in the dialogue Socrates takes it to be an instance of a dangerous relativism, and he crosses swords with the admirers of Protagoras. At the crux of the dialogue, Socrates asks one of these, called Theodorus, to consider Protagoras's own view, the Measure Doctrine. And he asks him to notice that nearly everyone else ('thick thousands', says Socrates, quoting Homer) regards it as untrue.

SOCRATES: Well then, perhaps we ought to say that your belief is true for you, but false for all these thousands of people. What do you think?

THEODORUS: It looks as though the argument leaves us no choice.

SOCRATES: What does all this entail for Protagoras? Isn't it necessarily the case that if he *didn't* believe in man being the measure, and if the common run of mankind didn't either (as in fact it doesn't), then this book of his, *The Truth*, would be true for no one? He *did* believe it, however, but most people don't share this belief. The first notable consequence of this is that the idea is more false than true, in proportion to the extent that the unbelievers outnumber the believers.

THEODORUS: That necessarily follows from the premises that its truth and falsity are dependent upon individual impressions.

SOCRATES: And there is a second consequence, which is exquisite. In saying that everyone believes what is the case, he is conceding the truth of beliefs which oppose his own; In other words, he is conceding the truth of the opinion that he is wrong.

THEODORUS: Yes.[1]

Theodorus is typical of the Socratic target, initially confident of some unexamined opinion, but eventually confined to confessing how completely Socrates has steamrollered him. A colleague once told me he had wondered how Socratic dialogues look without Socrates's own speeches, and the result goes something like: 'You've got me there, O Socrates,' 'Yes,' 'There is no resisting that, O Socrates,' and so on and so on.

Socrates's questioning is called the 'maieutic' method, which means the method of the midwife, merely assisting the patients to give birth to their own understanding – something that inevitably they have to do themselves. Education, as schoolteachers like to say, is a drawing out and not a putting in, a doctrine that Plato stretched to breaking point, arguing in the dialogue *Meno* that all learning is a matter of recalling what was once known in a previous existence.* At any rate, it seems true that Socrates's hearers gave birth very much more easily than the students most teachers of philosophy encounter. However, this in turn may be unfair, for there is room to argue that Plato, writing as a dramatist as well as a philosopher, is not simply recording Socrates's remarkable abilities to deliver other people, unresisting, of their embryonic thoughts. Plato may, for example, be inviting us to sympathize with the underdogs, perhaps seeing them as defeated only by methods which they, and the reader, can feel to be underhand, but where we cannot put our finger on what is wrong. Perhaps Theodorus was left inwardly seething. This is, incidentally, our first brush with something which will occupy us again: the

---

* The starting point is the idea that you cannot set about learning something unless you know what you don't know, a doctrine unhappily confirmed by those students whose infirmities include being unable to recognize why they are getting poor marks.

possibility of multiple and possibly indeterminate interpretations of what the writer of a text is doing or saying.

To return to our theme, the passage presents the classic 'recoil' argument, a judo-flip designed to discomfort the relativist Protagoras. The idea is that the relativistic position, supposed here to be exemplified by the doctrine that man is the measure of all things, recoils upon itself. It is advanced as something to be accepted, as something *true*. But that is somehow inconsistent with the doctrine's own import, its own denial that truth has the meaning that common sense ('thick thousands') gives to it. In a nutshell, if the Measure Doctrine is true, then it is refuted by its own truth. And this means it cannot be true.

In simple cases the recoil is a matter of straight inconsistency, simple self-refutation. 'In recent years, historians have discovered that there is no historical truth' (Have they? When?). 'We now know that all general statements are untrue' (That one as well?). But one is lucky to find an intellectual opponent innocent enough to fall straight into that trap. The recoil is often more indirect, more a matter of finding that the opponent is in some concealed way paying tribute to notions such as reason or truth in the very act of denying them. He may be submitting to the order of reason, even as he officially denies that there is any such thing.

The matter at issue between Socrates and Theodorus is one of authority: the authority of truth, rationality, objectivity, knowledge, science. Socrates aims to hold firm to this authority, believing there to be a stamp of truth, independent of us, and independent as well of our wishes, emotions and desires. Our proper role is to submit to this authority of reason. This is the authority of what the Greeks called *logos*, and I shall continue to use the Greek word, not as a technical term but rather as a signpost into the whole area, for *logos* can take very different shapes. Protagoras is presented as suspicious of any such authority, just as atheists and agnostics are suspicious of divine authority. This is, indeed, a comparison to remember, for it haunts these debates, with relativists frequently complaining that absolutists make a divinity of reason or a divinity of truth – a divinity that, like others, has an unhappy habit of remaining hidden just when it is most needed. To relativists, Plato's heaven, in which eternal laws of right reason or *logos* subsist, is a nowhere place, an unintelligible fantasy.

Protagoras or his pupil seeks to voice these suspicions and argue for them, and Socrates urges that by doing even this much he is submitting to the very kind of authority that he is bent on denying.

Now, blanket denials of authority are certainly apt to sound incredible to many of us. How can anyone deny the authority of observation, or of science, or mathematics or logic? At the beginning of the twentieth century the Cambridge philosopher G. E. Moore famously defended common sense against scepticism by holding out his hand and claiming that any argument that he did not know he had a hand would have to be rated much less convincing than his immediate certainty that he did.[2] We have brute, straightforward convictions. We trust unhesitatingly in the abundant delivery of our senses, and fairly obviously could not survive without doing so. The point is even more apparent when we come to mathematics and logic. However much Protagoras manages to confuse us, we will not stop believing that two plus two makes four, or that if everybody in the room is married and John is in the room, then John is married.

To proceed it is important to recognize Moore's point, but also to put it on one side. For the argument should not be about the *existence* of convictions such as these, but about their authority. It is about their status in the dimension of reason or *logos*. There is no evidence that Protagoras wants us to jettison everyday certainties, trying – in vain, of course – to live a life free of beliefs at all, although that may have been the radical prescription of the later philosopher Pyrrho and his followers, the Pyrrhonian sceptics. Rather, Protagoras can allow Moore to have his conviction, so long as he can take away its badges of honour, its decorations and signals of status. He can allow what was later called *natural belief*, where this is confidence that unfolds in natural human life. We return to this notion in connection with David Hume.

We should remember, as well, that Socrates is not a cardboard cutout absolutist. He does not roar and bawl the absolute across the hall; famously, he questions and questions but never dictates. He is not a dogmatist. This shows what we have already come across, that you can admit the authority of truth without immediately supposing that you possess it. The admission might precede a dark night of scepticism, whereby although truth, real truth, should be the target of our inquiries, we fear that we shall never achieve it.

So the situation is that Protagoras or his pupils seek to voice their suspicions and argue for them, and then Socrates urges that by doing even this much they are submitting to the very kind of authority that they are bent on denying. They are caught in a kind of inconsistency, and their position undermines itself. This is the recoil argument, a kind of judo-flip that turns the relativism against itself. Does it work?

2. Modern Judo

Before looking into Plato's own recoil argument a little more deeply, it will be useful to compare it with some recent followers. Hilary Putnam, one of America's most distinguished contemporary philosophers, asks us to consider a formulation of relativism put in terms of 'norms'. Since norms weave themselves into our story fairly pervasively, it will be good to explain them a little. Norms are thought of as rules or principles governing our activities, and in particular our activities of thought and speech. Norms govern what it is permissible to say or think, or what it is obligatory to say or think. They are invoked when we allow that something was right, or insist that it was wrong. Speaking and thinking are norm-governed activities in the minimal sense that sometimes we get things right, speaking and thinking correctly, and sometimes we get things wrong, thinking or speaking incorrectly. We can think or say that there is rain on the way when there is rain on the way, in which case we are right, or we can think or say that there is rain on the way when there is none, in which case we are wrong. Right and wrong here do not imply praise or blame, but they do imply success or failure, like the contrast between missing a target and hitting it.

As well as the norm of truth or hitting the target, there are norms of right procedure. These govern whether you have done your stuff properly: taken the right observations, made the right inferences, hedged in the right places, weighed the evidence carefully and, in short, made yourself immune to procedural criticism. It may not follow that you arrive at the truth. The evidence may be poor, or misleading, or the interpretation which everyone supposes reasonable may be based on insufficient science or general misunderstanding. A trial may be fairly conducted, yet unhappily arrive at the wrong verdict. Still, there is nothing better that we can do. We act under the conviction that our best procedures, although they may let us down, markedly increase the chance that we get things right. Provided there was nothing better which we should have done then we may be immune from charges of irrationality, negligence or carelessness. Our procedures accord with reason, and it is only bad luck that might stop us hitting the truth.

The dispute between Socrates and Protagoras can then be put as one about the status of these norms, the source of their authority. Do they have more than a local or conventional standing? Is the rule of reason more than the rule of conventions, or even a mob rule, a question of might rather than right?

Here is Putnam's argument that there is more to the authority of reason than just what we happen, at this place and time, to think. It is a pithy version of the judo-flip. The relativist Putnam imagines asserts:

A statement is true (rightly assertible) only if it is assertible according to the norms of modern European and American culture.

Putnam then neatly points out that this sentence is *not itself* assertible according to the norms of European and American culture. These norms do not demand that we make an equation between something being true and it being something we hold true or allow each other to hold as true. In fact our norms actually *forbid* the equation. For our standards allow that we are fallible. We may in principle sometimes all be wrong, and we may be disallowed from asserting things, although they are true. For example, perhaps it is not assertible according to our norms that there will still be a Gulf Stream in a thousand years' time, for doubts about global warming are supposed to make that highly uncertain; but it may happily be true, for all that.

Even if we reason carefully, by contemporary historical, medical, scientific or political standards with which our culture is comfortable, we may get things wrong. Conversely, there may be truths so outrageous and surprising that nobody would be able to assert them without causing dismay and ridicule. But truths, for all that.

So, the relativist's doctrine is not assertible by the norms of modern European and American culture. But if the relativist's sentence is not assertible by those norms, then *by its own lights* it is not true. Applying its own doctrine to itself, it comes out as untrue. Hence, if it is true, it is not true. But that means that it cannot be true, QED.

This is a nice knock-down argument, and it applies to other flamboyant statements of a similar kind. The equally illustrious contemporary philosopher Richard Rorty refuses to describe himself as a relativist, for reasons that we come to in chapter 6. But he is someone who has a robust debunking attitude to the norms of truth and reason. Indeed, he once wrote that 'truth is what your contemporaries let you get away with'. That is a shocking thing to say, outlandish even by philosophers' standards. In fact, it is shocking enough to be something Rorty's contemporaries wouldn't let him get away with (and unsurprisingly, they didn't). So again, if it is true then it is false – by its own lights it is false.

This judo-flip is certainly neat, and it locates a trap that the relativist must avoid. He had better not formulate his doctrine so that, applied to itself, it measures itself as being false. But does he have to do any such thing? Is it not a little hard to believe that this simple judo-flip settles the issue of relativism so decisively, so quickly?

Perhaps it depends what other formulations the relativist can find. If we return to Plato's text, we can see that Protagoras's actual doctrine is not really allowed to come very clearly into focus. Protagoras said that man is the measure of all things, the Measure Doctrine. As we go down the argument we see that this is taken to mean a number of things. First, that 'truth and falsehood are dependent on individual impressions'. Second (in Socrates's last speech), that 'everyone believes what is the case'. There is also supposed to be the idea that things can be more or less true, according to some kind of democratic vote. These seem to be rather different. The idea that truth and falsehood are dependent on individual impressions, for instance, may sound like a quite moderate kind of empiricism – the doctrine that the ultimate source of authority for any belief lies in sense experience. Far more lurid is the doctrine that 'everyone believes what is the case', that is, there is no such thing as false belief. For obviously according to common-sense ways of looking at things, there is plenty of false belief. Truth is a goal, and lies, mistakes, carelessness, muddled thinking, plain bad luck or the thickness of the surrounding darkness all interfere with the achievement of hitting it.

Perhaps Protagoras did not even accept this much. Perhaps he did hold the lurid doctrine. But wouldn't that be a lunatic position? How could anyone hold that 'everyone believes what is the case'?

3. The Variation of Subjectivities

We could imagine Protagoras coming to the Measure Doctrine by thinking along these lines. Try to think of us human beings as instruments, put into an environment. Things impinge on us. Just as a thermometer registers the temperature, so we respond to causal impacts: energies and photons and pressures of touch and sound. I, as an instrument, respond to this continuous causal flux one way – a way determined by the state of my sense organs and brain – and so do you. But if I respond one way, and you a different way, where is truth or falsity? I am an input-output device which gives one output, and you are a similar device which gives another. And isn't that all there is to it? What else does nature contain?

Suppose, for example, that I feel pain on touching a moderately hot surface whereas you, with hornier hands, do not. There is no question of right or wrong. The surface is painful to me, and not painful to you, and that is the end of it. Suppose I, being used to drinking reasonable wines, find Coca-Cola sweet and insipid, but you, with a different history of tasting things, find it quite tart and interesting. Where is there a right or wrong in either reaction? You are an instrument calibrated one way, and I am an instrument calibrated a different way, and that seems to be the end of it. We have different ways of responding. We have our different responses, our different subjectivities, but there is no question of fault or error. In our own time, of course, we can easily extend the argument to variations lying between one culture and another, or one gender and another, or one language or culture or historical period and another. What is salient to one culture need not be so to another. What our history and language make it easy to think in terms of, another might conceal, and vice versa.

This is always the central argument for either relativism or scepticism: we can christen it the argument from the variation of subjectivities. So, for example, in the classical world sceptical arguments took various shapes, finally coming together in the codification by Sextus Empiricus, writing at the end of the second century or possibly as late as the third century AD. The sceptical repertoire included the 'ten modes of Aenesidemus' and the 'five modes of Agrippa', Aenesidemus and Agrippa being shadowy earlier figures of whom not much more than their modes is known. Nearly all the modes argue from a variation of subjectivity to the impossibility of knowing things 'as they are in themselves'. They try to show that things appear differently to different sensibilities, that there is no neutral or authoritative decision procedure awarding victory to just one of these; hence that we should suspend judgement about things themselves. For example, the first mode of Aenesidemus stresses variation in animal perception ('oil is pleasant to men, unpleasant to bees'), the second mode stresses variation among human beings, the third contrasts the delivery of different senses in the same person, the fourth brings in the different circumstances of perception, while the fifth directs our attention to variations arising from distance and perspective. The sixth indeed breaks this pattern, at least at first sight, since it highlights the 'admixtures' always involved in perception. It tries to urge that even in the case of perceptions of a single object, since things do not have effects by themselves, the inference back from effect to cause is always fraught.[3]

The variations of subjectivity bolster the move to the sceptical suspension of judgement, the *epoche* that was the intermediate goal of classical scepticism, the overall moral aim being *ataraxia* or the tranquillity of mind that comes from suspending all judgement. In the Introduction and the last chapter I mentioned the licence that attaches to modern relativism, seemingly enabling people to believe anything they want. Whereas for the Greek sceptic, the variation of subjectivities had the opposite, chastening effect. Their motto '*Ou mallon*' – no more – seems highly appropriate when we are faced with the cacophonies of astrology, homeopathy, Mayan rebirthing ceremonies and the rest.

The somewhat more sophisticated modes of Agrippa take off from the same variations. The datum in the first two modes is again dispute and variation, and the last three detail the pitfalls that face us when we try to sustain one opinion against others. They can be given the form of a trilemma – an offering of three possibilities, none of which turns out to be very attractive. As Michael Williams presents it:

Of course, attempts to provide justification come to a halt. But how? The sceptic will say that we just run out of ideas: either we have nothing to say, or we find ourselves going back over old ground. As an implied claim to knowledge, then, every statement I make invites a new challenge; and in the face of these constantly renewed challenges, I can do only one of three things:

1. Keep trying to think of something new to say – i.e. embark on an infinite regress (Mode of Infinity)
2. At some point refuse to answer – i.e. make a dogmatic assumption (Mode of Assumption)
3. At some point repeat something I have already said – i.e. reason in a circle (Mode of Circularity).[4]

None of these is immediately appealing.

Now we return to Protagoras. We can imagine him insisting that an instrument calibrated one way responds accordingly, and an instrument calibrated a different way need be no better nor worse – just different. Obviously, the variation of subjectivities would not worry us much if we could easily tell that some subjectivities are better than others – better attuned to the truth. But the modes give a Protagorean plenty of scope for denying this. And if there is no such thing as better or worse, how can there be truth? If you are at one place you see the end of the rainbow in one field, and if I am in a different place I see it in a different field, and neither of us is in the least at fault. For that very reason, there is no one true place for the rainbow. A wide-angle lens gives a different result from a telephoto, but neither image is truer than the other. Even a cracked or clouded lens is obeying the same laws of physics, the same laws determining what output there is for any given input, as the lens that is not cracked or clouded.

Or imagine a strange calculating machine. Mostly when you tap the '+' key you get the sum of the two numbers you just entered. But sometimes you get something else. You might say that the machine is malfunctioning, and perhaps it is by your lights. But it might be functioning perfectly well by some other lights. For example, suppose it adds hours. Then if the sum of two inputs comes to more than 24, it subtracts 24 from the result. Or, suppose it is a navigator, adding compass bearings. Then if the result comes to more than 360, it subtracts that from the result. In itself there is nothing 'right' or 'wrong' about what the machine is doing. Such verdicts are imposed entirely from outside, from us who are the users or onlookers.

If we imagine a modern Protagoras arguing this way, we see that what he has presented is an image of human responses to the world, but responses for which all questions of right and wrong have been brushed out. There remains only the 'is' of actual response, not the 'ought' of the right or true way to respond. And a whole host of interrelated notions disappears along with that 'ought': notions of the *rational* way to respond, or the *objective* response, or the *required* response or the *better informed* response. In this picture the authority of reason or *logos* withdraws from the world. James's complaint to Clifford that 'objective evidence and certitude are doubtless very fine ideals to play with, but where on this moonlit and dream-visited planet are they found?' gets no answer. There are just the endless variations of different subjectivities voicing different responses; the Queen's dark forces of which we know nothing shape everything.

The word 'response' now loses some of its colour. Just because all notions of correctness have been bleached out, so has the very idea of a judgement. In this stark world, people make noises and do other things, but they do not express judgements, for judgements are essentially subject to correctness.

Historically, it is probable that Protagoras proceeded with a slightly different set of thoughts in his tool-kit. It is not at all clear that he really wanted a vision of a world without judgement at all. Nor is it clear that he wanted to proceed from the premise 'X seems cold to A', in the sense that A is inclined to judge X to be cold, directly to the conclusion that it is true that X is cold, even in some relativistic sense of true-for-A. He may have had a more complex set of thoughts in mind. Suppose you hold that at least in basic cases knowledge must be a matter of perception. You then face the problem of connecting how things appear in perception to how they are. But suppose you also hold the view that the best chance, or only chance, of bridging that gap is by a principle of identity: perception works when things that have properties pass them on into how they appear. Now the variation of subjectivities is really catastrophic, for we can infer from X appearing cold to its being cold (its coldness is the only thing that could account for it so appearing). And you can equally infer from its appearing hot to it being hot. But since nothing can be both hot and cold, the whole attempt founders, and the very notion of truth founders with it. We are left with no bridge from how things appear to how they are. Indeed (as the relativist, rather than the sceptic, would infer) we are left with no intelligible idea of a single 'way' things are, but only with the multitude of appearances, literally a plurality of worlds.[5]

4. The Moving Bull's-eye

The world presented in the last section was devoid of judgement. But now another trap awaits our Protagoras. He might try saying that there are as many truths as there are responses. Indeed, this is how Plato seems to have thought of the position – and as we have mentioned, one of the mantras of relativism is that everyone has 'their own truth', or everyone believes what is the case (for them). But this is an odd way to put things, and opens up another problem. For, as Wittgenstein said, if everything that seems right is right, that just means that we cannot talk about right at all.[6] In other words, there is something jarring about trying to retain some notion of truth, even if it is downgraded to 'truth for us' or 'truth for me, here, now', while at the same time trumpeting the disappearance of 'ought': the withdrawal of any conception of right and wrong. And this is one of the traps that Plato was setting for Protagoras in the extract from the dialogue. Protagoras seems to want to *hold* the Measure Doctrine, but at the same time to say that there is no question of right or wrong about either holding it or rejecting it. And this seems somehow inconsistent.

Here is a powerful analogy. Suppose you shoot arrows at a barn door, and every time an arrow lands, you paint on the door a target, with the arrow as its centre, and claim thereby always to score a bull's-eye. There is no success or failure in this game. But that does not mean that you score 100 per cent, an unbroken succession of 'bull's-eyes for you'. It only means that 'scoring a bull's-eye' has lost any meaning. Its meaning in normal archery comes along with the idea of an *attempt* to do something that can easily *fail*, and that can sometimes, but only sometimes, *succeed*. But here the possibility of failure has vanished. Only at a very uncritical first glance might that sound good, for we immediately realize that any conception of success disappears along with it. You cannot intelligibly play your archery this way, and hold on to the connotations of success by describing yourself as scoring a bull's-eye, even a bull's-eye for you.

Now the charge against the Protagorean relativist is that this is exactly what he is doing. He is pretending that truth is still a prize of sorts, even when there is no possibility, by his lights, of anyone missing it. It is like trying to maintain the value of a currency when everyone is allowed to print as much as they like.

The absurdity of the false bull's-eye is not always so apparent. A great painting is one that succeeds in ways in which other paintings fail. But when young children come back from school they proudly present their parents with works of art, and the parents proudly put them on the freezer door. The pictures are great, they say. All of them are great, and the ones brought home tomorrow and the day after will be great too. There is in fact no possibility of anything else. This is painting described in the spirit of our fake archery, but with the honorific connotations of 'great' apparently retained.

To be fair on parents, it may be that all they want to say is that it is great that their children are painting at all, and that may indeed be true. Perhaps the charge of absurdity fits the art establishment better, when the standards of greatness so effortlessly move to cover just whatever this season's favourites are doing: exhibiting dead pigs, blank canvases, soiled underwear, buckets of offal and innards.[7]

Faced with the problem of avoiding this absurdity, it seems as if Protagoras has a number of choices. He can withdraw any use of the word 'true'. He can admit that it is a word that can be used only in company with right and wrong, success and failure, and these have disappeared from his world view, which includes only the endless succession of responses that just happen, one after the other. Saying something would no longer be seen as a matter of trying to get something right, with standards of success that may or may not be met. It would be more a matter of putting something forward in the spirit of a rather flabby poetry-reading: a simple voicing of some words that work for me, here, now. If they work for you, well and good, but if not, that's fine too.

If Protagoras takes this option he does face the question: what is he doing not merely voicing, but actually *holding* the Measure Doctrine, or indeed anything else? If we consider only his action of voicing it, we might convince ourselves that he is simply trying to achieve celebrity, or get an income, or cut a dash. But by actually *believing* that man is the measure of all things, Protagoras seems to be involved in more robust norms and standards, satisfied that he has hit a bull's-eye that is not movable. He is not, in his own eyes, just repeating words in his head. He is giving us the words that *rightly* represent our place in the world. So how can he understand what he is doing while acknowledging no notion of failure, and therefore no notion of success either? He cannot *both* understand himself only to have hit a bull's-eye that is placed wherever his arrow falls, and as having achieved an insight or understanding, a true representation of how things stand.

5. Doing it Ourselves

Protagoras may choose to put more backbone into his account than this, but from a different direction. He can see conversation, the presentation of words, as an activity with political and practical implications. Words are deeds, and the deeds can be successful or not in a different dimension from any associated with *logos*. They have effects, both intended and unintended. They can be useful. In the social world they can seduce and offend, and sway law courts and mobs. So there is a dimension of success and failure, but it has nothing to do with hitting the bull's-eye of truth. It has to do with achieving our ends, such as maintaining friendly relations with our fellows, or bending them to our wills. This is in fact what Plato's most notorious opponents, the Sophists, thought, and it is the seed of the pragmatist tradition in philosophy. It is also the seed of one significant movement in our approach to history. It makes a lot of difference whether we think of the writers we regard as spokespersons for a culture as trying disinterestedly to say how things are, or whether we see them merely as deploying words as tools in particular contests and conflicts. This is the difference between the ordinary approach to people's sayings, and the Soviet Union's approach described in the last chapter.

On this line a poor remnant of the norms we talked about might still remain, a pallid, ghost-like remainder of a more full-blooded notion of correctness. For within a like-minded group deviations from some responses can provoke hostility. Walking around the market place, Protagoras need not be surprised at the phenomena of human disagreement. Rejection and exclusion await the maverick – that is, someone who is the equivalent of the navigating calculator or the person with the differently trained palate or the unusually horny hands. These rejections and exclusions can be voiced, and the appropriate vocabulary will be exactly that of right or wrong, rational or irrational, true or false. But if this is how we think of ourselves, man remains the measure, and the clouds of relativism still lower over us. All responses are indeed of the same status, so far as authority and reason are concerned. It is just that some commend themselves to our fellows, while others do not. Or, in a wider landscape, some enable us to cope better than others. But none has the stamp of truth, or unique accord with the way of reason.

This relativist can reinject standards into the world, regaining a pallid substitute for *logos*. He can say that there is not just the endless variation of subjectivities. There is in addition the possibility of endorsing and grading responses: there is agreement and disagreement, and the human activity of awarding marks from zero to 100 per cent. This will sound like a concession to absolutists. But the kicker is that this is 'just us', just one of our responses. Among our responses, says this Protagorean, there are responses to the responses of others, and especially our 'Yes!' and 'No!' responses. But don't think that these responses escape the variation of subjectivity. They are the creatures of happenstance and contingency, evolution and culture, just as much as how things taste or how things feel, or which art looks good.

To see how this would play out, let us return to the image of human beings as instruments. We noticed that even a lens that gives cloudy or what we would call distorted results is obeying the same optical laws as any other. But surely we can call it faulty? On this line, indeed we can, but that is simply relative to our own practices of endorsing and grading. It is no more faulty in itself than a mountain that stands in our way is at fault for doing so. If our aims changed it might be just what we wanted, just as soft-focus lenses are required for some kinds of portraiture.

The set-up now is delicate. The absolutist feared the bleached-out world of endless variations of subjectivity, with no 'oughts' visible. He held out for standards and norms, proper and rational judgements and arguments, better than their disreputable opposites. And now, under pressure from the moving bull's-eye problem, the relativist seems to have thrown in the towel, admitting some notion of success and failure, some standards and norms governing what to say. But then he snatches the towel back, by adding that it is just us.[8] These norms are of our own making. It is contingent and potentially variable whether we adopt them or impose them. They are one more expression of our subjectivities. And now the absolutist will complain that he wanted bread but has been given stones. He wanted *real* norms, *real* standards, *real* objectivity and *real* truth, and is given only a fake. Like Plato, he wanted the light of the sun, but he is given only that of a man-made lantern.

Here is an example of this argument at work in the history of philosophy. Ancient scepticism, as we have seen, relied heavily on the argument from the variation of subjectivity. When this sceptical tradition was rediscovered in Europe, at the end of the sixteenth century, it was rapidly realized that scepticism needed not only the fact that subjectivities vary, but also the view that each different subjective response was equally 'good'. However, critics complained, we can easily privilege some subjective responses above others – the impressions of those whose constitutions are sound as opposed to those who are sick, for example. So, at a stroke, the sceptic or relativist is silenced.

Unfortunately, this is convincing only if the sceptic is silenced in the *right* way. But here is the seventeenth-century French philosopher Gassendi:

who can be certain that the constitution that you call unsound gives rise to appearances that are less true than the ones framed by the constitution you consider legitimate and sound? Just as there are certain mad people who see things more clearly than those of sound mind, so those whose constitution departs from the normal pattern perhaps perceive things more clearly and truly than others.[9]

In other words, from the absolutist point of view, the problem is not that of finding *some* criterion for privileging some impressions above others. The problem lies in supposing that whatever criterion we hit upon is the *right* one. The absolutist wants it to be that of reason properly attuned to the world, that of *logos* itself. Otherwise, he complains, we are just making it up as we go along. It would be like declaring that the true position of the rainbow is where it is seen as being when viewed from the garden gate. It might give us a decision; but it is not giving us a discovery.

Let us sum this all up by saying that the absolutist wants a special validation, an independent seal of authority attaching to his opinions, which we have called *logos*. And the relativist claims that *logos* is silent: the absolutist's cherished authority is a fantasy. There is no such authority. All opinions are equal in the sight of *logos*. None is required by this alleged authority, and none is forbidden. There is no such thing as asymmetrical standing whereby my opinion gets more marks from *logos* than yours. But the relativist is happy to offer a substitute: a socially constructed, contingent, situated parade of words such as 'rational' or 'true'. They signify a propensity to criticize each other that is itself an expression of our subjectivity. And predictably, this talk of norms will sound, in absolutist ears, like a monstrous parody of the real thing.

We might compare the difference between Plato and Protagoras to that between two attitudes to justice and law. The tender-minded absolutist respects the majesty of the law. He may not literally think in terms of God's laws, but he does think of justice as almost divine, and in his mind human institutions such as law courts are altars to this divinity. He thinks in terms of a rigid set of laws of behaviour, an independent set of demands to which human beings and human societies must conform. Compared to this standard our own institutions and practices often fall short, but it is our duty to improve them until they become the best approximation we can manage to the ultimate true standard.

The relativist, tough minded as ever, mocks the ideology, what the Germans call a *Begriffshimmel*, or 'concept heaven', in which the immutable relations between rights, duties, justice and truth hold their eternal sway. He sees only human institutions, ways of coping with social mess, patchworks and fixes and compromises, some of which prove useful, some of which break down, all of which have in principle a lifespan which depends on us and the problems we meet. The relativist would not be surprised by a Lord Hutton, whereas the absolutist would be outraged.[10] The relativist would be happy to think that final legal authority rests with some sovereign, human, lawmaking assembly, such as Parliament. The absolutist will hold that when Parliament tramples on rights and transgresses against the moral truth, for instance by denying people the right to due process as contemporary parliaments in Britain and America are happy to do, its edicts are no laws at all, but only the commands of a gang that happens to have gained power.

I suggest that we can all understand the relativist attitude to law, whether or not we sympathize with it. Even if, with the absolutist, we worry whether it is in the end bleak and cynical, we are hardly likely to think it is self-refuting. Indeed, in the modern world from which God is markedly absent, we may have difficulty thinking any other way. What kind of reality could 'laws of justice' be supposed to have, if they are neither God's commands on the one hand, nor those of human beings on the other? These seem to exhaust the alternatives, so if we lack the first we must put up with the second. This is the problem of the status of law. The absolutist is holding out for something very grand, but while we may vaguely imagine such grandeur somewhere else, in a *Begriffshimmel* or Plato's heaven perhaps, we find it hard to discover it here on earth. But it is here on earth that we conduct our lives.

Now it is easy to understand Protagoras's position. Think of him as simply extending this view of law beyond the world of courts and judges to include laws of reason and right judgement across the board, covering our science and history as well as our laws and our norms of behaviour.

While this example may be useful, it may also make it sound as if, provided we are theists, accepting the existence of a deity, all is plain sailing for the absolutist. Justice is God's command. But it is well known that this is only a stop-gap, since it is very hard to understand how something could become true just simply by being commanded, however powerful or frightening the being that commanded it. A just practice would be commanded by a just deity, no doubt, but that throws the question back on to why we suppose our deities are just, and whether that judgement in turn could be more than an expression of our own subjectivity. Indeed, the vengeful and jealous and fearsome monotheistic deity seems very obviously to be exactly that.[11] So it is plausible to say that the boot is on the other foot: we think of a deity in this connection simply in order to flesh out and embody our longing for absolutes. We explore this idea further in connection with Nietzsche, in chapter 4.

We have learned, then, that the canny relativist must avoid simple formulations, such as the one Rorty provided, or the one Putnam considered. If these formulations are true, then they are false, which means that they are false – that is, they refute themselves. But we have suggested that this is not quite as devastating as it seems. The relativist can retain the spirit of his position without having to expose himself to the judo-flip. He does so by pouring cold water on the idea of reason as a kind of divinity, an external or alien authority guiding our minds. For this he substitutes rules of our own making, ways of carrying on which we privilege, perhaps only at particular places and times.

In the same way, he sidesteps the problem of the moving bull's-eye, by allowing in some socially constructed standards, something less than the absolutist's real thing. *Logos* is silent, and all opinions whatever are *logos*-symmetrical, but we have a serviceable substitute, he suggests, in norms and standards of our own making.

3

Ishmael's Problem and the Delights of Keeping Quiet

The human spirit (in its different dispositions in different men) is a variable thing, quite irregular, almost haphazard. Heraclitus well said that men seek knowledge in lesser, private worlds, not in the great or common world.

Francis Bacon, *The New Organon*, XLII, p. 41

1. Who Tells the Tale?

The relativist survived Plato's recoil argument. He also survived the charge that he is pretending to keep the concept of true judgement when all he has really left us is a world with just noise in it, but no judgement at all: the charge represented by the moving bull's-eye. He did this by substituting earth-bound human processes for the eternal laws of right reason. But he has to avoid yet another danger, the one we saw dangling in front of Sextus. He must not exempt his own position from the status he accords to others. He cannot shelter behind what the Australian philosopher David Stove nicely called the 'Ishmael effect'. At the end of Melville's novel *Moby Dick* the ship is rammed by the whale and sunk in the middle of the Southern Ocean. And telling of this the narrator, Ishmael, says that 'I alone escaped to tell the tale' – something that, given the tale he tells, it was impossible for him to have done. Equally, a relativist cannot say that all human beliefs are subjective – except the belief that all human beliefs are subjective. He cannot exempt himself from the fate to which he condemns others. But according to critics, this is what he is trying to do.

The canny Greek sceptics actually foresaw this charge. Sextus knew that his opponents (the dogmatists, usually Stoics) would sneer that he was trying to produce proofs that there are no such things as proofs, and was therefore caught in inconsistency. But rightly he was unperturbed. He could simply admit that the argument represents how things appear to him now; he could record how he is inclined to come to *epoche* or suspension of judgement, leaving it for others to work out how it strikes them. He need claim no greater status for his own argument than the diminished status that he offers to any other. And, dialectically, en route to refuting his opponents, he can say that the dogmatists are the ones who are really in trouble, since they want their certainties, and among them the very principles that are involved in Sextus's own arguments. However, when they are followed through properly, those principles disprove the dogmatists' certainties, so this puts the dogmatists themselves in an inconsistent position.

But the idea that there is something self-undermining about the relativist or sceptical tradition dies hard. So here is another major contemporary philosopher, Thomas Nagel, considering the claim that *logos* is silent. Nagel complains that any claim as radical and universal as that would have to be supported by a powerful argument, but the claim itself seems to leave us without the capacity for such arguments. The judgement he considers is the relativistic claim that our logical, mathematical and empirical reasonings 'manifest historically contingent and culturally local habits of thought and have no wider validity than that'.

Or is the judgment supposed to apply to itself? I believe that would leave us without the possibility of thinking anything at all. Claims to the effect that a type of judgment expresses a local point of view are inherently objective in intent: They suggest a picture of the true sources of those judgments which places them in an unconditional context. The judgment of relativity or conditionality cannot be applied to the judgment of relativity itself. To put it schematically, the claim 'Everything is subjective' must be nonsense, for it would itself have to be either subjective or objective. But it can't be objective, since in that case it would be false if true. And it can't be subjective, because then it would not rule out any objective claim, including the claim that it is objectively false. There may be some subjectivists, perhaps styling themselves as pragmatists, who present subjectivism as applying even to itself. But then it does not call for a reply, since it is just a report of what the subjectivist finds it agreeable to say. If he also invites us to join him, we need not offer any reason for declining, since he has offered us no reason to accept.[1]

This is a puzzling passage in several respects, but let us begin at the end. Nagel says that the subjectivist or relativist has offered us no reason to accept his position. But is that right? Relativists typically do advance reasons for their view: we have already mentioned two central kinds of reason. The first is the variation of subjectivities, and the second is the problem of status, of understanding what Plato's heaven could be, or in other words what could even be meant by the reign of *logos*. Why does Nagel think that relativists do not advance reasons for their position?

And, moving back, we should also worry about Nagel's view that if the claim of subjectivity (here taken as equivalent to relativism) applies to itself, then 'it would not rule out any objective claim, including the claim that it is objectively false'. The problem with this is seeing how it is supposed to upset the relativist. For, put in these terms, his view is that there *aren't* any objective claims (*logos* is silent). It cannot then be an objection that he fails to 'rule them out', any more than it is an objection to the quality of my boundary fencing that it fails to keep out unicorns. According to the relativist, when Nagel says that the relativist position is false, that is an expression of Nagel's subjectivity. If Nagel adds the words 'objectively false', then the relativist simply sees theatrical costume, a flimsy disguise for the subjectivity beneath (we get another glimpse here why these issues attract swirls of emotion). It is as if Nagel is saying: I simply won't listen to anyone unless they have *logos* on their side. And the relativist replies that in that case Nagel will not be listening to anyone, so it is no skin off his nose that Nagel won't listen to him, the relativist.

Quite apart from Sextus's own rebuttal of this kind of argument, a similar relativist response to an argument like Nagel's was in fact given nearly a century before by the pragmatist William James (we discuss pragmatism later). In James's setting the pragmatist or relativist is urging an account of truth as no more than truth-as-we-measure-it or truth-for-us. James knows he is going to be opposed by the argument that he is sheltering behind the Ishmael effect, standing where he says there is nowhere to stand. And he meets it with the splendidly spirited reply:

But can there be self-stultification in urging any account whatever of truth? Can the definition ever contradict the deed? 'Truth is what I feel like saying' – suppose that to be the definition. 'Well, I feel like saying that, and I want you to feel like saying it, and shall continue to say it until I get you to agree.' Whatever truth may be said to be, that is the kind of truth which the saying can be held to carry.[2]

In fact, he should have gone one further. To preserve consistency, whatever truth may be said to be, that is the kind of truth which the saying *must* be held to carry. In principle, indeed, it is possible that there should be just one belief forced by *logos*, and it should be the belief that no other beliefs are forced by *logos*. But this is surely indefensible: the Ishmael problem shouts at it. Why should this be the only belief that escapes the fate to which all the others are condemned? In fact, it seems a particularly unlikely candidate for an Ishmael-like exemption. If cherished results of reason, such as 'two plus two equals four' or 'if one event precedes another and the second event precedes a third, then the first event precedes the third', do not qualify for baptism by *logos*, then delicate and contested claims about the status of judgement and truth themselves are hardly likely to be better candidates. So I think we can safely say that James should go one step further. Whatever truth may be said to be, that is the kind of truth which the saying *must* be held to carry.

So, as James admits, the relativist must accept for his own doctrine, the Measure Doctrine or the claim of *logos*-symmetry, just whatever status he thinks remains once *logos* has gone silent. But then, as James also asks, where is the problem in that?

Here there surfaces a dangerous opportunity for the two sides to talk past each other. People of an absolutist disposition, such as Nagel expresses in the passage above, see relativism as essentially a *wrecking* position. It is supposed to undermine cherished categories of reason, objectivity and truth. And so they insist that once relativism applies to itself, it goes down with the wreck. It cannot escape the fate to which it condemns everything else.

To the relativist ear, all this is pointless abuse. To the relativist, relativism should not be a wrecking position. By insisting that all opinion is equal in the sight of *logos*, it merely strips away false masks and false statuses. So indeed it should stand naked and unashamed, with no more but no fewer dignities than it accords to any other human saying.

For an example of the twists and turns here, consider the position Bernard Williams called anthropological relativism or vulgar relativism in ethics, which is supposed to fall into the same trap.[3] This position starts from the observation that different societies accept somewhat different ethical standards – the variation of subjectivities. From this observation, together perhaps with some thoughts about what truth in moral matters could be, it concludes that none of standards is more 'right' than any other. It then further infers that because of this we have an absolute duty of toleration and non-interference, and must leave other societies to pursue their own paths, however repugnant we may find them. This overall package is straightforwardly inconsistent. The interim conclusion, that there is no absolute right or wrong, contradicts the subsequent conclusion, that there is an absolute duty of toleration and non-interference.

But why should anyone buy the overall package? A Jamesian repair is to hand. To restore consistency, the relativist just has to back down, presenting his conclusion without the word 'absolute' inserted. He does not want that: he just wants us to admit that we have a duty of toleration and non-interference. Now, to those of an absolutist disposition, it will appear that if we drop that word, then there is no reason, no 'real' reason as they might say, for the toleration and non-interference. The rug, they think, has been pulled out from under everything, including the obligation to tolerate others. But for the relativist this is not at all how it stands. He now presents the duty of non-interference not as an 'absolute' duty (enforced by *logos*), but just as a consequence that we here, or we in the West, or he himself or his audience, draw from the data about variations of standards. In James's terms, this is what he feels like saying, and he wants you to feel like saying it too, and perhaps he is prepared to preach and proselytize until you do. And very likely his plea will fall on sympathetic ears, for it probably is part of our current subjectivity that unless we think we can 'prove' to people that they are wrong, we have no business trying to get them to change their ways.

James himself insisted, surely correctly, that 'the *temper* which the relativist may show is an extra logical matter', meaning that there is no inconsistency in going on to campaign, perhaps fiercely, for the relativistic stand, and similarly there is no inconsistency in going on to campaign for the toleration and non-interference, if those appeal to us as consequences of the relativistic stand. Of course, it will indeed not be 'absolutely' true that they are consequences, but we may be minded to draw them, all the same.

At this point, the Jamesian relativist, if we can call him that without slandering James himself, is *practically* or *ethically* on a slightly different course from his Greek predecessors. For them, it was an admirable consequence of their scepticism that they lost conviction, lost enthusiasm as it were for holding one opinion rather than another. With *epoche* or suspension of judgement came the desired *ataraxia* or tranquillity. James is more strenuous, less inclined to give up the hurly-burly of ethics and politics. Not for him the country retreat of the sage.

If we now return to Nagel's passage, we should find that the ending is doubly problematic. The relativist has presented reasons as he understands them for his position, namely, he has provided words that, given the structure of our subjectivities, will sway us or might sway us towards saying what he says. To make this clear, we need labels for the different conceptions of reasoning on offer. So we can say that the relativist has provided what he conceives of as R-reasons, meaning reasons as the relativist conceives of them. The absolutist may hold that this is not his conception of reasons, not the real McCoy, not real reasons, which we can call A-reasons. Similarly the absolutist holds out for A-truth and A-belief, where you A-believe something when you hold it to be A-true. The relativist, of course, denies that we should work in those terms. There are only R-reasons, R-truth and R-belief. So now we have two different conceptions of what the relativist is up to when he gives his arguments. But it is premature for the absolutist to complain that he has not been given A-reasons for anything. In the context of this argument it is up to him to decide that. The relativist indeed presented what he himself took to be R-reasons (the sceptics of the last chapter present how things appear to them). If the absolutist gets struck, as the relativist hopes he will, by considerations such as the variation of subjectivities, or the difficulty of conceiving of Plato's heaven, then at the beginning he will suppose himself to be thinking of these difficulties as A-reasons for changing his mind about the status of truth and reason. For he thinks of all good reasons as A-reasons, and these reasons strike him as rather good. But then after he has changed his mind, he will then stop thinking in terms of A-reasons and A-truth. He will smoothly put aside the old conceptions, and begin to fit himself to the new ones. And from then on he will also think of his conversion differently. He will reevaluate it in the same terms as the relativist whom he has now joined. But the process is still the same in any event, and for all he has said thus far, it may result in an improvement.

It is like this: imagine a theistic absolutist, who works in terms of God's truth and reasoning as God would approve of it: G-truth and G-reasons. Nothing less will do. But he hears someone arguing against these notions, in fact against God altogether. Can he dismiss this point of view without listening to it? Well, he can, of course, but he may not be within his rights to do so. He may find that the heretic offers what seem rather good G-reasons for his position – perhaps as good as any other G-reasoning the theist has ever heard on the subject. He may then find himself getting convinced that there are no G-reasons and no G-truth, and at the end of the process this is how he will think. He will himself see the movements of his mind in the lesser terms, but, by then, he will see that as a gain. He has thrown off an illusion, and that is a gain, not a loss.

It is useful to think of all the varieties of the recoil argument in these terms. The absolutist is trying to show that somehow, in spite of himself, the relativist is bound to be involved with A-reasons and A-truth. This is because he sees everyday processes, such as the giving of reasons or a change of opinion, in these terms. And so he projects them on to his opponent and claims a quick victory, since his opponent is then revealed as inconsistent. The absolutist arguing like this is just like the theist who holds that whatever they say or think they believe, atheists really believe in God just like he does. He sees acknowledgement of God lying in everyday activities, such as avoiding lies or keeping promises. And then he can convict the decent atheist, who indeed avoids lies and keeps promises, of being steeped in God, up to his eyeballs, only refusing to acknowledge it. But in each case the victory is entirely hollow, for the atheist, and equally the relativist, simply rejects the interpretation of what he is doing that the theist or the absolutist offers. And he may be perfectly within his rights to do so. At least, if he is not, it will require more than the recoil argument or the need to avoid Ishmael's predicament to show it. It will require the hard work of showing that A-concepts are indeed unavoidable. It would mean showing that something beyond R-substitutes must form and guide our reasonings.

So when the absolutist complains that something is lost, the relativist can afford to laugh. He hears no criticism. What was lost was only a phantom, or only the masks and props with which the absolutist tries to avoid confronting the human reality. And the full-scale, Protagorean relativist thinks this is not only true of heavily contested areas like morals, but everywhere.

To see how plausible this might be, consider a case where there sounds to be something rather obviously right about cultural relativism. We know a good deal about our perceptions of fashion and their harmless variations over time and place – harmless, at least, if we abstract from evils such as the subordination of women or the valorization of vanity or anorexia. We freely suppose that the judgement that some style of clothing is chic or cool is contingent and conditioned and altogether dependent upon a cultural matrix that constantly changes. We, of course, see certain clothes of our time as chic and cool, and we see those, say, of the nineteen-seventies as gross; and we know enough to realize that could they have seen our fashions, the people of the nineteen-seventies, with their nineteen-seventies eyes, would have seen just the reverse. I cannot share those eyes, so there is a sense in which this symmetry claim is 'transcendental'. The two views are not equally available to us; it is not possible to flip from the one mode of perception to the other. But there is no inconsistency here, and if inconsistency enters when the relativist tries to generalize the model, we still have not been shown where it is.

There is one way in which you cannot transcend the way you see things, certainly. You cannot see fashion with nineteen-seventies eyes, and you cannot see the end of the rainbow except as in that field, there, but you can know all the time that in other eyes and from other positions things are otherwise. Our own slavery to our own subjectivity does not prevent us from noticing the variation in subjectivity that puts relativism on the runway in the first place.

We have been saying so far that in talking of truth and reason, one side, the absolutists, sees robes of state, symbols of authority, the majesty of accordance with *logos*. And the other side sees only props and disguises, delusory Platonic clothing, a mask invented to disguise the real politics of dissent and persuasion. According to the absolutist we need our dignities. We must see ourselves as lovers of the truth and servants of the good, so we must work to make the robes of truth, absolute truth, fit us properly. This is why it takes work, and in Plato's view education and good birth, to exit the Cave and to appreciate the norms or Forms as they need to be appreciated. The relativist reply is all too predictable, and when Plato's guardians return to the Cave, as they do, we can imagine the raspberries blown at them.

As usual in philosophy when conflict is polarized, we might want to worry whether there is a shared mistake each side is making. Here the obvious common factor is the view that truth and its handmaidens are indeed *clothing*, whether masks or robes. But suppose they are not? Less metaphorically, suppose there is nothing in the notion of truth, or even absolute truth, to be contested. Suppose truth is, as it were, too *small* to sustain the battle? This is the beginning, but only the beginning, of the first truce in the truth wars, or if we prefer it, the first intimation that whichever side we were on, we may have been fighting phantoms.

2. A Gestalt Switch

There is one very good reason for thinking this. Consider common sense, and well-established science. On the one hand, it seems absurd, a mere folly, to question the reality of the objects of common sense and of core scientific theory. On the other hand, seeing ourselves as getting things absolutely right might seem to depend upon the idea of a mythical God's-eye view, whereby we step outside our own skins and comment on the extent to which our best theory corresponds with an independent reality. Scepticism about any such idea is famously voiced by Thomas Kuhn, whose work *The Structure of Scientific Revolutions* did much to batter mid-twentieth-century confidence in the objectivity of science and the linear nature of its progress:

There is, I think, no theory-independent way to reconstruct phrases like 'really true'; the notion of a match between the ontology of a theory and its 'real' counterpart in nature now seems to me illusive in principle.[4]

This characterization of 'realism' is found at least from William James to the present. In this way of setting things up the issue of whether theory matches the real world can be judged only from outside theory. But if theory includes all of our best empirical and scientific understanding of the world, then the 'outside' position is necessarily transcendental: we could never get nearer to the feat of occupying it, whatever the length and success of our empirical and theoretical inquiries.

This kind of complaint is often directed at something called 'the correspondence theory of truth'. This is the idea that truth can be understood and explained in terms of correspondence with the facts. It is not merely the idea that 'true' *means* 'corresponds with the facts'; that may just be a harmless synonym. It makes no difference whether you say that the witness was unreliable, or that what he said failed to correspond with the facts. But for the phrase to work as a philosophical explanation of truth, more is needed. It is needed that 'corresponds' means something on its own, and 'facts' are identifiable in some special way, and then we can put them together and see correspondence with the facts as a special kind of success. And then it is argued that this requires exactly the idea of 'stepping outside your own skin' – on the one hand making a judgement, and on the other hand obtaining a God's-eye or 'sideways' view of both the judgement and the facts, and measuring how well they match.

Well, what is wrong with that? Philosophers of an absolutist or 'realist' temper often like to compare the art of the theorist with the art of the map-maker. The analogy has many virtues, and I shall be exploiting some of them later. And you *can* go and check a map against a landscape. You can find that a cartographer was more or less accurate, more or less thorough, more or less honest about the extent of his knowledge, and more or less diligent in his observations. There is, similarly, the activity of checking theory against observation. This is how science advances. But what Kuhn disliked was *not* this everyday processes of observation, nor, of course, the idea that these are integral to good empirical scientific research. What he disliked was the idea that this checking can be conducted *without* the use of our best theories and best understandings. It is this idea of a distinct point of view on ourselves, taken as it were en bloc, a measurement of how well we are doing, such as God might make, that is to be avoided.

According to one of his pupils, Professor Elizabeth Anscombe, Wittgenstein was fond of a German saying that translates as 'You cannot shit higher than your arse', which encapsulates the same point.

The point comes better into view when we think of an example. Currently the temperature of the earth's atmosphere is a cause of great anxiety to many people. It is measured in several ways. Ordinary mercury thermometers scattered around the land surfaces of the earth are one. Measurements of microwave energies of oxygen molecules by satellites passing over regions of the atmosphere are another, since physical theory holds that such energies vary exactly with temperature. Then there are radio balloons with their own instruments, and a great number of other 'proxies': tree-ring growth, or the ratio of deposit of various isotopes in ice samples, for example, which are used to measure historical temperatures. When the measurements do not agree we know that something has gone wrong, but we may not know what. When this is our situation, there is no 'skyhook' – no way of peeking round the corner, looking over our own shoulders, asking God – and discovering what the temperature really is, or what it really once was, independently of the techniques of observation that are on trial. We can soldier on, perhaps with new theories and new techniques, if we can discover them, and that is all.

3. You Tell Me, or Down with Pilate

Perhaps these thoughts knock firmly on the head the very idea of a comparison between our best theories and the truth. Any useful idea of 'correspondence with the facts' becomes thought of as naive and simplistic. Then, in some circles, any talk of truth will sound suspect. It is felt to be a notion that only absolutists like: all truth is A-truth, and if we do not like that notion, we must do without truth itself. People sneer at notions such as the historical truth, let alone the moral or the aesthetic truth. Richard Rorty once said that only old-fashioned metaphysical prigs talk of truth any more. But this reaction might also be a mistake.

For in our everyday practices of advancing claims and then either accepting or rejecting them, we do not raise the temperature by talking of truth. If someone tells me that the price of petrol is rising, and I reply 'that's true' or 'that's right', I am simply expressing agreement. I am not suddenly doing metaphysics, or taking sides with Plato against Protagoras. I am not trespassing against Wittgenstein's injunction not to try to 'shit higher than your arse'. I am not even adding an extra pat on the back to the original remark, any more than someone who, like the tabloid press, tells me that the price of petrol is rising and then adds 'And that's a fact!' really adds anything to the first piece of information. If I don't believe the original remark, I can say that it is not true, or that we have to wait and see. If I do this, then we have to set about determining whether the price of petrol is rising, and it may turn out either way. We do not *in addition* have a different question on our plate, namely, whether it is true that the price of petrol is rising. Our only problem is set by what we say. It is the issue that is the issue.

Why does this make a difference to the debate? The idea is that the battle between the absolutist and the relativist is sustained by a conviction that there are two issues, when in fact there is only one.

For this battle to be joined, there must first be an ordinary issue, say, whether the price of petrol is rising. But second there is a further, philosophical or reflective (second-order) issue: whether there is a truth of the matter, or an absolute or 'real' truth of the matter, that the price of petrol is rising. The absolutist says yes, but apparently at the cost of buying into a mysterious world of norms and Forms, or a mysterious unmeasurable relationship between our sayings and the truth. The relativist will not pay this cost, and so says no. But now we meet someone who is deaf to their problem. There is only the issue of whether the price of petrol is rising, full stop. If we hammer this out, and decide one way or the other, then we do not increase the theoretical temperature by adding 'what's more, that's true'. This just repeats whichever conclusion we came to: that the price of petrol is (or is not) rising, which is the issue with which we started.

People who think that the last paragraph expresses just about everything we need to know about truth are called minimalists or quietists.[5] They think we should leave truth alone. We should not enter the fields of meta-theory or philosophical reflection, to try to say something more, to gain a 'conception' of truth, as both absolutists and relativists have been presented as doing.

We might put the attractions of minimalism in terms of explanation. Suppose we think it is true that the price of petrol is rising, and true that Tony Blair is a fantasist. Someone might ask: what is in common here? What explains why each of these is true? To the minimalist, this would be like asking why each passenger is on an aircraft. You can ask it if you wish, but there may be no one answer applicable to all. You can ask it individually, one by one, but then you may well get a different reason in each case. There need be no one reason covering all of them. There might be, if they are all flying to the same conference, for example. But there need not be. And in the case of our assertions, there cannot be. For whenever we say different things, different things also make them true.

So a good way of thinking of minimalism and its attractions is to see it as substituting the particular for the general. It mistrusts anything abstract or windy. Both the relativist and the absolutist are impressed by Pilate's notorious question 'What is Truth?', and each tries to say something useful at the same high and vertiginous level of generality. The minimalist can be thought of turning his back on this abstraction, and then in any particular case he prefaces his answer with the prior injunction: *you tell me*. This does not mean, 'You tell me what truth is.' It means, 'You tell me what the issue is, and I will tell you (although you will already know, by then) what the truth about the issue consists in.' If the issue is whether high tide is at midday, then truth consists in high tide being at midday. If the issue is whether Blair is a fantasist, the truth lies in Blair being a fantasist or not. We can tell you what truth amounts to, if you first tell us what the issue is. But to do *that* you must already know enough to be able to say what truth amounts to yourself. If you don't know what the truth of the matter consists in, then you cannot have really framed and understood an issue at all.

The *point* of these disappointing-sounding minimalist responses is not to tell us something we did not know. We *knew* that this kind of answer could come along, just as soon as we understood the issue. The *point* is to discourage us from looking for anything more general, anything, as it were, that there might be in common between Blair being a fantasist and high tide being at midday. These are different things, judged in different ways, and need have nothing in common. They do not share a subject matter, do not say the same thing about different subject matters, and are not established in anything like the same way. And so it is across the whole spectrum of judgement. We can say, of course, that each judgement is true, if that is how we think. But saying that is no more than saying that Blair is a fantasist and high tide is at midday. It is not coming across some shining absolute property, nor some dark and socially constructed, sinister property, that they share.

There is a very powerful argument for minimalism about truth, due to the great logician Gottlob Frege.[6] First, we should notice the *transparency* property of truth. This is the fact that it makes no difference whether you say that it is raining, or it is true that it is raining, or true that it is true that it is raining, and so on for ever. But if 'it is true that' introduced some substantial, robust property of a judgement, how could this be so? Consider, for example, a pragmatism that attempts some equation between truth and utility. Then next to the judgement 'it is raining' we might have 'it is useful to believe that it is raining'. But these are entirely different things! To assess the first we direct our attention to the weather. To assess the second we direct our attention to the results of believing something about the weather – a very different investigation. And if we go further, up to 'it is useful to believe that it is useful to believe that it is raining', we introduce a yet different and more complex claim. These claims are sufficiently different that our verdicts on them might even come apart: it might be useful to believe that it is not raining (e.g. for certain purposes) although it is, and it might be useful to believe that it is useful to believe that it is raining, although in fact it is not useful to believe that it is raining. If William James did think that truth was some kind of expediency, as seemed possible in chapter 1, this refutes him.

In general, a robust or substantial property will introduce a new *topic*, as we ascend from making an initial judgement to making the second-order comment that the initial judgement had the robust property. But the phenomenon of transparency means that there is no new topic introduced by talk of truth. Hence, we have to be minimalists, on pain of distorting our account of our own intellectual practices.

Let us return to Pilate. Where does minimalism about truth leave him? It suggests that when he asked his question, he was *distracting* himself and his audience from his real job, which was to find out whether to uphold certain specific historical charges against a defendant. Thus, if I am innocent, and I come before a judge, I don't want airy generalities about the nature of truth. I want him to find that I did not steal the watch if I did not steal the watch. I want him to rub his nose in the issue. I want a local judgement about a local or specific event, supposed to have happened in a particular region of time and space. It might be that the charge against me is badly drawn, so there is no one issue or no clear issue, in which case there is no such thing as the issue to be settled, and the case should be dropped and I should get off. But otherwise, there is an issue, and it is the duty of the judge to rub his nose in it. Of course, if I am guilty I might be relieved if the judge amuses himself with distractions instead, and I might hope my counsel can confuse him enough to make him do so.

If we feel like making peace, we might concede that in the original, polarized debate, each got something right and each got something wrong. Let me take a difficult moral issue to make this plain. Suppose we are discussing the rights and wrongs of capital punishment. Then the Platonist or absolutist was right that it takes some work to decide whether capital punishment should be allowed. It requires thinking hard about rights, revenge, deterrence and the powers of the State, and these are confusing and contested matters. It is not a judgement that ought to come tripping off the tongue. The relativist was right that anyone's verdict on such a matter will be a function of a good many factors in their background, including, for example, recent history, and other cultural determinants of who to admire and what to reject.

But neither of them was right that second-order reflection, focused on worries about truth, either precedes or helps or hinders decision about whether capital punishment should be allowed. To come to an opinion about that, your gaze must be firmly fixed on capital punishment and the confused factors suggesting either that it is, or is not, a process to advocate. And once you have thought about such matters, you may be inclined to take a stand. You might then say that capital punishment should not be allowed. Or, for it is the same thing: it is true that capital punishment should not be allowed. Or: it is really true, a fact, that capital punishment should not be allowed. Or: capital punishment should not be allowed; you had better believe it. Or even: it corresponds to the eternal normative order that capital punishment should not be allowed. For none of these says any more than what you started with. We might have thought there was an ascending ladder here, with ever more bold theoretical claims made at each stage But the ladder – which I like to call Ramsey's ladder, in honour of one of the first philosophers to see these things clearly, Frank Ramsey of Cambridge – is horizontal. It takes you nowhere. There is no more and no less involved at the last stage than at the first.

One consequence of minimalism is that it is no longer *important* to insist that 'there is such a thing as moral truth'. Anybody can say that. All you do is find a moral remark you stand by. Assert it. And then say: there is an example, for *that*'s a moral truth. This does not raise the temperature at all. Ramsey's ladder being horizontal, there is no different or better view of anything gained by climbing it.

There is a tendency to think it is terribly important to assert or deny that there is such a thing as moral truth, and even that it has implications for such matters as politics or law. If this were so, it would have to be because minimalism is wrong. The one thing you should not do is protect your right to talk of moral truth via minimalism, and then insist that it is terribly significant and important that there are moral truths.

In morality whatever is different conflicts. And minimalism does nothing to diminish the chance of moral conflict. It does not help us to decide issues just one way. So it does little to reassure us about *the* moral truth, the *right* normative order, the operating manual of the universe. In science we expect convergence on the one true theory of this and that (not necessarily the one true theory of everything, which strikes most of us as too ambitious). In ethics we do not, and for this reason we can expect relativism to stay in business.

4. *Moral Relativism*

However, minimalism does give us the germ of an answer to moral relativism, the most tempting application of Protagoras in the contemporary world.[7] So suppose I believe that foxhunting is cruel and should be banned. And then I come across someone (Genghis, let us call him) who holds that it is not cruel, and should be allowed. We dispute, and perhaps neither of us can convince the other. Suppose now a relativist (Rosie) comes in, and mocks our conversation. 'You absolutists,' she says, 'always banging on as if there is just one truth. What you don't realize is that there is a plurality of truths. It's true for you that foxhunting should be banned – but don't forget that it's true for Genghis that it should not.'

How does Rosie's contribution help? Indeed, what does it mean? 'It's true for me that hunting should be banned' just means that I believe that hunting should be banned. And the opposite thing said about Genghis just means that he believes the opposite. But we already knew that: *that*'s why we are in disagreement! Perhaps Rosie is trying to get us to see that there is no real disagreement. But how can that be so? I want people to aim at one outcome, that hunting be banned, and Genghis wants another. At most one of us can succeed, and I want it to be me. Rosie cannot stop us from seeing each other as opponents.

Perhaps Rosie is trying to get us to respect and tolerate each other's point of view. But why should I respect and tolerate another point of view *simply* on the grounds that someone else holds it? I already have my suspicions of Genghis: in my book he is already looking cruel and insensitive, so why should his point of view be 'tolerated'? And in any case, I should be suspicious of any encouragement to toleration here. The whole point of my position is that hunting should not be tolerated – it should be banned. Tolerating Genghis's point of view is too near to tolerating Genghis's hunting, which I am not going to do.

Rosie has to avoid skating on the thin ice we have already mentioned. She has to avoid the Ishmael problem. Suppose she gets ruffled by what I have just written: 'Look,' she says, 'you must learn that Genghis is a human being like you; respect and toleration of his views and his activities, are essential. If you did not fetishize absolute truth you would see that.' I, on the other hand, say that 'toleration of Genghis is just soggy; it is time to take a stand'. If Rosie thumps the table and says that tolerating Genghis is *really* good, then isn't she sounding just like the fetishists she mocked? She has taken the fact that there are no absolute values to justify elevating toleration into an absolute value.

Rosie has to avoid that contradiction (and we gave her space to do so, above). So perhaps she needs to say that she has her truth (tolerating Genghis is good) and I have mine (tolerating Genghis is bad) and that's the end of it. But that amounts to bowing out of the conversation, leaving Genghis and me to go on arguing exactly as before. In practice, Rosie's intervention hasn't helped at all. She hasn't made foxes, or those who hunt them, look one jot more or less likeable. Her intervention seems just to have been a distraction.

Perhaps Rosie wanted to stop the conversation: she is like someone asking, 'Will you two just stop bickering?' This can be a good thing to say. Some conversations are pointless. If you and I are in an art gallery, and I say Rembrandt is better than Vermeer and you say Vermeer is better than Rembrandt, and we start bickering about it, the best advice may well be that we stop. Perhaps we can agree to differ, because nothing practical hangs on our different taste. It is not as if we have enough money to buy just one, and I want it to be one and you want it to be the other. (On the other hand, it does not follow that our conversation is *useless*. We might be forcing each other to look closer and see things we would otherwise have missed, or to reconsider what we find valuable about art in general.)

But however it may be in the art gallery, in moral issues we often cannot agree to differ. Agreeing to differ with Genghis is in effect agreeing to tolerate foxhunting, and my whole stance was against that. Moral issues are frequently ones where we want to coordinate, and where we are finding what to forbid and what to allow. Naturally, the burden falls on those who want to forbid: in liberal societies, freedom is the default. But this cannot be a carte blanche for any kind of behaviour, however sickening or distressful or damaging. It is just not true that anything goes. So conversation has to go on about what to allow and what to forbid. Again, Rosie is not helping: she seems just to be a distraction.

So why do people like to chip in with remarks like 'It's all relative' or 'I suppose it depends on your point of view'? What you *say* of course depends on your point of view, and whether another person agrees with it depends on their point of view. But the phrase is dangerous, and can be misleading. The spatial metaphor of points of view might be taken to imply that all points of view are equally 'valid'. After all, there is no one place from which it is right to look at the Eiffel tower, and indeed no one place that is better than another, except for one purpose or another. But when it comes to our commitments, we cannot think this. If I believe that O. J. Simpson murdered his wife, then I cannot at the same time hold that the point of view that he did not is equally good. It follows from my belief that anyone who holds he did not murder his wife is wrong. They may be excusable, but they are out of touch or misled or thinking wishfully or badly placed to judge. I have hit a bull's-eye, which they have missed.

It is only if I do not hold a belief at all, but am just indulging in an idle play of fancy, that I can admit that an inconsistent fancy is equally good. If I like fancying Henry VIII to have been a disguised Indian, I am not in opposition to someone who enjoys fancying him to have been Chinese. But that's just the difference between fiction, where the brakes are off, and history, where they are on.

If relativism, then, is often just a distraction, is it a valuable one or a dangerous one? I think it all depends. Sometimes we need reminding of alternative ways of thinking, alternative practices and ways of life, from which we can learn and which we have no reason to condemn. We need to appreciate our differences. Hence, in academic circles, relativism has often been associated with the expansion of literature and history to include alternatives that went unnoticed in previous times. That is excellent. But sometimes we need reminding that there is time to draw a line and take a stand, and that alternative ways of looking at things can be corrupt, ignorant, superstitious, wishful, out of touch or plain evil. It is a moral issue, whether we tolerate and learn or regret and oppose. Rosie the relativist may do well to highlight that decision, but she does not do well to suggest that it always falls out the one way.

We can put the matter in terms of our hidden dark forces. It might undermine either me or Genghis to remind us that we are the products of dark forces in our genetic and cultural environments. It might undermine us to the point that we give up the debate. But there is no reason for it to do so. For even if we accept that this is what we are, there is no reason yet to suppose that my dark forces are worse than Genghis's dark forces. No doubt by luck and by forgotten or unknown pressures in my background, I have got to be like I am, and the same for Genghis. But then the question is: should we be proud or ashamed of how we have turned out? If for a moment we took our eye off the original issue, and started instead to discuss whether the dark forces that lead Genghis to approve of hunting are more or less worthy or admirable than the dark forces that lead me to disapprove of it – well, we are no further forward. To decide which dark forces were the ones to be proud of is pretty much the same as deciding whether foxhunting should be banned, and back we go to the original problem. Once more, the relativist intervention was just a distraction, and the issue remains the issue.

5. Man the Measurer

In the last chapter we used the doctrine that man is the measure to introduce the vision of man as an instrument taking inputs and delivering outputs, but for which any conception of success or failure, truth or falsity, correctness or incorrectness is stripped away, leaving us only sameness or difference of output for a given input. But measuring implies a little more than simply responding, passively, as it were, in the same way as an instrument responds to a causal flux. Measuring in the human world is an activity with a purpose and a result, and it can be pursued more or less successfully. We may *react* to photons bombarding our eyes, or sound waves bombarding our ears. Reaction is a casual notion: it depends on forces impinging upon us, including perhaps the Queen's dark forces.

But what we *measure* are aspects of the world of which we are aware. Measuring is an activity, under the control of reason and intelligence. Indeed, one of the things we sometimes measure is whether a mismeasurement has been made – we go back and check, or we think of new instruments or new approaches to the problem.

As the example of the temperature of the atmosphere shows, measuring is a complicated art. Science took great leaps forward when we first measured the circumference of the earth, the distance to the sun or the speed of light. It took judgement, practice, technique, theory and trust in the testimony of others or the readings of instruments.

How does this affect the debate? Well, suppose the issue is a nice one of measurement. What time is high tide at Dover tomorrow? I could have an opinion about that, but unless I have done my homework, it would not be worth much. Homework here means consulting tide tables. Or, if it is my business to produce tide tables it may mean something more direct, such as doing some calculations, or perhaps going down to Dover with a measuring rod and a clock. It is true, of course, that a particularly awkward customer may dislike this measurement process, and it is open to him to argue for another. Like any human process, even simple measurement is fallible and may be conducted more or less well. But at the end of the day either the water stops rising at a given time, or it does not.

Tide tables have their prestige. Good sailors make a point of carrying them. This is not because of social and political machinations, or dark cultural or psychological forces like the grip of myth and superstition, but because they are reliable, and in turn that enables you to do things with them. Were there a competition, a market place for rival tables, success would eventually winnow out those that work from those that do not. Hence, Protagoras got only part of the way. Man indeed makes the measurement, but that does not mean we can conduct the measurement any which way. If we do, our ships run aground, and our projects are thwarted.

When I said above that the issue is the issue, this is what I meant. To make an assertion at all is to put a view into public space, up for acceptance or rejection. That public space will be replete with more-or-less articulate norms determining which things count for acceptance or rejection. In the case of the height of the tide, those norms determine what counts as an answer and what counts as a reason for an answer. There is no question either of putting on a mantle of robes of state, or of seeing the same mantle as nothing but a tawdry prop or mask. There is just the question of when it is high tide at Dover, and our best methods for settling it.

Here, as with ambiguous figures seen first one way and then another, we meet a sudden gestalt switch, a change of view that makes everything look different. We find that the relativist, at first blush a tolerant, relaxed, laid-back, pluralistic kind of person, can suddenly seem to be a kind of monster. If I look it up and say that high tide this afternoon at Dover is at two o'clock, I do not want to be met with the patronizing question 'Who's to say?' or the patronizing response 'That's just your opinion' or 'If that works for you that's great'. That might be appropriate if I had just said something that strongly suggested I was mad, or if I were uttering the sentence in something like the spirit of a poetry recital, not as something to be accepted or rejected, but perhaps as something to be tasted and savoured. But this is not what I am doing when I voice some commitment. I expect my audience to engage with the commitment itself. To hear my saying just as a symptom, perhaps of my class or race or history, is failing to do this. It is regarding me as a patient. It is to think of me, in Peter Strawson's wonderful phrase, as someone to be 'managed or handled or cured or trained'. It is relativism itself that is here dehumanizing.

This is why the 'science wars' generate such heat. The science wars arose when scientists found sociologists and historians of science apparently rubbing a lot of the bloom from the scientific enterprise itself. In good relativistic fashion the sociologists and historians and cultural critics bracketed science's claims to objectivity and truth, and regarded the enterprise purely in an anthropological spirit. Scientists became a tribe whose structures of authority, of peer group acceptance, of prestige and funding, were to be investigated in the same spirit as those of the medicine men of the Azande or the Navajo. This proved not to be an attitude that went down well among people actually engaged with forming scientific opinion, any more than a parallel attitude would go down well with the conscientious navigator directing the vessel out of the harbour.

None of that suggests that real challenge, in a specific context, is impossible. There might be reason for fearing that the tide tables are wrong or were wrongly consulted (they are actually quite difficult to read; it is not impossible to make mistakes). But a real challenge *itself* focuses upon the issue. It needs to put forward a specific doubt about whether the procedures were executed properly, which means in this case whether the sources of information indeed put us in a class with a better chance of being right about high tide than those who have not followed them. But this kind of challenge is essentially local: it is about this issue, here and now. It does not derive from highly abstract reflection on 'the nature of truth'.

The point is that the comparison between man and a measuring device does not have to mean that everything everybody thinks is equally true, 'true for them'. Some measurements and techniques of measurement may be better than others. Perhaps Protagoras had forgotten that. Or perhaps it was his very own point, and Socrates was putting an unfavourable gloss on Protagoras's intentions, as so often happens in debate, and especially when one side writes up how the debate went. But if Protagoras becomes as docile as this, does his relativism disappear entirely? Is there anything left to worry about?

I fear that there is. We have given the minimalist argument that 'it is true that p' and 'p' mean the same. And we may accept the minimalist insistence that the issue is the issue. But we have not shown that minimalism takes *everything*. That is, we have not shown that there is nowhere for reflection to stand. The absolutist and relativist were presented as offering different conceptions of reason. They think of themselves as having distinct and rival conceptions of what is happening when we debate and argue and accept and reject our sayings or those of others. We have not yet shown that there is no room for those different conceptions, nor that their rivalry is bogus.

We have not shown, for instance, that reason has the same nature, the same command, in each area of discourse. We have not shown that cherished truths may not concern the real world at all, but only a world of fictions or imaginings or illusions, 'constructions' of our own making, or denizens of our virtual realities. We have not shown that our cherished ways of carrying on, intellectually, are more obligatory than our cherished ways of carrying on in matters of etiquette or dress.

6. Summary

So far so good. What have these chapters told us, and where have they left us?

First, we have presented the conflict as a conflict about the nature of authority, the authority claimed by words such as truth, rationality, objectivity and knowledge. The absolutist holds out for an authority we christened that of *logos*. The relativist claims that such authority is an illusion: there is no deity and no authority to offer any such stamp of approval.

Second, we have peered into the abyss opened up in front of us by the vision of human beings as nothing more than devices for registering impacts from their environment, and delivering outputs of action, including the saying of words, in ways which may vary one from another. This led to the argument from the variation of subjectivity, but it also led to the problem of the moving bull's-eye.

Then we allowed the relativist to escape this problem. He should not try to maintain both that truth is an achievement and that it is guaranteed by the simple fact of someone's tendency to hold something. This in turn motivates the cunning relativist to admit certain kinds of norms, separating things he wants to say from things he wants to deny. It is just that those norms do not have the awful majesty attached to the authority of *logos*. They are our norms, just as much as the rules of football or chess.

Fourth, we discovered that less lurid kinds of relativism avoid the recoil, the judo-flip. As general doctrines about truth and reason, they must apply to themselves, but with sufficient care they can do this. 'Truth is what contemporary Americans and Europeans let you get away with' is not all right, since as Putnam pointed out it is not itself something that contemporary Americans and Europeans let you get away with, so is not true according to its own standards. If true, then it is not true. But the cunning relativist does not have to say anything so lurid.

We have also discovered the uncomfortable number of ways in which the relativist will insist on inserting subjectivity back into absolutist claims. He will not, it seems, be unduly surprised or discomfited by what he can hear only as absolutist roarings and bawlings. The absolutist cannot win simply by reaching for his cherished words of truth, rationality, objectivity and knowledge. For the relativist is poised to yawn, hearing only subjectively allowed statuses, postures dignified with the constructed masks of authority.

Finally, however, we have begun to sympathize with the minimalist rejection of the whole debate. Perhaps we do not need a conception of truth, but only a conception of the particular truths in the plural, the ones that make issues for us from time to time. If we do this we turn our backs on the Platonist or absolutist and the relativist equally.

We just get on with judging what we have to, as issues arise and become important.

Socrates is usually presented as the ordinary chap, with an ordinary respect for common-sense ways and unvarnished truth. His victory over Protagoras is no more than a small but inevitable triumph for common sense. But writing the dialogue, Plato was not above putting a little metaphor, poetry, rhetoric and spin on what happened. As so often, the victory for unadorned, unvarnished truth needed a quantity of adornment and varnish to be told as it should be. Our own preferred judgement on relativism, that it is a distraction, scarcely gave any victory to absolutism.

So can you, the reader, shut this book now, having learned of a minimalism that sees off the relativist as a distraction, and thereby undercuts the entire debate? Not quite. For minimalism did not address itself to the nature of judgement itself. It did not speak to the kinds of thing we might be doing as we frame our words. And it did not speak to the variation of subjectivities, or the adequacy of our words themselves or the ways they might let us down. If you thought that *logos* was silent before, you may still think it now.

Neither have we done much to halt the contemporary stampede to weird faiths and strange cults. Consider the issue of whether flying saucers abduct people, which so exercises the minds of many. We can now talk unblushingly of this in terms of its truth or falsity. But we have not done much to help believers to put the brakes on, get the epistemology straight or listen to reason. We have not done much to help Clifford or silence James. To pursue this further we must turn to the looming icon of postmodernism and the most significant modern descendant of Protagoras: Friedrich Nietzsche. And although Nietzsche is a frequent target of recoil arguments and seems highly vulnerable to the Ishmael problem, we have not shown in advance that he is making a flap about nothing.

4

Nietzsche: the Arch Debunker

Men associate through talk; and words are chosen to suit the understanding of the common people. And thus a poor and unskilful code of words incredibly obstructs the understanding. The definitions and explanations with which learned men have been accustomed to protect and in some way liberate themselves, do not restore the situation at all. Plainly words do violence to the understanding, and confuse everything; and betray men into countless empty disputes and fictions.

Francis Bacon, *The New Organon*, XLIII, p. 42

1. Facts or Interpretations?

In the Introduction I remarked that the saying 'There are no facts, only interpretations' could serve as a motto for the relativist movement. It comes from late notes of Friedrich Nietzsche, probably the greatest figurehead for that tendency since Protagoras.[1] We jump to Nietzsche rather than following the historical course of ancient and modern scepticisms, for several reasons. First Nietzsche, more than any philosopher from the nineteenth century or before, is still with us. He is currently the most influential of the great philosophers. It is an axiom of many academic schools and programmes that he has something supremely important to tell us about truth. He is the patron saint of postmodernism. But secondly, the bewildering varieties of Nietzsche interpretations perfectly illustrate the battles of the last two chapters. He appears quite wilfully to put himself in the firing line for a self-refutation charge, or the charge of sailing in Ishmael's boat. And the interpretive problem is worse given that he entirely throws over the sober conventions of philosophical writing. Reading him can feel like listening to a great drunken bellow, a huge gust of wind attempting to blow down ancient forests, including those that shelter the rest of us. And one of the shelters he rattles is the shelter of truth. But which direction is the gale blowing from?

Above all other modern philosophers, including Wittgenstein, Nietzsche is irresistibly quotable. Seeing disguise and falsity as endemic to human nature, the weapons that in our case substitute for teeth and claws, he writes:

In man this art of simulation reaches its peak: here deception, flattering, lying and cheating, talking behind the back, posing, living in borrowed splendor, being masked, the disguise of convention, acting a role before others and before oneself – in short the constant fluttering around the single flame of vanity is so much the rule and the law that almost nothing is more incomprehensible than how an honest and pure urge for truth could have arisen among men. They are deeply immersed in illusions and dream images; their eye glides only over the surface of things and sees 'forms'; their feeling nowhere leads into truth, but contents itself with the reception of stimuli, playing, as it were, a game of blind man's buff on the backs of things.[2]

At first sight this is a fine expression of what is known as Nietzsche's denial of truth. And of course, it opens him to the charge of self-refutation, via some version of the recoil argument. Nietzsche holds or believes, and he wants us to hold or believe, that there is no truth. But as we saw in the last chapter, to hold or believe anything is plausibly just the same as holding or believing that it is true. And you cannot consistently present it as true that there are no truths. Nor can you sensibly join Ishmael, and condemn as false all other sayings than the saying that there is no other truth than this one – the saying that everything else is false. 'Truths are illusions that we have forgotten are illusions,' says Nietzsche in the same essay. Well then, is it true that truths are illusions, or is that too an illusion, in which case why say it?

He is also liable to less direct recoil arguments, when his confident pronouncements about the presence of illusion jar with the fact that if illusion were as universal as he thought then he could be in no position to proclaim it. Knowing a mistake implies knowing the truth. Again, there is an uncomfortable air of an Ishmaelite self-exemption around.

It is not just immediate self-refutation that faces Nietzsche. In his philosophy as a whole there are many assertions about the world and about human life and human nature. Nietzsche is most famous as a culture critic, and in the course of his criticism he maintains many specific things. He holds that Christianity is a slave morality, founded in the resentment of the weak or ignoble in face of the superior powers of the strong or noble. He holds that the idea of personal immortality is *impertinent*.[3] He holds that the French revolution was a gruesome farce.[4] He holds that even powerful people bowed before saints, but only because they recognized an equivalent power, so that 'they honoured something in themselves when they honoured the saint'.[5] He holds that in a commercial culture a person appraises things according to the reactions of the consumer, even in order to determine their value in his own eyes.[6] There are hundreds of other comments on culture and morality and history, quite apart from the highly general doctrines for which he is most famous, such as the omnipresence of the will to power. In sum, Nietzsche comes across as one of the most opinionated men of all time. He had no volume control, let alone a mute button, so it is only his extraordinary acuteness that stops him qualifying as the pub bore of philosophy. And although some of his sayings may have the status of aphorisms – tossed off to stimulate thought rather than as representations of how things are – clearly in many cases Nietzsche advances these assertions as true.

And even aphorisms betray presuppositions. You cannot say that English philosophers are vulgar and the French do no better than imitate them, even as an aphorism, unless you believe that there are places such as England and France and that philosophers have lived there. Furthermore, even when we find Nietzsche delighting in self-contradiction, first putting forward *p* and then putting forward its negation, not-*p*, this is far from proving a postmodernist contempt for truth. It is just as plausibly the work of someone who cares passionately about truth, but by tossing the reader to-and-fro confronts him with the insecurity in his own grasp of it. And in many places Nietzsche actively asserts the existence of truths and of methods for determining them: he says, for example, that the personal strife of thinkers at last led to procedures 'so acute that truths really could be discovered and the aberrations of earlier procedures exposed for all to see'.[7]

How can he coherently say these things while at the same time railing against truth? Is he as badly off as the historian in chapter 2, who said that historians have discovered that there is no historical truth?

This question of self-refutation is the central problem in attempting to understand Nietzsche. One option, obviously, is to suppose that he was simply inconsistent. Perhaps he courted paradox as a prick to understanding. Or perhaps he was caught in some kind of unfinished business. So, for instance, the German philosopher Martin Heidegger thought that Nietzsche tried to deny what Heidegger calls Being, which is a grounding for life and thought, something like the *logos* of chapter 2.[8] Heidegger however wanted to insist on the importance of seeing human beings as tending the flame of Being, which may be more or less disclosed or withdrawn at any given time. Indeed, one of the reasons people enter the purgatory of trying to read Heidegger is because they join him in fearing that in a modern, frenetic, technological, consumerist age Being is pretty much absconded and keeping itself hidden. We have left the Garden of Eden. Nietzsche is second to nobody as a culture critic, but we are about to see that he also blows raspberries at Being, so it is convenient for Heidegger to see him as fundamentally in thrall to the mysteries of metaphysics, although officially denying them. Thus in Heidegger's view Nietzsche's struggles with metaphysics (with Being) gave him an honorary place in a process that eventually had to overcome such contradictions in order to understand the search for Being properly, which unsurprisingly meant understanding it as Heidegger did.

Then there is a family of 'postmodernist' interpretations that admits that Nietzsche was inconsistent, but salutes him for it.[9] Derrida, for example, holds that Nietzsche is no worse off than anyone else.[10] His idea is that metaphysics is so intimately bound into language that you cannot attack it, as Nietzsche is taken to be doing, without employing it. You are bound to use the concepts of metaphysics even as you attack metaphysics. Scepticism itself cannot help the 'implicit postulation of precisely what it seeks to contest'. So it is not that Nietzsche failed to think hard enough, or that we need to get beyond him, nor indeed that we need to rescue him from his own inconsistencies. It is precisely through contradiction and self-refutation that he operates, wilfully (but insightfully) playing one position off against another. His midwifery works by jerking us from one point of view to its opposite. Similarly Paul de Man holds that we can 'show' the limits of rational thought by *showing* its basis in power, rhetoric and metaphor. But this cannot be simply *asserted* without self-contradiction. So Nietzsche is doing as well as human sceptics can do. His work should be read as a 'symptom of a set of instincts, values, and ultimately health or illness, rather than a revelation of Being'.[11]

Such interpretations may offer valuable insights into Nietzsche's methods, and they help us come to terms with the aphoristic, mobile, elusive style of many of the writings, but they only postpone the principal paradox. As I have said, to make aphorisms about English and French philosophers you have to believe that there are countries such as England and France, and believing that is the same as believing it to be true. So how can it 'increase health', or indeed serve any purpose at all, to rail against truth while in the same breath you assert it?

2. *Twilight of the Idols*

To find our way here we need to understand something of Nietzsche's attitude to the strange subject of metaphysics. Fortunately, Nietzsche himself gives us a wonderful sketch of the entire progress of metaphysics since the time of Plato. The sketch occupies one short section of the text *Twilight of the Idols*, the last work that Nietzsche himself published. It has some claim therefore to being seen as an authoritative summary of his thought. By the time it appeared, in 1889, Nietzsche had finished his productive life, and had become insane.

The subtitle of *Twilight of the Idols* is 'How One Philosophizes with a Hammer', which might seem to accord with one popular conception of Nietzsche as a purely destructive force, a kind of stormtrooper for nihilism and atheism or even Nazism, a prophet of all that has been godless and destructive since his time. The caricature is wrong, and the subtitle should not be taken to support it. Nietzsche's hammer is a tuning fork: his philosophizing is destructive only in the sense that he thinks that civilization has taken the wrong turnings, as any critic of a contemporary culture must think. His hammer is really offering only a rigorous testing of what is in tune and what is not.

Here is section four of *Twilight of the Idols*:

1. The true world – attainable for the sage, the pious, the virtuous man; he lives in it, *he is it*.

   (The oldest form of the idea, relatively sensible, simple, and persuasive. A circumlocution for the sentence, 'I Plato, *am* the truth.')

2. The true world – unattainable for now, but promised for the sage, the pious, the virtuous man ('for the sinner who repents').

   (Progress of the idea: it becomes more subtle, insidious, incomprehensible – *it becomes female*, it becomes Christian.)

3. The true world – unattainable, indemonstrable, unpromisable; but the very thought of it – a consolation, an obligation, an imperative.

   (At bottom, the old sun, but seen through mist and skepticism. The idea has become elusive, pale, Nordic, Königsbergian.*)

4. The true world – unattainable? At any rate, unattained. And being unattained, also *unknown*. Consequently, not consoling, redeeming, or obligating: how could something unknown obligate us?

   (Gray morning. The first yawn of reason. The cock-crow of positivism.)

5. The 'true' world – an idea which is no longer good for anything, not even obligating – an idea which has become useless and superfluous – consequently a refuted idea: let us abolish it!

   (Bright day; breakfast; return of *bon sens* and cheerfulness; Plato's embarrassed blush; pandemonium of all free spirits.)

6. The true world – we have abolished. What world has remained? The apparent one perhaps? But no! *With the true world we have also abolished the apparent one.*

   (Noon; moment of the briefest shadow; end of the longest error; high point of humanity; INCIPIT ZARATHUSTRA.†)

In this sublime thumbnail sketch, the origin of Western metaphysics is, as usual, traced to Plato.[12] And the Platonic doctrine that matter is the opposition between the merely 'apparent' world, the world of Plato's cave, the world of the senses and of things that change, the world of everyday life, on the one hand, and a 'true' world, the world

---

* Königsberg, now Kaliningrad, on the Baltic coast, was Kant's home town.
† That is, Zarathustra arrives or begins his ascendancy.

of the enlightened, the world of those who ascend to the sun, of those who understand timeless unchanging truths, on the other hand. In Plato reason has its credentials only because we ourselves once dwelt in the higher world, and have brought what we learned there with us into this one. Relativism is avoided, because we retain traces of the absolute within us.

In the second stage this Platonic opposition is Christianized, along the lines of St Paul's saying that 'Now we see through a glass darkly, but *then* we shall see face to face.' So ascent to the true world now becomes more widely available. In Plato only those of exceptional natural ability and who have studied immensely (mathematics alone for nine years) can hope to glimpse the 'Forms', or the true norms governing reality. Christianity de-intellectualizes Plato, and offers heaven all round, but only as a tantalizing promise, and again one that must be earned, although now it is only those who have faith or listen to the priest or exercise a particular set of slavish virtues such as humility who can expect the reward.

Kant is next beautifully placed as a kind of pallid lapsed Christian, not really pious, but maintaining at least the view, implicit in both Plato and Christianity, that it takes an understanding outside the ordinary, or even a kind of deity or supernatural vision, to give us true standards, and imperatives of conduct, and thereby to protect morality (and reason).

Then dawn breaks. We get a gradual realization that the idea of a metaphysical world is not needed even for this. The supernatural vision is useless, the 'true' world can be abolished. Does this leave us saying that there is only the 'apparent' world? No, for 'true' and 'apparent' live off each other. If one dies, the contrast dies with it. We should no longer go about pitying ourselves for being condemned to a superficial world, a world of mere appearance. For the idea of any other kind of world has been destroyed. The metaphysical contrast introduced by Plato is abolished, and the new man, the man who fully partakes in this revolution, the prophet of a new way of grasping life, Nietzsche's imagined hero Zarathustra, emerges. It is now up to us to give our lives meaning ourselves, and this creation means not only being human (which might mean, to remain in the grip of phantoms and fantasies) but being all-too-human: a being that fully and joyfully accepts the challenge of living in the full power of its faculties, the challenge of *healthy* living.

Among other things, Nietzsche is supremely sensitive to the cultural and political aspect of ideas, the pervasive influence that they exert although they may be inarticulate, or even when they are denied. So in this story, the trans-worldly metaphysics of Plato functions rather like a virus, or what Richard Dawkins called a meme. It has shown a kind of Darwinian cunning enabling it to mutate and change and insidiously infect our minds, passing from one mind to another in different forms in different moral and political and intellectual climates. Nietzsche thinks of it in terms of denigration of the world of time and change, together with hostility or cruelty towards the senses or towards the merely animal. Just before the quoted passage, he claims that any distinction between a 'true' and an 'apparent' world is a suggestion of decadence, a 'symptom of the decline of life'.

We might now think that interpretation of Nietzsche ought to be straightforward. The 'truths' against which he rages would be metaphysical truths as conceived by Plato, truth about the world as it really is, Being, contrasted with truth about the everyday world. Far from needing Heidegger to come after him, rescue him, and complete his work, he would have pre-empted the possibility of standing anywhere near the position that Heidegger or similar other-worldly metaphysicians wish to occupy.

We could follow that interpretation out in two different ways. The first would be to imagine Nietzsche diminishing the *scope* of his denial of truth. On this line, it is only certain kinds of sayings that are illusions, such as metaphysical sayings. The thesis itself is then exempt: provided it is not a metaphysical statement it does not fall within its own scope. It relegates metaphysical sayings to the ragbag of illusion, but keeps itself preserved outside. The denial really takes the form 'All X statements are illusions,' but this itself is a Y truth, not one of the contaminated kind X. There is notorious logical trouble when Epimenides, the Cretan, says that everything Cretans say is false. But there is no problem when someone from somewhere else says it. Similarly Nietzsche can stand outside metaphysics and mock its illusions, and he can go on and make pronouncements about human life, provided these too do not fall within the contaminated class.

The second, related suggestion plays a variation on this interpretation. In this variation we do not stick with denying the existence of an M-world but we suppose that there is a corresponding conception of truth – M-truth, truth whose status is certified by the way of that M-world. And it is this conception of truth that is under attack. This variation affects not the scope but the *nature* of the denial. This would fit Nietzsche into the armour we offered the relativist in reply to Nagel in the last chapter. Mankind is enslaved by the idea of A-truth and A-reason. The task is to replace that conception by R-truth and R-reason. Perhaps, for example, philosophers and cultures have thought of truth in some specific and grandiose way (Correspondence with Reality, again). And we now have to learn to think of it as something different and lesser.

Although there may not seem to be very much difference between diminishing the scope of the denial and diminishing the nature of the denial, they need to be kept distinct. This is because while we can say true things about many different subject matters, it does not actually follow that in each different application we deploy a different conception of truth. Truth about France is truth in the same sense as truth about Germany. And discovering that there is no subject matter of a particular type is not really making a discovery about truth itself. When we learn that there was no such place as Atlantis, we learn some ancient geography, but nothing about truth.

On the first option, truths about metaphysics, or Being, or the Absolute are supposed to be true in the same sense as truths about physics or golf. And when we avoid them, or believe that they have no subject matter, it is like finding that Atlantis or Zeus does not exist. But abolishing the M-world is more plausibly taken to have an impact on the nature of truth than abolishing Atlantis, or France. While we are immersed in the Platonic or the Christian world view, or perhaps even that of Kant, M-truth will be whatever underlies and grounds the A-truth of the absolutist. Absolute truth is precisely that which is underwritten or guaranteed by way of the M-world. We might even say that beefing up our conceptions of reason and truth is precisely what the metaphysical world is *for*. Its function is not to sketch out a new geography of the cosmos, but to underwrite our convictions with *logos*.

And this in turn makes it plain that what looks at first sight like a piece of superior geography – with the Platonist, the Christian and even Kant claiming new regions with new denizens for themselves – is actually nothing of the sort. Geography cannot have the function that the metaphysics of Plato and his followers was designed for. It is the conception of truth that matters, not how much of it there is. It is precisely the will to absoluteness and authority that drives the metaphysical show.

On this interpretation it is, however, a little optimistic to say that if we abolish the 'real' or metaphysical world, we also abolish the apparent one. What is happening is that we are abolishing the absolute conception of truth, the giver of holidays. And that leaves us with *something*, but unfortunately something that may not satisfy our hunger. It leaves us with the R-truth, the apparently pallid and insubstantial substitute for the Real Thing that even Protagoras was able to cook up. Presumably, by this late stage in his life, Nietzsche is counselling us to be satisfied with what in more robust times would have seemed contemptible.

On either of these accounts, whether he presents it as the denial of a metaphysical realm or as the denial of the metaphysically certified conception of truth, Nietzsche is safe provided that he presents the denial as straightforward, ordinary, everyday truth (it may also be a personal confession, hiding moral or immoral intentions, but that is fine as well). By dividing the place he is attacking from the place he is standing, he avoids any threat of a recoil argument. The boat he is sailing in is not Ishmael's impossible boat, but a perfectly ordinary, seaworthy, R-understanding of the everyday way of the world. This Nietzsche can claim that the abolition of the true/apparent contrast, as it is used to support a wholesale metaphysics of the Platonic or Christian kind, requires no countervailing metaphysical doctrine, but merely a healthy attitude towards life in the here and now, life as it is lived.

This is roughly the view of the scholar and translator Walter

Kaufmann, who more or less single-handedly reintroduced Nietzsche to philosophers in the USA and Britain in the middle of the last century. In Kaufmann's view, Nietzsche holds solidly to a view of truth as correspondence to reality. And he holds that his own views are true in this sense. Nietzsche's apparent denials of truth are really denials of the Kantian thing-in-itself, or the Platonic supersensible world. Nietzsche's own doctrines, such as the pervasive presence of the will to power, or the story of the history or genealogy of morals, are empirical truths, and therefore exempt from his scepticism.

Unfortunately, with Nietzsche, nothing is straightforward. And this simple picture, while it undoubtedly contains much of the truth, and may often be uppermost in Nietzsche's own mind, is certainly confounded by other elements in his thought, meaning that the damage cannot be so easily contained. Illusion and fiction spread wider than metaphysics, and do not die with it. Nietzsche says enough to show that he regards illusion not as a metaphysical add-on from the infancy of thought, but as part and parcel of thought itself.

3. Perspectivism

Nietzsche often laments the apparent inevitability of illusion, as in the quotation from 'Truth and Lies' at the beginning of this chapter (p. 75). However, the essay from which this comes is an early one, and it has been doubted whether it represents an opinion held by the mature Nietzsche.[13] Nietzsche's writing career lasted only some sixteen years, from 1872 until 1888, ending with the onset of insanity the following year, but there is no doubt that he changed his mind freely within the period. But I doubt if he ever obtained a stable view of the relation between truth and illusion. One of the most famous passages is from the late *Genealogy of Morals* (1887):

Henceforth, my dear philosophers, let us be on guard against the dangerous old conceptual fiction that posited a 'pure, will-less, painless, timeless knowing subject'; let us guard against the snares of such contradictory concepts as 'pure reason', 'absolute spirituality', 'knowledge in itself': they always demand that we should think of an eye that is completely unthinkable, an eye turned in no particular direction, in which the active and interpreting forces, through which alone seeing becomes seeing *something*, are supposed to be lacking; these always demand of the eye an absurdity and a nonsense. There is *only* a perspective seeing, *only* a perspective 'knowing'; and the *more* affects we allow to speak about one thing, the *more* eyes, different eyes, we can use to observe one thing, the more complete will our '*concept*' of this thing, our '*objectivity*', be. But to eliminate the will altogether, to suspend each and every affect, supposing we were capable of this – what would that mean but to *castrate* the intellect?[14]

Here we have the omnipresence of *perspective* – one of the doctrines for which Nietzsche is best loved or most hated, perspectivism.

The idea of us trapped inside a perspective or a 'version' might lead to the melancholy thought that our knowledge of things is only *partial*, but how is it supposed to imply that it is not knowledge at all, but only fiction or illusion? Other philosophers than Nietzsche have found it easy to make this jump: here is William James making a rather similar kind of claim:

Reality 'independent' of human thinking is a thing very hard to find. It reduces to the notion of what is just entering into experience and yet to be named, or else to some imagined aboriginal presence in experience, before any belief about the presence had arisen, before any human conception had been applied. It is what is absolutely dumb and evanescent, the mere ideal limit of our minds. We may glimpse it, but we never grasp it; what we grasp is always some substitute for it which previous human thinking has peptonized and cooked for our consumption. If so vulgar an expression were allowed us, we might say that wherever we find it, it has been already *faked*.[15]

It is that last word that ought to grate. James is here warning us against what later became known as the 'myth of the given', or the idea that reality is just nakedly present in our minds. He insists on the omnipresence of beliefs and conceptions, or what Nietzsche would have called interpretations. They give us our perspective. But how does the idea of fakes (falsifications or illusions) feed on this idea of perspective?

It is a big step from the omnipresence of perspective to the omnipresence of *illusion*. You and I see the world from literally different points of view, but on the face of it we can each be right about what we see. We are in different places, that is all. Indeed the very metaphor of perspective seems a poor springboard for any general scepticism. Perspective is a notion from the science of sight. It conceives sight is a transaction between a thing at one place in space, and another thing, a perceiver, at a different place in space, but one at which she can receive energies from the first. It is therefore essential to it that the perceiver is located in a space of stable objects on which she has a point of view. If the perceiver had no location, or was able to shift instantaneously from place to place without a speed limit, the information would not be better, but worse. It would smear and blur and fail when the displacement exceeded the speed of processing. It would stop being information at all. Hence we do not lack knowledge of the Eiffel tower because we can see it only from one place at one time, or with one set of eyes at a time. It is because of this that we know about it, by sight, at all.

Furthermore, in spite of the inverted commas, the further facts about sight that Nietzsche offers are exactly what we would stress to reassure ourselves about the objectivity possible to vision. We can walk around the Eiffel tower, and in doing so we interpret what we see in terms of its invariant shape and form. We are not confined to a single glimpse, when, indeed, we might not quite know how to interpret what we see (a small object nearby? A big object a long way away?). We can compare what we see with what we saw yesterday, or with what other people see: if we need reassurance that the Eiffel tower is not a delusion or a ghost, these are the methods to follow. Throughout everyday life their results cohere together perfectly, and it is only if they do not that fears of delusions, the pure effects of deceived or malfunctioning subjectivity, assail us.

Perspective might alert us to the *partial* nature of our truths, but this is scarcely frightening. It is not so very radical to insist that we manage to gain only part of the truth, or that there is always more to be said. Consider, for instance, the not-so-radical thought that history is always written from a point of view, or with one or another sets of interests and categories. As a result, an economist's history of a decade might look different from a political theorist's and different again from that of a linguist or a historian of science or feminist. Then the natural, reassuring thought is that it is nice to read them all, or have them put together like chapters in a book. The economy was doing this, the political affairs were thus, while the language was changing in these ways, and science did this and that, while the lot of women changed in these other ways. If you send a dozen historians off to the archives with the instruction to write a narrative of some ten years, you will get a dozen different stories. But that is no reason to conclude that any of the stories is illusory.

There is a philosophical temperament that sometimes surfaces here, that indeed thinks that anything less than the *whole* truth must be not only partial, but just because of that somehow false. The so-called British Idealists of the nineteenth century liked this idea (which they took from Hegel). It derives from Plato's idea that the lover of wisdom, when he gets out of the cave into which the rest of humanity is confined, not only learns *more* but also learns that what the others take for truth is in fact illusion. The Platonist Iris Murdoch was an artful exponent of this implausible line, constantly denigrating everyday life in the name of Something Higher.[16]

One way to see its implausibility is to concentrate on falsity rather than truth. We recognize the norm of avoiding falsity, without confusing ourselves with the thought that anything less than the whole falsity is somehow less than false. Bernard Williams quotes Clemenceau's riposte to those who asked what future historians will say about the First World War: 'They will not say that Belgium invaded Germany.'

Perspectivism derives from Kant, who applied it to our most general theory of the world as spatially and temporally extended around us. The 'idealism' or perspectivism holds that 'It is only from the human standpoint that we can speak of space, of extended things.'[17] But the 'human standpoint' here is something very slippery. It is transcendental, because it is something whose own relation to the view we obtain from it cannot itself be an object of understanding. Any attempt to understand it would mean having a view of the world as it is in itself, without that view being the view of subjects with a perspective. But that is impossible: all we get, if we as it were lift the veil to see the world as it is in itself, is another human view. It is in effect because of this that Nietzsche exultantly strides on to the final act in the section of *Twilight of the Idols*, where along with the real world we abolish the apparent world, finally overcoming Kant's duality.

Kant agrees with common sense when it says that some facts do not depend on us. But casting a shadow over this agreement is the attempt at a second-order or theoretical commentary that tries to say, in a different voice, that they do depend on us, in something like the same way that views depend on the properties of the viewer. This different voice needs to identify a sense for its terms, and it is not clear that it can do this. It is everyday dependencies and independencies that give us our feel for the very notion. So at least for the sake of argument we can sympathize with Nietzsche's dismissal of Kant. But where does that leave perspectivism?

If we think of vision, there is no room for reality itself being perspectival: a spatial configuration of objects cannot be 'really' wide-angle or long-distance, although a representation of it can be.[18] But this makes it an unpromising starting point for a theory trying to insist that the reality of some area is itself essentially perspectival. Not only is this extending the metaphor perhaps unrecognizably, but also it is vulnerable to destructive questions. For instance, suppose we are to reconcile ourselves to ethical or mathematical reality by insisting that ethical and modal descriptions of things are themselves conditioned by our perspectives. We must ask: on what do we have these different perspectives? A non-ethical and non-mathematical world? Visual representations are not perspectives on a non-spatial world! An ethical or mathematical world? But this leaves the metaphysics untouched, for it gives us no sense of our perspectives playing any role in constituting or creating the facts.

If the analogy with visual perspective is to help Nietzsche's purpose, he must want us to discard just the reassuring aspects of visual experience. The remaining image might be one of us occupying just a *single* point of view, bolted as it were to the ground and unable to import other information or to take in other views. In other words, the idea must be of us *trapped* within a static perspective, unable to appreciate that the objects of our belief are also capable of being seen in other ways, by different subjectivities. We can only measure things with our own measuring sticks, unaware that there may be others. In one familiar way of putting this, which we return to in chapter 8, we possess only a single conceptual scheme through which our experience is shaped and organized – but there could be others, more diverse than we can imagine.

So the metaphor of perspective needs not just one, but three, tonic shots to get us to anything remotely as pessimistic as relativism or scepticism. First, as already described, we would need to jettison one feature of the usual notion: the fact that we can change perspective on things at will, simply by moving around. We would need instead to think that we are trapped in one perspective, and only able to think one way at a time or at best to move our thoughts very, very slowly. We must imagine our subjectivity in terms of a permanent lens through which we are condemned to take our view of things. Second, we would need the idea that although there are many such different lenses, their results cannot simply be conjoined to give us a comprehensive view that maintains the insights of each. And third, we would need that there is no possible way of ranking them as superior or inferior, in point of truth or accuracy, than one another. And then, if we cling on to the idea of one true way that reality is, we will be drawn to scepticism. And finally, if we discard that idea, leaving only a reality partly created by our perspective, a world-as-it-is-for-us, we will be drawn to Protagorean relativism.

Nietzsche often writes as if the missing argument is self-evident: from first to last he finds it easy to move from the omnipresence of perspective to the denial of truth.

Formerly, alteration, change, any becoming at all, were taken as proof of mere appearance, as an indication that there must be something which led us astray. Today, conversely, precisely insofar as the prejudice of reason forces us to posit unity, identity, permanence, substance, cause, thinghood, being, we see ourselves somehow caught in error, compelled into error.[19]

If we are universally compelled into error, then we have an unbridgeable gulf between appearance and reality. Yet this passage occurs in *Twilight of the Idols* only a couple of pages before the section quoted, where the contrast between appearance and reality is allegedly overcome. Nietzsche sounds the same note in other works.

Here and there we . . . laugh at the way in which precisely science at its best seeks most to keep us in this *simplified*, thoroughly artificial, suitably constructed and suitably falsified world – at the way in which, willy-nilly, it loves error, because, being alive, it loves life.[20]

Whatever philosophical standpoint one may adopt today, from every point of view the *erroneousness* of the world in which we think we live is the surest and firmest fact that we can lay eyes on.[21]

Notice that here it is the erroneousness of the *world we think we live in*, not the erroneous of some Platonic vision or M-world that Nietzsche laments (or celebrates).

The first of these quotations contrasts interestingly with the doctrine from 'Truth and Lies', quoted above. There, it was the senses that seemed to introduce error, crawling only over the surfaces of things, as in a game of blind-man's buff. The idea was that of the unstable world of appearance and the senses, with a hidden order behind it, which it would take something else to apprehend. Relying on the senses is not enough. But here he puts into the dock the 'synthesizing' role of reason, the part that smoothes over the unutterable particularity of things, finding similarities and resemblances that are sufficient for the purposes of memory and prediction.

It is an implication of the Kantian heritage that surrounded Nietzsche that understanding of both the self and the world required the cooperation of both the senses and reason.[22] But it is not part of the Kantian world that the result is *erroneous*. So where did the further pessimism come from?

As suggested above, things would liven up if we could import the idea that what is seen from different perspectives is not just *complementary* but *contradictory*. If it is the first, then in principle we can imagine the view from different perspectives conjoined, like chapters in a book. Only if it is the second does a more radical scepticism or relativism rear its head. If it is the second, then the plurality of views cannot be unified. There cannot be a synoptic vision, incorporating the insights of all. There cannot be a coherent book, created by conjoining the chapters. That might be all right if just one chapter came with the stamp of authority, but it will not be all right if there is nowhere to stand from where to rank them.

4. Adequate Words

There are, however, other streams feeding into Nietzsche's philosophy. The passages I have quoted contain echoes of two Greek doctrines. The first prominent idea is that language works by smoothing over difference and change: 'Every concept originates by our equating what is unequal.'[23] The idea is that the intellect abstracts from differences, and *thereby* falsifies things. By calling something a horse you identify it with other horses, and thereby ignore or suppress or distort the fully particular fact: the particular nature of its very own horsiness, as it were. This is part of why Nietzsche finds it evident that we live in a simplified, artificial, constructed and eventually falsified world.

At first sight there is not much to be said for this idea. If I classify something as a horse I need not be denying that it is unlike other horses in all kinds of ways. It is just that for the purpose in hand I am not interested in them. If I am interested in them, I can go on indefinitely: a small, dappled, friendly, three-year-old, four-legged mare with a long tail, perhaps. The right degree of detail depends on the purpose in hand. If I am selling it, what would otherwise be a boring recitation of a whole lot of its properties may be needed. If I am simply reassuring you that it is not a bull and dangerous or a sheep and edible, it is not. But by no stretch of philosophy does it become *false* that it is a horse or an *illusion* that it is a horse, just because the detail is left out.

Nietzsche's thought might seem more attractive when we try to throw the net of language over phenomena that differ in many subtle and concealed ways, or ways that we do not quite know how to think about. Social phenomena and historical periods provide salient examples. Suppose, for instance, someone poses the question of whether Charles II was a liberal. It is easy to think that the word 'liberal', as we now have it, comes trailing a whole history of thought and whole centuries of experience. The ideas it contains have been rubbed up against ideologies unheard of in Charles's time, and its implications may be very different. The more we delve into the complexity, the less adequate will a one-word verdict appear. A clear-cut decision one way or the other would seem inferior to a bigger picture painted in various shades of grey, and that in turn will leave out detail that a yet bigger picture would include. Moral language in particular works too much in terms of black and white.

This example should enable us to sympathize a little with Nietzsche's interest in an idea worked over in Plato's dialogue *Cratylus*, that in order to be a vehicle for truth language must not name things by convention, but by nature. Nietzsche considers the conventionality of language a significant step to his denial of truth:

And, moreover, what about these conventions of language? Are they really the producers of knowledge, of the sense of truth? Do the designations and the things coincide? Is language the adequate expression of all realities?[24]

At first sight this too is unconvincing. What could be more obvious and more harmless than the conventional nature of the relationship between words and things? Why else are there so many languages, and such changes in the languages we have? And surely we can divide and conquer. We can distinguish between the brute and conventional association of a term with a property which supplies its meaning, and the subsequent description in which the property is said to hold of something. The former can be as conventional as we like, while the latter, applying properties to things, putting them under descriptions, brings in correctness and incorrectness, truth or falsity. It is conventional that the word 'horse' refers to horses, but once that is fixed, it is information, true or false, that the animal over there is a horse. Perhaps the whole discussion gets off the ground only because Plato muddles these two very different things together under the idea of the 'giving' of names to things.

I doubt if this gets to the heart of the matter, if only because it is taking the objectivity of properties for granted. What is at stake is not so much the superficial and obvious conventionality of words, but the underlying possibility of language being *adequate* or not to the phenomena. In *Cratylus* Socrates urges that naming things is a *techne*, an art or skill, and the central part of the dialogue is taken up with suggesting that our ancestors who first forged the language did it well enough for it to be worth paying close attention to the etymologies of our words.[25]

This will not strike us as right when we think only of naming children at the font, or naming properties at the font, as it were, in the way that modern colour science provides diagrams that name specific shades of colour that previously had no names. But it might strike us as right when we think of whole vocabularies: the vocabularies that enter into our theories. These are not quite arbitrary. Or rather, they are in the sense that different combinations of sounds or letters could do the same job, as they do in other languages. But they are not, in the sense that there is a job to be done, and anyone who would gain the same understanding of the subject matter must have some vocabulary to do it. These are terms that translate, since other people can speak other languages but still have the same theories. Whereas arbitrarily given names do not – Germans and French call me by my English name, but they have their own words for my various properties. To find a vocabulary in which to conduct mathematics or physics or chemistry, or in which to think about ethics or politics, is indeed a skill. The emergence of the right way of talking about things is also the emergence of the right way of thinking about things.

Bringing things under a description may easily generate illusions of understanding. We may think we understand a human phenomenon better when we have netted it in words, although in fact we do not. Medicine is especially addicted to this vice. I once had a bad reaction to a cartilage operation, and sneaking a look at the notes at the end of the bed found that it was PUO. This afforded reassurance, since the doctors evidently had things under control, until I also found that it stood for 'Pyrexia' – that is, a fever – which I knew already – 'of unknown origin', which scarcely helped. Perhaps the relatives of people who die suddenly may be comforted to know that it was SUAD (sudden adult death syndrome). A rather more serious example as I write is the label 'Munchausen's syndrome by proxy', which was a description invented by a British paediatrician for a 'condition' in which mothers harm or kill their babies in order to gain attention for themselves. By insinuating the quite false idea that science had 'discovered' this 'condition', and therefore in some sense was on the way to understanding it, and then by ceding power to 'expert witnesses' who could pronounce upon its presence, the medical profession assisted in the conviction of many innocent mothers whose babies had died of natural causes. This is not to doubt that sometimes mothers do harm or kill their children, although it may be doubted that they do it 'simply' to gain attention. The point is that in the absence of more theory, for instance connecting such a crime to other patterns of action, or even to organic or neurological abnormalities, the impressive-sounding label simply added nothing by way of understanding, and merely served to direct power and prestige to those who invented it and deployed it.

It may be peevish of me to cite it, but another example also illustrates the point. Just at present almost all university activities in Britain are described in the language of accountancy. So even an activity such as philosophy is described not in terms of hopes and insights, understanding and despair, which at least seem to capture much of it, but in terms of deliverability, production targets, output monitoring, measuring, auditing, appraisal, value-added point-of-service strategic resource allocations, and other horrors adapted, perhaps, for measuring the delivery of coal or the production of landfill, but grotesquely unfitted to describing attempts to understand the world.

A radical, postmodernist Nietzsche would now mock the idea of a language adequate to the nature of things. He might suppose that 'Munchausen's syndrome by proxy' is a good illustration of our general plight. We try to capture reality in the net of words, but are left only with words. Understanding is a delusion. Nietzsche certainly sounds that note:

'Explanation' is what we call it, but it is 'description' that distinguishes us from older stages of knowledge and science . . . how could we possibly explain anything? We operate only with things that do not exist: lines, planes, bodies, atoms, divisible time spans, divisible spaces. How should explanations be at all possible when we first turn everything into an *image*, our image![26]

Nietzsche's general view is that the classificatory categories we hit upon earn their keep insofar as they enable life to go forward, but never by corresponding to the nature of things.

It may be easier for us to get a purchase on Nietzsche here if we think in terms of historical understanding:

Historia Abscondita – Every great human being exerts a retroactive force: for his sake all of history is placed in the balance again, and a thousand secrets of the past crawl out of their hiding places – into *his* sunshine. There is no way of telling what may yet become part of history. Perhaps the past is still essentially undiscovered! So many retroactive forces are still needed![27]

Historia abscondita is, literally, history obscured or lost sight of. That implies a historical reality, but one perhaps veiled by time. The more radical idea implied in the passage is that there is no one reality.

Here it is not so much the innovative historian or scientist who begins a new way of classifying things, or a new perception of connections that were hitherto hidden. The great human being who changes our perceptions may do it simply by initiating great events. A social upheaval or a war or a massacre causes us to look at previous upheavals, wars and massacres, and then new connections and new understandings are made (I should guess that fanaticism became a much more popular historical category after 11 September 2001). New understanding emerges, and if the word 'understanding' is by now problematic, at least new things get said.

If we ask if the changes brought in are improvements, winds of Protagorean relativism may start to blow. They are different, and new ages will find differences again. But why suppose that they represent progress? If we had confidence, as Hegel had, that the whole process of history represented a progress, then we might think that the telling of history was also progressive. We could even satisfy ourselves by thinking in terms of a final point, a *focus imaginarius*, the descriptions given on the Day of Judgement on which the last word could be spoken and on which a complete historical truth could be written. But if we see only revolutions and changes with no direction, the very idea looks like a self-deception. And then the idea of objective historical truth, as something that would be part of what was written on the Day of Judgement, starts to dissolve in front of our eyes. Perhaps there will only be different versions, more or less striking at different times, serving different purposes in different climates.

It is good to stand in the bracing wind of Protagorean relativism, but this is not the last word either. Nietzsche himself provides part of a defence:

Can we remove the idea of a goal from the process and then affirm the process in spite of this? This would be the case if something were attained at every moment within this process.[28]

There can be 'better' and 'worse' without an endpoint. 'Better' does not have to mean: 'nearer to God's truth, truth written in the book of the world, truth told in the right vocabulary, truth leaving nothing more to be said'. It can mean something less than this, but still give us an idea of progress – more accurate, more adequate, better fitting the data – or so Nietzsche here implies. This would mean that we could build on our predecessors, as well as overthrowing them. And if we look carefully at the previous quotation, we will not see Protagorean relativism, but a more modest kind of faith in improvement. Nietzsche thinks in terms of new *discovery*. Perhaps he is not presenting us as condemned to wallow in a plurality of perspectives or versions, so much as lamenting that a dawn may still be in front of us. The result would not be relativism but scepticism, whereby Nietzsche is resigned to the partiality of the understandings we now possess or ever will possess, but he is not denying the very idea of understanding and its improvement.

It would be a satisfyingly conservative interpretation of Nietzsche, but it is certainly not the whole story. Maybe 'discovery' here does not mean uncovering new knowledge, something that lay there anyway, just waiting for the light to be shone upon it. Perhaps it is meant more in the sense of invention, like discovering a new way to write blank verse or to play Hamlet. If this is in his mind, however, it is odd that Nietzsche talks about the past being essentially undiscovered. It would seem better to say that there is no essence about it: there is just the endless succession of new interpretations and versions. The past as it really or essentially was, the past as it must be described, the past as it was in itself, retreats, even as an idea.

The worry about this is not that discovery becomes too difficult, but that it comes too cheaply. New ways to play Hamlet can indeed be invented, and so can history. But whereas the ways to play Hamlet do not answer to a pre-existing real person with real doings to his name, history does. We discuss how, in the final chapter.

5. Heraclitus and the Flux

The second Greek influence on Nietzsche is a little more specific than the doctrine that reality is so unutterably particular that descriptions falsify it. And it is a little more radical than the warning to be careful that our preferred classificatory schemes are adequate to the nature of things. The further ingredient is the Heraclitean doctrine of flux and its impact on the quest for truth. We have already seen that Nietzsche supposes that substance – something that remains unchanged through other changes – and permanence itself are among the categories that introduce universal error.

Heraclitus believed that everything in the universe is changing, the doctrine encapsulated in the famous saying that you cannot step into the same river twice, for new waters are ever flowing upon you. This might initially seem to be merely an amusing paradox, for we classify or 'type' rivers in full knowledge that the same river will contain different waters at different times: that's what makes it a river, not a long pond. But paradoxes have a nasty way of biting back, and certainly the Greeks took them very seriously. In the *Theaetetus* Socrates argues that at bottom Heraclitus's doctrine that all things are in flux is actually equivalent to Protagorean relativism. So what are the connections here? What has change got to do with different perspectives or different vocabularies suiting different people at different times?

Plato himself, a Heraclitean about the physical world, confined real knowledge to the world outside the cave, the world of unchanging Forms. He knew that the ordinary world was stable enough for us to describe it, but he thought that such descriptions could only achieve the status of *doxa*, or opinions, being permanently subject to revolutions of time. The contrasting, eternal world of the Forms (something like the A-world of chapter 2) ushers in the first act of the section from Nietzsche's *Twilight of the Idols*, quoted earlier in this chapter.

We can see at least dimly a connection that must have impressed Plato and Nietzsche. One is that if everything changes, then human beings change as well. Among the new rivers that flow in upon us are rivers of thought. Our responses and categories are impermanent, perspectives change, and even our best understandings have only a finite shelf life, waiting like us to go to their grave and be replaced by new generations. Perspectivism is a simple consequence of Heracliteanism.

Our own age finds little problematic about scientific truth, truth about the world as it is, but is intensely bothered by truth about how things ought to be. In our day, Protagorean relativism first grips people when they think about values. Plato understands things the other way round. Heraclitus stands in the way of knowledge (as opposed to opinion) about the physical world, but the eternal and unchanging nature of the Forms, or norms of justice and reason, makes them fitting objects for knowledge by those who are suitably prepared. From Heraclitus's point of view, this must be just a fudge, since however we hymn the eternal and unchanging nature of norms of justice and reason, the human perspective on them will be as mutable as anything else, so that if this mutability denies our title to knowledge, we will not find knowledge here either.

We can flesh out further the profound point that universal change is hostile to stable understanding. Science must proceed by finding the permanent among the impermanent. Put slightly more formally, a science will understand the change in state of a system by finding constant 'state equations' or descriptions that the system follows over time. If we swing a pendulum or roll a ball down a plane, we can calculate eventual velocities and positions only because the length of the pendulum or the inclination of the plane, and the gravitational force, can be taken as fixed. If in turn they become regarded as changeable, something else will need to be taken as constant, such as the rate of change or the direction it takes. The shape of scientific laws must also remain fixed. Newton tells us that bodies attract each other with a force inversely proportional to the square of the distance between them, and this is why we can calculate planetary orbits and make predictions about eclipses. Were the function of distance to change, everything would be unpredictable, at least until some further constancy became discernible behind the change. Physical understanding, and indeed scientific understanding *in toto*, depends upon constant laws and constant magnitudes. The issue became visible in the early nineteenth century, when the geological record was first being unravelled. 'Catastrophists' interpreted the geological record in terms of devastating upheavals such as Noah's flood. They were rebutted by 'Uniformitarians' such as one of the most eminent geologists of the time, Charles Lyell:

When we are unable to explain the monuments of past changes, it is always more probable that the difference arises from our ignorance of all the existing agents, or all their possible effects in an indefinite lapse of time, than that some cause was formerly in operation which has ceased to act . . .

Our estimate, indeed, of the value of all geological evidence, and the interest derived from the investigation of the earth's history, must depend entirely on the degree of confidence which we feel in regard to the permanency of the laws of nature. Their immutable constancy alone can enable us to reason from analogy, by the strict rules of induction, respecting the events of former ages, or, by a comparison of the state of things at two distinct geological epochs, to arrive at the knowledge of general principles in the economy of our terrestrial system.[29]

Lyell's principle is again gloriously flouted by those fundamentalists who think, for instance, that the Grand Canyon is the result of

Noah's flood, perhaps not realizing that the same principles could just as well lead them to believe that the Bible was written last week, or indeed that they themselves may be no more than one day old.

Uniformity is, incidentally, why the idea of a 'social science' – the kind of science of history that was aspired to by Marx, or in general a science of human beings in their social and political aspects – is such a problem. People in societies act according to their deliberations and their understandings of themselves and their situations. Perhaps that much is indeed constant. But after that, in the human world, very little else seems to be so. There are rule-of-thumb generalizations, perhaps: people prefer pleasure to pain (but we go in for self-sacrifice and painful rites of passage), people act to meet their needs (but we know of anorexics and smokers), people reward good with good and ill with ill (but some are ungrateful and some turn the other cheek). Such broad generalizations are far from lawlike, and such as they are they do not help us begin to predict the social, political or moral understandings that will belong to us in the future. Hence, they do not help us to predict the kinds of actions that those understandings will generate. A generation ago, nobody would have predicted that reputable professors of philosophy would think of themselves as managers and their faculties as cost-centres.

If Heraclitus were right, even the constants upon which science depends would have a shelf life. Practically, that might not worry us too much: a landscape does not have to be unchanging for us to be able to find our way about in it. It just has to change slowly, in human terms, so that things are constant enough for us to rely upon them. We may mistake anything that changes this slowly for permanence. (In *D'Alembert's Dream* the great French Enlightenment figure Diderot christens this mistake the 'fallacy of the ephemeral', giving the lovely illustration from Fontenelle, of the rose who said that as far as any rose could remember, no gardener had ever died.) But Heraclitus may be right that change dints confidence in our *understanding*. If there is change in everything, however slow, we could have no conception of cosmic order, of stable forces governing the whole show. All hope of absolute truth, absolute understanding, final realization of the way things are and must be, would vanish. We would be alienated from our only possible sources of understanding the world.

It may be that by some standards it does not even take time and change to induce this sense of bafflement. When cosmologists come upon final fixed points in their science, such as the magnitude of fundamental forces, it is not only the idea of actual change that often proves unsettling, but also the idea of being faced with an inexplicable constancy. If, for all we can make out, it is even possible that such a magnitude should change, or that it should have been different, we are left feeling victims of a giant accident, a contingency on which our understandings get no foothold. And then if we look for A-truth, it seems we have to turn our gaze outside the physical cosmos altogether (although we may at the same time continue to hope for more physical understanding to help us. The arbitrary nature of fundamental constants in the 'standard model' of particle physics is the strongest motivation for trying to uncover yet deeper theory). Perhaps it is only Zeus, or justice, or the will of something unimaginable – something sublime in the way of an absolute – that holds everything together. Alas, that only postpones the problem, for we will have no understanding of what perpetuates the stable reign of Zeus or justice or anything else, in which case we should settle for one full-stop in front of our understandings rather than two. There is no hope for an alchemy that turns the humility of cosmological silence into the arrogance of religious doctrine.

In the dialogue named after him, Cratylus (who was a teacher of Plato) is presented as holding that there is a right and wrong about what you call things, as does Socrates. He even seems to hold that each thing has a uniquely correct description, a name as a kind of superior identity card, which separates out and identifies its essence, distinguishing it from anything else. This is a much more radical and surely unsustainable doctrine, although one that dominates much mythology, for instance in the religious idea that it is blasphemous to utter the true name of God or, in the fairytale, that by discovering Rumpelstiltskin's name, you gain power over him. But at the end Cratylus is shown veering towards a Heraclitean doctrine of change. And we know that historically this is what happened, in spades.

Aristotle tells us that Cratylus eventually outdid Heraclitus, holding that not only can you not step into the same river twice, but also that you cannot step into the same river once. This splendidly Zen-like remark means that any use of language falsifies the reality it is trying to capture. Slippery reality escapes as you try to hold it stable with your words. It is not possible to speak correctly of anything that is 'always becoming and never is'. This consequence of his Heracliteanism upset Cratylus so much that according to Aristotle he was reduced to silence, eventually communicating only by wagging his finger.[30]

A related Heraclitean thought is about change itself. If change were discrete, perhaps discrete words would be adequate to describing it, but Nietzsche constantly emphasizes the continuous nature of change. Nature has no boundaries, and the suggestion is that language falsifies it by imposing artificial boundaries upon it.

Perhaps an example will help. Consider the continuous change of the year. We divide it into four seasons. This was a practical achievement, of undeniable utility. It would enable us, for example, to pass on instructions, for when to sow or when to harvest. But was it a cognitive achievement: one that improves our understanding of things, or gives us insight or knowledge into the process itself? Presumably not – we would surely have no quarrel with a culture that divided the year into five or seven seasons. We should not think that we had got something right that they had mistaken, although it is not too hard to imagine diehards who *would* think this. Our language gains points for utility, but none at all for adequacy to things. I suspect that Nietzsche thinks that it is always like that. A 'dismemberment' of the flux can earn its bread, but it cannot advance our understanding. It can only give us the illusion of understanding. A related thought is that where the causal flux is dense, with innumerable factors flowing down the river together, any separation and dissection, carving out just one or two as 'the' cause, is at best of some practical utility, but never a gain in real understanding.

Nietzsche certainly thinks that describing processes in terms of cause and effect arbitrarily splits up and falsifies the indefinitely rich flux of events:

The suddenness with which many effects stand out misleads us; it is a suddenness only for us. There is an infinite number of processes that elude us in this second of suddenness. An intellect that saw cause and effect as a continuum, not, as we do, as arbitrary division and dismemberment – that saw the stream of the event – would reflect the concept of cause and effect and deny all determinedness.[31]

It would deny, that is, the view that one event is conditional upon another. We may be inclined to retort that it is precisely by careful separation and analysis, finding hidden constancies in the apparently shapeless flux, that real science progresses. And we might also respond until this 'real understanding' comes along, or until we are given a better idea of what we are missing, the facsimile that Nietzsche is denouncing will do perfectly well. It wins by enabling us to predict and sometimes to control the way things fall out.

6. The Darwinian Element

This last remark suggests pragmatism, but although Nietzsche is often hailed as an honorary pragmatist, he himself speaks differently. 'Truth,' he says, 'is the kind of error without which a certain species could not live.'[32] He explains what he means elsewhere:

Innumerable beings who made inferences in a way different from ours perished; for all that their ways might have been truer. Those, for example, who did not know how to find often enough what is 'equal' as regards both nourishment and hostile animals – those in other words, who subsumed things too slowly and cautiously – were favoured with a lesser probability of survival than those who guessed immediately upon encountering similar instances that they must be equal . . .

In order that the concept of substance could originate . . . it was likewise necessary that for a long time one did neither see nor perceive the changes in things. The beings that did not see so precisely had an advantage over those that saw everything 'in flux' . . . no living beings would have survived if the opposite tendency – to err and *make up* things rather than wait, to assent rather than negate, to pass judgement rather than be just – had not been bred to the point where it became extraordinarily strong.[33]

There is here no equation between utility and truth. On the contrary, the necessary errors and fictions are admittedly useful, but this does not stop Nietzsche from calling them illusions. Here as well we gain a more secure purchase on Nietzsche's association between perspectivism and error. Again, there is a Heraclitean background: the conviction that our perspective imposes order on something that is essentially changing and fluid. But the dominant note is that survival forces us to pattern our world. It makes us find things equal, so we can make the same reactions, and, since we have survived where others have not, these will be adaptive. They will be useful. Our inherited wisdom is a patchwork of devices that work. It is not so much a journey of understanding, as a journey of competition and survival. We perceive what is salient for our needs and ignore the rest; we theorize in ways that give us usable patterns of response and action, and not in ways that do not serve our ends. We see change only at a rate that matters to us, and ignore change that does not matter. In other words, the selection mechanisms that dictate the nature of our perspectives are not there for uncovering the way things are, but for suggesting to us how to act.

Nietzsche is surely right that in many circumstances an adaptive illusion will do just as well as truth. Philosophical theory can lead us to think that way. A nice example is the Cartesian doctrine that although pains actually occur in the mind, which is located somewhere in the brain, it is a very useful illusion that they occur somewhere else in the body. If, when we burn our finger, we were to feel the pain anywhere else, we would be slower to jerk the finger itself out of harm's way. Hence, it was good of God to provide us with a system of sensations that located the pain at the place of the injury. In secular post-Darwinian terms, it was adaptive for this to be the way the system works.

On the other hand, the risk of self-refutation has not disappeared. How can Nietzsche possibly claim to know about the pervasiveness of error? How does he know that the adaptations that result in our beliefs and perceptions distort and falsify the real world? We usually suppose that our senses are useful because they enable us to appreciate things that are really going on: horses appearing, buses departing, people looking at us and so on without end. If we do not suppose this, what other explanation of our success is on offer? And how did Nietzsche himself learn of it? Could he alone peek behind the information given by the senses and reason, and mark it down on grounds of truth?

Some commentators suppose that very late in his (sane) life, Nietzsche began to see the danger here.[34] As we have noticed, the last act of section four of *Twilight of the Idols* (quoted above, p. 80) sees him abolishing the distinction between 'real' and 'apparent'. That might mean simply the abolition of Plato's world, the world of objective Forms or norms, and the guarantor of absolute conceptions of truth. But perhaps he is also repudiating the more ordinary mistrust of science and the merely 'apparent' world that leads to the association between perspectivism and illusion.[35] It is hard to tell – as we have already seen, contradictory passages from *Twilight of the Idols* are only pages apart. But what is clear is that Nietzsche leaves us wanting a better understanding of the credentials of science and scientific realism. We probably want to turn our backs on him, and maintain our conviction that the senses and reason together enable us to detect the different kinds of things in our world accurately enough for us to determine their causal powers, to understand them and thence to make use of them in the struggle for survival. We will want to jettison the constant association between pragmatism and illusion, or perspective and error. So why should we not remain good, conservative, scientific realists – whatever that might mean?

5

The Possibility of Philosophy

But much the greatest obstacle and distortion of human under-standing comes from the dullness, limitations and deceptions of the senses; so that things that strike the senses have a greater influence than even powerful things which do not directly strike the senses.

Francis Bacon, *The New Organon*, L, p. 45

1. Getting Puzzled

In chapter 3 we met strong arguments for minimalism about truth. We met the argument that theorizing involves an impossible activity of stepping outside our own skins and pretending to a 'transcendental' point of view, a standpoint from which we can survey the relationship between our thoughts and the facts, without using the very forms of thought whose relation to the facts we are hoping to describe. And we met Frege's argument from the transparency of truth, seemingly forcing us to deny that truth could be a robust or substantial property. But in the meantime we have also been exposed to the sceptical torrent of Nietzsche, apparently forcing us to query whether our words can ever be adequate to things.

In this chapter I want to approach, from a slightly different direction, the kinds of discomfort and upset that generate worries about truth. We have already sketched highly general thoughts, images almost, of language as the expression of mere subjectivity, of language as abstract and therefore untrue to reality, of our linguistic practices being the upshot of mere pragmatism and practicality, and for those reasons inadequate to the awful duty of representing the world as it is. But in specific areas there are more immediate problems, problems of getting a grip on the kinds of *fact* that we seem to be talking about. Some kinds of fact seem very elusive: what are they, how do we know about them – and why do we care about them?

Philosophical reflection arises when we don't know our way about. We find we have lost our grip. Consider the perennial conundrum of free will. We live our day-to-day lives doling out responsibility and praise and blame, without worrying too much about excuses. We believe ourselves to be happily in control, sometimes. But then something gives us pause. We find we can't quite keep together our picture – there seem to be bits missing, or bits that don't fit. We cannot keep together our conception of ourselves as free agents, motivated by thoughts and reasons, with an alternative but equally powerful conception of ourselves as creatures of nature, part of the everyday causal flux. We need to restore harmony, and this is where the philosophy becomes hard.

Let me give a different example. Consider the absolutist's norms of morals and reason, the norms of *logos*, as we have been meeting them in previous chapters. What kind of facts are we talking about here? What makes it so that there are duties either to behave or to think in particular ways? Some people find the idea of God's commands helpful. This is a simple example of what philosophers call a reductive account. You get to understand one kind of fact by identifying it with another that you think you understand better. Here, you might hope to understand the moral law in terms of orders or commands, and similarly you might understand human law simply as the command of the sovereign government. Unhappily, as Plato pointed out, in the case of morals the account gets off the ground only if the lawgiving God is not arbitrary, but wills the right things. His or Her fiat is unable to generate real laws of morals or reason unless we suppose that He or She is tuned to the good and the right, in which case we face the same problem: what kind of fact is that? There is also, of course, a problem of knowledge: how do we know of God's commands, and how would we know if God changed His or Her mind, perhaps at weekends? And there is also a problem of motivation. For why should I be motivated, except perhaps by fear, to conform to this alleged legislation? Yet it is not fear that keeps me reasoning as I do or even obeying the principles I do. It is the belief that this is the way to do things, the only way that makes sense.

In the case of human law the parallel problem is that we don't like to think of law as the command of just any old gang that happens to have power. It ought to be the command of a properly constituted authority – but then, what kind of fact is it that some group of people makes up such an authority? How do we recognize it and how much should we care if something we should like to see in place (for example, democratic election) is missing?

When it comes to reason itself, perhaps the fact that some rule of reasoning obtains and must be followed is of some strange metaphysical nature. But then, again, how do we know about it? And why should knowledge of it be motivating? If the fact is strange enough, it seems we should be able to ignore it without penalty. It is everyday things that we cannot ignore, not the mysterious rainbow of *logos*.

Here is a very different example. Suppose you believe in probabilities, such as the probability of a child being born with six fingers. What kind of thing is a probability, or if we prefer to put it a different way, what kind of fact is it that a probability obtains? Perhaps, with your feet firmly on the ground, you say that it is simply a matter of the observed frequency of this condition. But that does not seem quite right. Over history the observed frequency might be one thing, but it may be that just now the chance or probability is higher or lower than it used to be, perhaps because of other changes such as diet or lifestyle. Perhaps in answer to this you say that it is not the actual historical frequency that matters, but where it is tending: a hypothetical frequency, the 'limiting frequency in the long run' as the jargon has it. But now a pincer movement starts up. First, the epistemology becomes difficult. It is fairly easy to know about nice actual historical frequencies: those are what the hospital records tell us. But how on earth could we know anything about hypothetical frequencies in the long run? And the motivational problem looms as well: why should we be interested in it? As the economist and philosopher John Maynard Keynes famously said, in the long run we are all dead. Probabilities determine how we act now – how much we should pay for insurance, for example. Why go all the way to infinity, only to come back again with something whose point of application is the here and now?

So perhaps we should start again. Perhaps probabilities aren't really frequencies at all. Perhaps the values we put on them measure something like objective dispositions or powers. In our example, that might be the disposition or power of the mother–baby system that issues in the frequencies of six-finger births that we observe. But now we might worry if we have a real conception of what kind of thing *that* is. It begins to sound a bit ghostly, something like a theorist's fiction rather than a part of living nature. After all, how are we to think of the connection between the existence of this thing and the observed events? Was it inevitable that they occur, given the dispositions? Probably not: there is slack between chances and frequencies, since probable things sometimes fail to happen, and improbable things do so instead. So – heaven forbid – is there another chance at work: the chance that the system with the first power in it issues in whatever results we find? Might these two come apart, so that while there is a high chance of any birth being six-fingered, fortunately there is a low chance that this high chance is ever manifested? And what has all this to do with practical affairs, such as the rate it is reasonable to pay for insurance against the problem?

These twists and turns, and others like them, make it very hard to keep things in harmony, and therefore very hard to come to a stable view about the nature of probabilities. And in fact different philosophers have chased down the alleys signposted above, but with little consensus. Of course, if we have little appetite for problems, we might just shrug off our difficulties. However, difficulties have a way of biting back – a claim of negligence and huge lawsuit might depend on the difference between acting under uncertainty (good) and taking an objective risk (bad), just as judgements of responsibility determine what is done with offenders. While we don't know our way about, our practices will risk being muddled and unjust.

2. *Four Responses*

Suppose then we consider some set of commitments that we hold, and that make up our views in some area of thought. The area might be quite local, if we are considering some specific practices of judgement: mathematics, morality, probability, ethics, aesthetics or descriptions of the world in terms of ordered laws of nature. Or, the area might be more general, so that we might be considering, as a block, the commitments of science or of common sense. In any event suppose we become puzzled by some aspect of the area, and are motivated to theorize about it. What kinds of options face us?

Any map of alternatives must be provisional, but there is good reason to attempt to draw one. In the chart overleaf the central topic is described as our area of discourse and commitment. In other words, the phenomenon about which theories cluster is the fact of our sayings and thoughts. It might seem odd that this is so: why don't philosophers just get on with it and talk about the facts themselves – probabilities, norms, numbers, whatever? Why move to talking only of what we say about them? The answer may be evident already. The very existence of 'the facts themselves' is up for grabs. It is plain that we talk of probabilities or duties; it is not plain, yet, whether there exists anything corresponding to this talk. It is the facts themselves whose status is on trial. Whereas it is a datum that we talk and think in the terms that we do.

Eliminativism
(Get rid of it!)

Realism
(Get it right,
then talk of truth,
ontology, reality, fact . . .)

AREA OF DISCOURSE
AND COMMITMENT

Constructivism
(Keep on playing, but . . .)
also fictionalism,
instrumentalism,
pragmatism,
expressivism . . .

Quietism
(No contest)
Soggy pluralism

There is no great significance in the ordering, but we might think of it like this. *Eliminativism* is heavily involved with what we should actually do with the first-level commitments. We should get rid of them. Eliminativism magnifies the power of the philosopher. We can comment on practice, and sometimes sufficiently drastically to counsel changing it or even abandoning it. This is diagonally opposed to the view that most diminishes the role of philosophical theory, which is *quietism*, a kind of generalization of the minimalism about truth that we have already met. *Realism* is the darling of absolutists and believers in *logos*. It stands proudly on real facts, and it is hoped, real knowledge of them, and real authority for those with that knowledge, but it proves a surprisingly slippery fish, and a major theme in what follows is the difficulty of distinguishing it from any pallid shame-faced imitators. It is diagonally opposed to the various options suggested by the label of *constructivism*, which in their various ways emphasize what James called 'the trail of the human serpent', or the potentially diverse subjectivities we bring to things. Constructivism sees things in a Pythagorean or Nietzschean light.[1]

3. Eliminativism

The easiest of these options to understand is the first, eliminativism. On this view reflection goes further than merely prompting puzzlement about the area; it goes far enough to prompt rejection. In some respect or another we have fallen into error. Perhaps the area is defined by a cluster of theoretical views, and enough of those theoretical views are false to prompt rejection of the entire subject matter or 'discourse'. We are not to think in those terms; just as most of us suppose that we should not think in terms of astrological or alchemical categories. Some of us might wish to see religious language simply disappear. Perhaps the commitments voiced in it are subject to objection, and it would be better if we did not go in for them. How much better it would be, and what, if anything, needs to go in their place, obviously depend on the gravity of the error and the availability of options.

Writing some thirty years ago, the influential philosopher John Mackie argued that ethical claims can be made with their ordinary significance only if we believe in the existence of 'objectively prescriptive facts' – card-carrying elements of *logos*, denizens of Plato's heaven – but, alas, there cannot be any such things.[2] Mackie thus joins Thrasymachus and Gorgias and the sophists of Plato's day in having a dismissive attitude to the very possibility of 'moral truth'. A curiosity of the book is that, having argued this, Mackie himself went on to make an assortment of ethical claims. It is not as easy to eliminate elements of our thinking as philosophers sometimes like to suppose.

Eliminativism is not the same as scepticism. This is properly the denial that there is knowledge to be had in some area, or perhaps more strongly the denial that we can even have any justification for beliefs in the area. More subtly it may be the view that while we might have knowledge, we cannot know that we do, or while we might have reason for our beliefs, we cannot be sure of that either. Either way, one could think those things, yet still be resigned to the necessity of holding on to the area, and continuing the commitments that make up its way of thought. This is in fact Hume's characteristic position. There is no prospect of us doing any better than thinking, for example, in terms of a spatially external world of independent objects. Nature forces us so to think, and it would be absurd to recommend otherwise. Yet we may have no reason whatsoever for supposing that the thoughts we then have are true: indeed we may even have good reason to suppose them false. Scepticism thus does not imply eliminativism, although, as the example of Hume shows, the cost of holding one and not the other is a pessimistic view of the place of knowledge and reason in human life.

Eliminativism is not motivated by the idea that there are truths that can be couched in the terms in question, only for some reason lying beyond our powers of determination. An eliminativist about theology does not lament how little we know of the nature of God. He laments us thinking in these terms at all: he wants us not to think of hidden truths of that kind; he wants us to change the subject.

The cost and benefits of eliminativism are obvious. The benefits are that whatever intellectual puzzles the area generated are shrugged off. The cost is that it is not so easy to shrug off an entrenched way of thought. Sometimes the attempt is of doubtful coherence, as when eliminativists in the philosophy of mind counsel us to think of ourselves as never really thinking, or those in the philosophy of ethics counsel a way of life, or ethic, with no ethics, as John Mackie appeared to do. Recoil arguments are set to strike such naive suggestions.

Part of the motive for eliminativism can come from the other doctrines mapped here. We may become convinced that some area demands a certain kind of theory, but then also convince ourselves that the relevant theory cannot possibly be true. A nice example of this comes from the view that psychological ascriptions can be true only if there exist particular computational states, which have a geographical location literally inside us, doubtless in our brains. The philosopher Stephen Stich once argued that nothing answers to our ordinary conception of a belief. For that conception requires that a belief can both explain a saying (hearing the dog under the bed, I say 'The dog is in the bedroom') and a doing (I reach down to heave it out).³ But, Stich urged, neuroscience tells us that areas of the brain responsible for sayings are distinct from areas of the brain responsible for actions. Hence there is no one 'state' corresponding to believing anything. Hence, as scientific philosophers, we need to ban talking of 'beliefs' altogether. We have shown, according to this argument, that such states of mind are pre-scientific 'fictions' whose shelf-life is due to expire. When we find implications unacceptable, we need to abandon the discourse that demands them.

Philosophers, however, can seldom carry many disciples with them when they purport to turn their backs on a way of thinking. Mathematics, talk about possibilities, ethics, psychology, all have their ways of creeping back. They seem more firmly in our repertoire than any purely philosophical reflections that end up asking us to go without them. So a better response is to query the philosophy, and seek to explain how the facts are less demanding than they might have seemed. For example, to avoid this last argument of Stich's it would be enough to find a different account of what is being spoken of when we talk of people's beliefs. Roughly, we are not attempting to count their areas of cerebral activity but to make sense of the whole cluster of their reactions to their perceived environments. Hence, it is fine if lots of different things are happening in the brain when we come to believe that there is a dog under the bed, just as it is fine if there are lots of different things happening in the engine when it is running. It does not mean that we should 'eliminate' talk of the engine running, or think of its running as an unscientific kind of state, one that is unfitted, for instance, to explaining why it is heating up or making a noise.

This shows that the motive for eliminativism is not solely fear of realism in these cases: it is realism coupled with a particular imagining, a particular conception of the kind of fact needed to make true the commitments. By changing the conception we may be able to avoid the pressure to eliminativism.

4. Realism

If eliminativism is easy to characterize, the next option is certainly not. The difficulty arises because much of what people who think of themselves as realists characteristically say may turn out to be sayable from the two southerly corners as well. So cross-purposes abound.

But to begin with the idea of realism is clear enough. Realists believe themselves to be offering a view about the area of discourse. They have a story, they believe, and the story invokes some relation between the commitments in the area and a reality to which they answer. It is this confidence in a genuine and illuminating story that marks off an '. . . ism'. The story goes something like this:

(Story) The commitments in question are capable of strict and literal truth; they describe the world; they answer to or represent (independent) facts of a particular kind; there is a way in which the world is that makes them true or false. These facts are discovered, not created, and they have their own 'ontological' and 'metaphysical' natures, about which reflection can inform us.

So far so good. But realists also need to hold that this *is* a story. It is a real philosophical commentary, a bulwark against flabby relativists and postmodernists. It is where the action is. So the realist should also sign up to:

(Meta Story) The terms of Story themselves mark out *the* substantive philosophical position, or theory about the area; they are the terms in which to define the best view of it. There are bad people out there who oppose Story, but they are wrong.

Anyone holding both of these is a *real* realist, an industrial strength, meat-eating realist. This is Realism with a capital 'R'. It has affinities with what some philosophers call 'metaphysical realism'. But that label has become contaminated by various doctrines, and is best avoided.

There is one slightly tricky requirement in Story. This is that the facts or aspects of the world that make commitments true or false be 'mind independent', or not of our own making. I discuss this further when we come to the constructivist corner, but it is a little awkward to include it universally as definitional, since the kinds of fact that might concern us include those of psychology, and these are not mind-independent in anyone's book. What is important to realism is that any common-sense independence of facts from our minds is preserved. A realist will want to stress that we do not create planets or stars, icebergs or oceans, historical persons, or tigers or rocks. On the other hand, a realist can cheerily acknowledge that we do create other things: lasers, radios, even stable electrical currents are all man-made, but they are real enough for all that.

Realism also says that we must get the discourse right before we philosophize about it. This is intended to cover the issue we already touched upon, of reductionism. According to reductionism the facts about an area can be grounded in or 'reduced' to facts that are at first sight of an entirely different kind. In our example, moral facts were reduced to facts about the commands of a lawgiver. Other philosophers might hold that biological facts reduce to or are grounded in chemical facts, or that chemical facts reduce to or are grounded in facts of physics. Some hold that psychological facts consist in facts about dispositions to behaviour. Others have held that facts about numbers reduce to facts about sets, or facts about mathematical formalisms.

Realism as I have described it is silent whether the commitments of an area are reducible, so that the facts to which they answer 'consist in' something characterized in other terms, or whether they are *sui generis*. Reductionism is not as popular in philosophy as it used to be, and this is part of my excuse for adopting a terminology that sidelines it. I am however departing from historical usage, in which debates are often mounted as if the only options are realism versus some kind of reductionism. Certainly reductionism has been the traditional escape route for philosophers nervous about finding their way about. If scratching our heads about the kind of fact found in some area has started to hurt, it is a great relief to be able to identify them with the kinds of fact found somewhere that is apparently less itchy.

There is no need to quarrel about whether reductionists remain realists. We could reserve the term 'realist' for what we might call a '*sui generis* realist': someone holding that no reduction can be given, and that Story and Meta Story are the things to say. The issue of reduction crosscuts this one. If a reduction is accepted, then *either* the area is cleaned up, so that the motivating puzzles disappear, *or* (alas) the motivating puzzles reappear when we turn to thinking about the area from which the reduction was provided, in which case the four options I have exhibited reappear. In the usage I am adopting someone meets the conditions for realism even if she provides a reduction, provided that after the reduction, she adopts a realist theory of the assertions to which the original is reduced, or the facts that the original facts 'consist in'.

Another issue that crosscuts Story and Meta Story is that of confidence. This too is deliberate. A realist as defined here need not be over-confident about the truth even of central and cherished commitments in an area. The issue of confidence is apt to muscle its way in: in the Introduction I associated absolutists with the roaring and bawling of conviction. And there are plenty of definitions of 'realism' that associate it with confidence. Michael Devitt, for instance, defines scientific realism as holding that 'most of the essential unobservables of well-established current scientific theories exist mind-independently, and mostly have the properties attributed to them by science'.[4] This means that the realist is pretty optimistic about the discoveries of science. But the central issue is the way in which commitments answer to the world, or whether they do so, or whether the world they answer to is suitably independent of us and our perspectives. This is an issue of how we take our commitments, or of what they purport to give us. It is independent of the degree of confidence we have in them. Thus scepticism ought to be compatible with realism: one might think that realism is right about the nature of our commitments but, perhaps for that very reason, be pessimistic about our prospects of knowing or gaining reasonable belief about the aspect of the world in question, and think that confidence ought to be diminished as a result. We can become overwhelmed by the difficulty of obtaining real knowledge. Indeed, a standard objection to realism is that it properly leads to scepticism, since our access to the needed facts is hazardous.

Conversely, if we find that a position falling short of realism is attractive in some area we might, for that very reason, be content that cherished commitments in it deserve absolute certainty. We might think, for example, that if numbers are real Platonic objects which our mathematics struggles to represent, then we could never be sure we had got them right; by comparison, if they are man-made constructions, then we are in control and what we say goes, just as what we say goes about the rules of tennis or chess.

The second clause, Meta Story, has a concealed place in these debates that leads to total confusion. Why add such a clause in this definition of realism? Because there is all the difference between merely asserting what is claimed in Story, on the one hand, and regarding it as making up a theory, or as having a distinctive content, on the other. It is this distinctive content that is threatened with being 'metaphysical' or even transcendental, dependent on the illusory external standpoint. This is most obvious if we reflect that the words of Story might come very cheaply – so cheaply that anybody who voices commitments in the area can say them. They might represent no second-order theoretical stance, but simply be available as a high-flown way of expressing ordinary commitment within the area. In this case, they are available to anybody except the eliminativist. Devitt's own definition of realism, quoted above, is open to this charge. If I write down the book of science – all that is taught in physics, cosmology, biology, chemistry and all their progeny – and then add a preface saying 'most of the things I am talking about exist', I don't really create a theory *about* the area. I just express mild confidence within it.

This should be obvious if we remember the trivial property of words like 'true' and 'fact': the 'transparency' property that 'p' and 'it is true that p' amount to the same thing. In the terms of chapter 3, Ramsey's ladder raises you nowhere. This means that the original area of discourse must be thought of as *itself* containing the commitments in Story. They are part of the game, not part of a loaded description of the game. We should think of the central topic – the Area of Discourse – as itself large enough to hold the clauses of Story (in a north-east corner of the central box, as it were). If we hold this thin view of the terms in Story, we will not, by using them, generate a thick theory or locate a thick issue. In chapter 7 we return to work out in detail the way this affects issues of realism in connection with science and common sense.

5. Deconstructing the Issue

Deconstruction is the aim of the quietist. On this option, the whole attempt to mount a theory is wrong-headed; it involves trying to take up the standpoint that cannot be had: a 'sideways perspective' on language and the world: one that pretends to step outside our actual commitments and estimate from some 'neutral' standpoint whether they are doing well or badly at delineating the world. Arguing that there is no such standpoint the quietist plays the sequence 'p' – 'it is true that p' – 'it is really true that p' – 'there is a fact of the matter that p' – in reverse. Suppose we are lost about whether some commitment p really corresponds with the world in such a way as to be literally true. The content of the worry deflates, all the way down to the worry whether p. And that can be solved, if at all, only by the methods of the area in question. If p is an ethical commitment, we need ethical argument, if mathematical, we need proofs, and so on. Each area stands on its own feet, and no second-order commentary helps or hinders it. The terms that marked out a thick concept for the real realist are actually insufficient to take us out of the original area. They do not take us to philosophical commentary *on* the area, but only show us affirming confidence *within* the area.

Quietism brushes off the issue of whether commitments in the area are capable of 'strict and literal' truth. That would be an issue if we have some thick notion of literal truth as opposed to some facsimile, and just this is denied by quietism. The options are squeezed down to a north-west to south-east line: eliminate an area, or put up with it.

And what of the puzzles that lead us not to know our way about? Clearly there is a choice. It may be that they retain their power and have an impact on first-order confidences. It may be that the worries that initially struck us as undermining the notion of truth, for instance in ethics, deserve playing again in the lower key, and appear as ethical problems demanding ethical solutions. For instance, when people wonder whether there is no truth to be had in ethics because they are impressed by the divergence of standards in different communities, they might be seen as voicing a twenty-first-century ethical insecurity – an anxiety about dealing with other people – rather than seen as having a distinctive philosophical, second-order problem about truth. The cure would be a course in ethical poise and confidence. In the same way Bertrand Russell's paradox may not strike theorists as providing a problem about mathematics, but only as presenting a problem within mathematics.* Crises that have led philosophers to worry whether

* In set theory, it is plausible that some sets are not members of themselves – the set of bananas is not a banana, for example. Others may be: the set of all numbers might itself be a number. Russell showed that naive set theory allowed us to form the set of all sets that are not members of themselves, but this generates contradiction, when we ask whether it is a member of itself, and find that if it is, it is not, and if it is not, it is. The question is how to avoid the contradiction, and the issue raised in the text is whether this is a 'philosophical' question, as it appears to be, or a purely mathematical or technical question, which it has generally been tackled as being. The so-called semantic paradoxes, such as the Liar, are often thought to generate horrendous complexities in the theory of truth. My excuse for not treating them in this work is not only that adequate discussion would double its length, but that a plausible approach suggests that what they throw into doubt is not so much our conceptions of truth, but our naive conviction that every apparently well-formed sentence introduces a proposition, or issue, about which questions of truth and falsity arise.

quantum mechanics should be taken as really describing a very strange quantum reality, are actually physical problems that, if anything, should lead to doubt whether it should be taken at all. If this is the true pict-ure, then we are not at any point philosophizing *about* an area, but must always reason *within* it.

The most common diagnosis here will be that which we applied to Stephen Stich, above. The puzzles arose from a muddled imagining that one kind of fact must be reduced to another or somehow modelled on another, and it is when the attempt to do this fails that we are wrongly led to look for advanced, second-order theory, when none can actually be had. This is the diagnosis we gave of Stich's argument about the unscientific nature of the concept of a belief. Similarly, for instance, perhaps the problem with ethical truth seems urgent only if we mistakenly look for a kind of spatial model (norms laid out in some Platonic heaven), and the solution is to abandon any such model. People worrying about the relationship between mind and the world may be in the grip of a spatial model of the mind, as a kind of gaseous or glassy or gossamer presence in the head, and their difficulties may arise from that image (not that a gaseous or glassy or gossamer thing stretching some way outside the head would be any better: the whole spatial vocabulary needs uprooting). The cure is to show that the fears were inappropriate. This liberates us for a joyful immersion back into the words and thoughts we naturally use.

How would a quietist cope with the difficulty of finding a coherent picture of probability, given the Pandora's box that seemed to open when we tried? A principal quietist strategy will be to rely upon what is given by the everyday, by the first-order theory itself. A quietist will point out that ordinary statistical techniques bring their own epistemology with them. If you make enough of the right kinds of measurement, as determined by one or another school of statistical theory, you can claim a value for a probability, indeed, you might even get to write it down in a book of physical constants, such as one detailing the half-lives of different sub-atomic particles (which are probabilities). If you keep up the nagging thought, 'Yes, but what *are* probabilities?' you need to be cured, not answered. If we know how to get to infer them from data, and we know how to use them, for instance in making predictions or buying insurance, then we understand their *function* in our thought. And what more should we want?

Obviously the quietist finds it easy – too easy, perhaps – to trot out Story. And if saying those things defines realism, then a realist is what he is. But he denies Meta Story. And anyone accepting Story but denying Meta Story is at best a pallid realist. This will include quietists of various brands, and even, as we shall shortly see, some fellow travellers from the final south-westerly corner. Just because the terms of Story are transparently thin they are freely available to anyone with commitments in the area.

Quietism is a close cousin of the minimalism we already met in chapter 3; indeed it simply takes minimalism about truth and generalizes it to minimalism about any of the terms we might use to conduct the truth wars: representation, fact, objectivity, authority. We should notice that all by itself it implies one local eliminativism. It wants to eliminate certain kinds of attempts at philosophical theory, or certain kinds of reflections on our practices and the world. In particular, it wants to eliminate the kind of thinking that leads either to *real* realism, or to the constructivist views that offer alternatives to that; it wants not reflection, but silence. In terms of chapter 1, it thinks there is no difference between theology and onto-theology.

And then the question will arise whether one can be a determined quietist across the board. Even if we suppose that *some* philosophical problems arose from misunderstanding the kinds of fact our words point towards, can we really claim in advance that *all* of them do? Quietists may need to become rather noisy to convince us of that. Some problems are disquieting enough to prompt the thought that you can ignore them only by feigning general paralysis of the brain.

6. The Constructivist Corner

The challenge to present a real theory is taken up again in the final corner. Here one agrees with the realist against the quietist that theory is needed, and agrees with the realist that the discourse is in order and theory about it can be had. But one disagrees with realism by rejecting Meta Story. Either it misdescribes the role of these commitments, or it is as the quietist alleges: a mere facsimile, a parade of flummery, the fake façade of a theory. What is needed instead is a better understanding of the role of commitments in the area. This understanding shows that the realist is wrong in what he takes the terms to do. We are not in the business of representing an independent layer of reality, but of doing something else.

There ought to be space for such a suggestion. After all, the quietist gives a very flat-footed account of our thinking in any area. He says that just as talk of chairs describes chairs, so talk of duties describes duties, talk of probability describes probability, talk of possibilities describes possibilities, and so on in an endless mechanical and unilluminating list. The realist who embraces Meta Story is even worse, suggesting in addition that these plonking descriptions are really explanatory, exciting, theoretical assertions.

But perhaps sometimes we can see the discourse we are investigating in an entirely different light. We have already met this interpretation of religious sayings, in chapter 1. Perhaps our commitments have a function other than that of describing or representing a particular corner of reality. They may serve as instruments governing the flow of confidence among other, genuine descriptions of the world. Or perhaps they function as expressions of intellectual or emotional habits or attitudes. Perhaps they function as prescriptions, blueprints for a framework within which more ordinary descriptions of the world can be provided. Perhaps they give us only 'models' of reality, or useful fictions. If so the real realist was wrong in the Meta Story part of his claim, and the quietist was wrong because there are after all theory and explanation to be had.

Even on the face of it, language has more contours than are allowed by quietism. There should be norms of acceptance and rejection of utterances of ordinary sentences, which exist because there are other ways of going right or going wrong than by simply describing things truly or falsely. Thus, in principle a commitment illustrated by the assertive utterance of some sentence might be objectionable for all sorts of reasons. We might start with fiction. The natural thing to say, at least about writing fiction (as opposed to reporting on established fictions), is that the sentences written do not deserve calling true or false, because the author's intention is not to describe the real world, at least in terms of the names employed or the events represented as having happened. But that gives the obvious opening for anti-realist theorists to suggest that the same may be true, for instance, of simple expressions of emotion or attitude, or even of some scientific theorizing. Another pertinent example will be acceptance or rejection of metaphors. These are typically couched in ordinary-looking indicative sentences, certainly governed by norms of appropriateness and found in complex thoughts, yet certainly not intended or evaluated as straightforward cases of truths or falsehoods. This is how theorists in the south-west say it is in more controversial examples, such as talk about whether we ought to do something, whether something is beautiful, or God is all-seeing, and so on. These commitments may illustrate dispositions to movements of thought or attitudes. There will be norms for acceptance and rejection of them, but these norms will not simply be read off from the world, or from what these sayings are 'describing'. The norms will be down to us, rather than down to anything else.

There are labels for theories from this corner: projective, non-cognitivist, expressivist, instrumentalist, fictionalist; there are also names that are derived from famous champions of the approach: Humean, Kantian, Ramseyan. The essence is that such a theory seizes on an illuminating story about the *function* for commitments of the kind in question, and uses that to explain our attachment to them. But the function is contrasted with that of describing or representing fragments of reality.

Now, however, a dismal point stares us in the face, and will be trumpeted by the quietist. The point is that words like 'describes' or 'represents' belong with the terms of Story, since being true is equivalent to describing or representing the world properly. So the quietist will deny that there is any point in searching for a non-descriptive role for commitments. 'X is good' describes X's value, 'X is probable' describes its probability, 'if p then q' describes a hypothetical fact, and so on. Just as he goes minimalist about 'truth' so the quietist goes minimalist about 'represents' or 'describes'. No materials are left out of which to make contrasts or theories.

I believe that while one may eventually end up saying these flat-footed things, there are very different routes to becoming comfortable with them. Those in the south-west believe that for some specific areas we can start earlier. We do not have to presume a descriptive function in order to understand the place of some commitments in our thought. As for the point in starting further back, that will depend on the motives for seeking an understanding. It depends on why we did not know our way about.

It has become evident that any such approach faces a choice. The commitments we make will typically be propositional in form. That is, they will be expressed by normal indicative sentences that appear to describe an aspect of the world, and this has consequences for the range of our thought, such as our comfort in talking of knowledge, or proof or objectivity. Anyone in the south-west must decide how much of this appearance he can tolerate. One natural worry is that if things are as he says we ought really to express ourselves differently – we ought not to talk as we do of truth or knowledge in the area, or ought not to say things in the area that we then treat as explaining other things, or treat the commitments as being independent of us and our investigations. The general drift is that we are cheating or deceiving ourselves by talking 'as if' there is a corner of reality that we are describing. Suppose, for instance, that a theorist of this kind persuades us to see ethics in terms of prescriptions and commands, then surely it would be better if it wore that on its face, and instead of saying 'We have duties to our children' we went around saying 'Look after your children, or else!' If the function of talk of probabilities is that we mention them simply in order to express degrees of confidence, then instead of saying 'The probability of the coin falling heads is .5' perhaps we ought to say 'Bet on heads at evens – I would.'

Anyone holding this line will have eliminativist leanings. He will believe that ordinary thought embodies a mistake, and that a preferable mode of expression would avoid it. There are distinguished suggestions of this kind in the history of philosophy. Kant, for example, held that when it considers things like infinitesimals, the mind gets muddled because we take 'regulative' principles for 'constitutive' descriptions of things. We have already met John Mackie holding that ethics is shaped as if it describes a strange layer of intrinsically authoritative fact, when there is no such thing, and that therefore the whole subject needs reform. The Italian mathematician Bruno de Finetti held that a substantial number of things we say in terms of probability arise from mistakenly supposing that probabilities are aspects of the world that we describe, whereas in fact they are mere fictions, reflecting ways in which we must distribute confidence in more worldly things.[5]

A different view is that we can explain why we give our discourse its propositional form: why a form of thought meeting our needs would naturally and justifiably come to have the shape we actually find. I have called the enterprise of explaining the propositional surface from the starting point that rejects working in terms of description and representation, the enterprise of quasi-realism. The quasi-realist will have no opposition to the Story component of realism. He can perfectly properly share the minimalist view that Ramsey's ladder is horizontal. So, once he hears himself saying p with a good conscience, he can say the rest. He differs from the realist not by avoiding these terms, but by denying that they are the ones that give the needed theory of our thought. He is uncomfortable with Meta Story. But he differs from the quietist in thinking that a theory is needed, and indeed that he can provide one.

Here too emotions run high and truth warriors clash their weapons. For a realist will dislike hearing the quasi-realist say that there really are facts about ethics, probability, possibility or whatever the area is. He thinks of that as private property, a theoretically loaded remark that he alone should be making. He does not want others to trespass on his personal territory, and still less to issue fakes and fictions ('McFacts') as if they were the real thing, his truth, real truth. But perhaps he is deluded. The essence is that it is not what you *end up* saying from the Story menu, but how you *defend the right to say it*, that defines the philosophical options.

7. The Example of Wittgenstein

We met Wittgenstein telling us that we cannot step outside our own skins, cannot survey our own practices on the one hand and the world on the other, and get a view of how they are related. So he is often taken to have been a quietist, who thinks that there is nothing in general to say about how language relates to the world. We just immerse ourselves in our different language games – pursuing ethics, mathematics, science, religion or whatever it is – and when we come up with various sayings, then they are true in just the same, minimal sense. 'Reference to an objective reality' is not a special distinction belonging to some class of sayings but not to others. There are no debates to be had.

Wittgenstein certainly held a minimalist or deflationist theory of truth. So he can pass without cost from any assertion p to 'p is true' and to 'p corresponds to the facts' or 'p says how things are'. Nothing is added by these locutions, so Wittgenstein can say without hesitation all the things that define the Story part of realism. He can do this across the board. He can say that there really are values, numbers, possible worlds, rules, intentions, but he does not agree with our *real* realist, the meat eater who goes on to Meta Story, that these sayings are laden with theory. They go without saying, or rather, they go with saying, the things that get said in the respective areas of discourse. It is also plain that Wittgenstein had no sympathy with eliminativism or error theories. He was deeply suspicious of philosophical theory and its pretensions to cosy acquaintance with *logos*, and the idea that such theory could have the authority to dismiss any area of human activity (even, as we saw in chapter 1, religious activity) struck him as almost impious. Reflection must take off from where we stand.

This has led to Wittgenstein being celebrated for teaching the denial of differences, the celebration of the seamless web of language and the soothing away of distinctions. On this account, there is nothing interesting to be said about the contrast between empirical science and mathematics, or fact versus value, or any other significant kind. What is left is a smooth, undifferentiated view of language, in which all sentences perform the same function: that of saying how things stand. Wittgenstein is frequently presented as a patron saint of quietism. This bizarre misreading would not be worth taking seriously were it not practically universal in the philosophical community.

So is Wittgenstein bent on flattening out even these common-sense distinctions? Far from it. He works in the south-west, not the south-east. Even at a cursory glance, his later work is shot through with warnings against taking surface uniformity as a safe guide to linguistic function. He wrote that 'We remain unconscious of the prodigious diversity of all the language games, because the clothing of our language makes everything alike.'[6] He said that 'The basic evil of Russell's logic, as also of mine in the *Tractatus*, is that what a proposition is illustrated by a few commonplace examples, and then presupposed as understood in full generality.'[7] The idea that the words don't determine the language game in which the proposition functions infuses his entire philosophy of mathematics, and might almost serve as a motto for it. He actually told his friend Drury that he had thought of using as a motto for the *Philosophical Investigations* a quotation from King Lear: 'I'll teach you differences.'

And he does. In *every* area that Wittgenstein considers in detail his weapon of choice is to look carefully at what we are *doing* with language (another motto he liked was from Goethe: 'Im Anfang war die Tat' – in the beginning was the deed). And, he shows, in many cases there are much more illuminating ways of going about this description than saying that we simply represent how things stand, how reality is configured. Indeed, he is consistently scornful of going about it this way. He thinks that precisely *because* minimalism about truth is correct, trying to understand a piece of language by insisting on the facts it purports to represent is either useless or positively misleading. Here are some examples of this way of thinking.

In the 1929 'Lecture on Ethics' Wittgenstein's central and repeated claim is that no statement of fact can ever be, or imply, a judgement of absolute value.[8] He considers the 'book of the world' as it might be written by an omniscient person, containing 'all relative judgements of value and all true scientific propositions and in fact all true propositions that can be made' (note especially the last clause). Even if we make sure that our book describes all human feelings 'there will simply be facts, facts, and facts but no Ethics'. 'Ethics, if it is anything, is supernatural and our words will only express facts; as a teacup will only hold a teacup full of water and as if I were to pour out a gallon over it.'

Considering statements of absolute value he urges that 'no state of affairs has the coercive power of an absolute judge', and goes on to consider various states of mind lying in the region of the ethical (wonder, fear, or a feeling of safety or of the miracle of existence) en route to the idea that a certain misuse of language runs through all ethical and religious expressions. It is as if they are similes, but 'as soon as we try to drop the simile and simply to state the facts which stand behind it, we find that there are no such facts'. Finally, what it (ethics) says 'does not add to our knowledge in any sense. But it is a document of a tendency in the human mind which I personally cannot help respecting deeply.'

Notice that he is not merely contrasting ethical facts with scientific ones. For he explicitly adds that the book of the world contains not only all scientific truths, but all truths, yet still no ethics. And the thrust of the lecture must surely be that it is from a different standpoint than that of description that ethics is found. It is found when it is felt, or perhaps even when we think not of description but of feelings and the will, and this explains the elusiveness, even the threat of vanishing, of the ethical proposition. Now Wittgenstein was still moving from his early to his later philosophy in 1929, and some might suppose that his minimalism or quietism was not at the time fully fledged. But Wittgenstein never gave any indication of changing this view. It is not as if later he said, as a quietist ought to say, 'Of course my lecture was hopeless: ethics describes facts – ethical facts.'

What does happen later simply reaffirms the disengagement of ethics and facts. In a conversation of 1942, Rhees reports, Wittgenstein considers an ethical dilemma: 'Someone might ask whether the treatment of such a question in Christian ethics is right or not. I want to say that this question does not make sense.'[9] If we imagine deciding which solution is right and which is wrong, he complains:

But we do not know what this decision would be like – how it would be determined, what sort of criteria would be used and so on. Compare saying that it must be possible to decide which of two standards of accuracy is the right one. We do not even know what a person who asks this question is after.

And in 1945 we find:

Someone may say, 'There is still the difference between truth and falsity. Any ethical judgement in whatever system may be true or false.' Remember that 'p is true' means simply 'p'. If I say 'Although I believe that so and so is good, I may be wrong': this says no more than that what I assert may be denied.

Or suppose someone says, 'One of the ethical systems must be the right one – or nearer the right one.' Well, suppose I say Christian ethics is the right one. Then I am making a judgement of value. It amounts to adopting Christian ethics. It is not like saying that one of these physical theories must be the right one. The way in which some reality corresponds – or conflicts – with a physical theory has no counterpart here.

Here Wittgenstein not only turns his back on the appeal to a moral reality, serving to make one opinion 'the right one'. He explicitly contrasts the case with that of physics where, he says, there is a different way in which reality does correspond or conflict with theory – the very antithesis of a 'minimalist' view.

One thing that is very obvious in this passage, and in others, is a dismissive attitude to the introduction of truth, reality or fact, as somehow containing the key to the use of the language game, ending the philosophical story. Here a minimalist or deflationary theory of truth is indeed exposed. His constant, characteristic stand is against using facts and the rest as a separate element in our description of the things we do with language – the 'language game' – something that we can use to 'place' or understand the activity of judgement, or that we can use as a constraint in any such attempt.

This is very important. An anti-realist about an area is likely to be met with sage rebuttals of the form 'Well, I happen to think that it is a *fact* that . . . It is a *fact* that honesty is a virtue, or a *fact* that energy is conserved in many physical processes' as if this settled the matter against the expressivist, or against an instrumentalist or fictionalist view of this part of physical theory. Whereas all it illustrates is commitment to the claims in question, which, of course, the anti-realist shares (he is *not* an eliminativist). It doesn't take us to a meta-level of special philosophical interpretation, and Wittgenstein is rightly impatient with views that pretend that it does.

A second area in which Wittgenstein certainly visits the south-west is that of mathematics and especially its necessity: the feeling we have that 7 + 5 not only *is* 12, but *must be* 12. What is it for necessities to obtain, so vast that they span not only this world but all possible worlds? Here are some of his sayings from *Remarks on the Foundations of Mathematics*:

Let us remember that in mathematics we are convinced of *grammatical* propositions; so the expression, the result, of our being convinced is that we *accept a rule*.

Nothing is more likely than that the verbal expression of the result of a mathematical proof is calculated to delude us with a myth.[10]

Why do you want always to consider mathematics under the aspect of discovering and not of doing? It must influence us a great deal that in calculating we use the words 'correct' and 'true' and 'false' and the form of statements. (Shaking and nodding one's head) . . . There is no doubt at all that *in certain language games* mathematical propositions play the part of rules of description, as opposed to descriptive propositions . . . But that is not to say that this contrast does not shade off in all directions. And *that* in turn is not to say that the contrast is not of the greatest importance.[11]

To be practical, mathematics must tell us facts. – But do these facts have to be mathematical facts? Why should not mathematics instead of 'teaching us the facts' create the forms of what we call facts?[12]

In other words, according to Wittgenstein the language game of mathematics is better described in many ways than by just saying that it is the one in which we attempt to describe the mathematical facts.

On the necessity or inexorability of mathematical truth he also has this delicious remark:

We say: 'if you really follow the rule in multiplying, it must come out the same'. Now when this is merely the slightly hysterical style of university talk, we have no need to be particularly interested. It is however the expression of an attitude towards the technique of multiplying, which comes out everywhere in our lives. The emphasis of the 'must' corresponds only to the inexorability of this attitude, not merely towards the technique of calculating, but also towards innumerable related practices.[13]

For Wittgenstein 'it is not a kind of *seeing* on our part; it is our *acting*, which lies at the bottom of the language game'.[14] Seeing would imply a relationship to something else, but this is exactly what cannot usefully be invoked when we are trying to understand, for example, basic mathematical certainties.

Wittgenstein adopted the same approach in his discussion of the foundations of knowledge. In *On Certainty*, a text put together from his last writings, he ruminates on the nature of 'hinge' or 'framework' commitments that define our whole intellectual landscape – such things as the existence of the earth, or the fact that there were people around before I was born, that motor cars do not grow on trees, that the words coming out of my mouth are English words that I understand. Propositions of this kind, he suggests, are not ordinary empirical propositions, for there could be no activity of verifying or falsifying them. We could not bring anything more certain to bear; for they themselves determine the whole roster of what is certain and what is by contrast relatively doubtful. Such commitments do not have the same status as more ordinary ones: 'one can lay down such a proposition and turn it from an empirical proposition into a norm of description.' Wittgenstein holds that 'there is something misleading' about applying truth or falsity to such matter-of-course backgrounds to all our living and thinking. 'Really "the proposition is either true or false" only means that it must be possible to decide for or against it. But this does not say what the ground for such a decision is like.'[15] The problem here is that someone seriously doubting such propositions is not so much making an assertion with which one disagrees, but ruling themselves out of the game, putting themselves beyond the pale. We can know in advance that argument and evidence will be hopeless: what is required is something more like a drug or a bang on the head, a conversion. But that in turn is a question of attitude:

What does it mean to say: 'But that's no longer the same game!' How do I use this sentence? As information? Well, perhaps to introduce some information in which differences are enumerated and their consequences explained. But also to express that just for that reason I don't join in here, or at any rate take up a different attitude to the game.[16]

Wittgenstein applies the same set of thoughts, the same reinterpretations, to the activity of philosophy itself. Like Kant, he was constantly preoccupied with the strange nature of philosophical reflection and its dubious claims to give us knowledge. As an activity, it is fine, but we are constantly in danger of misunderstanding the nature of the activity. For instance, we might suppose it to give us descriptions, but at a more 'deep' or 'necessary' level than those of more normal science or history. But, Wittgenstein holds, it is or should be nothing but an assemblage of 'reminders', a grammatical inquiry into the forms of thinking embedded in our language. Even reflection is not quite what it seems.

Another area where Wittgenstein invokes a south-westerly approach is that of our own descriptions of our own minds. We might think that when we say 'I believe . . .' or 'I intend . . .' we know our own minds through some specially privileged intimacy, an inner view which we have and nobody else has. Wittgenstein invites us to see the sayings instead not as descriptions, but as avowals: '"I intend" is never a description, although in certain circumstances a description can be derived from it.'[17] He presents this idea as helping to show us how intentions 'fit' actions, the implication being that if they just sat in our minds as 'mental states' (analogous to the state of our digestions) this fit would be mysterious. A food might fit the state of our digestions in one sense, but surely not in the same sense that an action fits my intention to do it. In fact, Wittgenstein thought that it was by misunderstanding these things that mind–body dualism gets such a hold on us. He does, however, notice that the approach makes descriptions of the intentions and beliefs of other people, or indeed of our own past selves, problematic:

Don't take it as a matter of course, but as a most remarkable thing, that the verbs 'believe', 'wish', 'will' display all the inflexions possessed by 'cut', 'chew', 'run'.[18]

His idea is that 'I intend to come to lunch' is an avowal, rather like issuing a threat or a warning or a promise. This unfortunately leaves it obscure what we are doing when we come up with slightly more complex sayings, such as 'I intended to come to lunch' (past tense), or 'He intends to come to lunch' (third person). Although Wittgenstein notices the problem, he does little to suggest how he would solve it, and this remains the principal problem with this part of this thinking.

Wittgenstein does not take these reflections to impugn the notion of truth. As a minimalist he cannot do any such thing. What they do is to show us what the activities, which include saying things, rest upon. In ethics, for example, we cajole and insist, feel emotions such as shame or guilt, coerce, judge, condemn and prescribe. If we could not see these practical activities at the centre of ethical moral practice, just announcing that with ethical remarks we describe ethical facts would be useless.

Wittgenstein's pluralism shows us that what goes for one area need not go for all. There is absolutely no reason for uniformity. One may be a perspectivist about some things, a realist about science, a *sui generis* realist about physics, but a reductionist about minds. One might be a quasi-realist about ethics and an eliminativist about theology. Any such combination will simply need to defend its own contrasts, and this is part of the interest. For this reason we should beware of framing the issues too generally, as issues about Language and the World. Even if that abstract issue ceases to enchant us, the loss of a global question is not the global loss of a question.

6

Observation and Truth: from Locke to Rorty

After the human mind has once despaired of finding truth, everything becomes very much feebler; and the result is that they turn men aside to agreeable discussions and discourses, and a kind of ambling around things, rather than sustain them in the severe path of inquiry.

Francis Bacon, *The New Organon*, LXVII, p. 56

1. Paradise Lost

Analytical philosophers are apt to suppose that the wild writings and licentious thinking of relativism and postmodernism have nothing to do with them. We like to think that these perversions are the preserve of a 'Continental' tradition where strange cults grow up around strange names. We draw in our breath in horror when, for instance, the Belgian intellectual Luce Irigaray calls $e = mc^2$ a 'sexed equation' since it 'privileges the speed of light over other speeds that are vitally necessary to us'.[1] We much enjoyed the famous Sokal hoax, when the journal *Social Texts* published an essay of what turned out to be deliberate gibberish, evidently taking it for profound commentary on the relation between science and politics. Analytical philosophers can use the terms 'truth' and 'reality' without putting them into sneer quotes.

Yet we should look to our defences. For although we maintain our sanity, it is fair to say that almost all the trends in the last generation of serious philosophy lent aid and comfort to the 'anything goes' climate. From Wittgenstein to Quine, through Sellars to Kuhn, and Davidson to Rorty – the brand-name philosophers of the last fifty years – any hope for a genuine vindication of knowledge and rationality went into retreat. *Logos* in the last generation was as absent in Harvard or Oxford as it was in Paris or Tübingen. In this chapter I shall introduce some of the ways this happened.

Let us begin by sketching a lost paradise. What would really enable us to turn on licentious thinkers and cultists, those abusers of their own minds and enemies to ours, and show them to be wrong?

How should we answer James's question to Clifford, when he asked where on this moonlit and dream-visited planet are objectivity and certainty to be found?

First, there should be a right way of gaining experience: a proper use of the senses in observation and the gathering of data, to provide the foundations for theory in experience. Then there should be method, or a canonical set of proper ways to take the data: not necessarily a handbook for theory construction, since that might well involve imagination rather than rules, but at least a handbook for the winnowing out of good from bad theories and systems. To help with this there should be an authoritative, foundational logic, telling us the implications of our views, or what may be inferred from what. And finally, we should be able to trust the words with which we frame our knowledge and pass it on. There should be a way of fixing meaning, so that we know what has been said and where we stand.

This is the Garden of Eden, the paradise whose last members were (perhaps) the logical positivists of the nineteen-twenties and thirties.[2] Our expulsion from it makes grim reading.

2. First Impressions

For a time, in the seventeenth century, ordinary, everyday empirical belief may have seemed fairly easy. The ideas in our minds come from impressions, and impressions come from the impact of the world upon us. John Locke compares the understanding to a 'closet, wholly shut from light, with only some little opening left, to let in external visible resemblances, or ideas, of things without'.[3] The senses are trusted messengers, and what they inform us of, by means of the impressions they make on the original blank tablet of our minds, is the world outside the mind.

It was not long before Berkeley saw the problem with this. Far from showing how the world is open to our observation, Locke gives us a picture in which it is entirely shut off from it. If we are stuck in his closet, we will be condemned to scepticism, since we will have no way of making a legitimate inference from these 'ideas' to the nature of things in the world. Claiming a 'resemblance' as Locke naively does, is claiming something we could not possibly know about, without having a view of both the ideas in the mind and, separately, the qualities of objects, in order to compare them. But this is a position that is banned by the theory. We can never do any such thing, since investigation delivers only more ideas, but no separate acquaintance with their source. Locke's realism remains 'transcendental'.

In fact, even the idea of a 'resemblance' between an idea and something that is not an idea seems preposterous: how does our idea of solid things resemble them? How does our idea of spatial distance resemble spatial distance? Berkeley responded by ditching the realism, bringing the nature of things in the world back into being the same thing as the nature of ideas in the mind: subjective idealism. Following Berkeley there is the 'phenomenalist' tradition in philosophy, a reductionist position in the sense of chapter 5, which regards physical objects as nothing but permanent possibilities of sensation. In the early twentieth century, deploying with great artistry the concepts of modern logic, philosophers such as Rudolf Carnap explained how everyday thought, apparently about objects independent of us and at a spatial distance from us, could be 'constructed' or abstracted out of similarities in experience. A building in the path leads us to expect various experiences, so why not *identify* it with that set of experiences?[4]

Following Locke and Berkeley, Hume despaired that the whole thing remained a muddle, in which we inconsistently recognize sometimes that our ideas and impressions are fleeting denizens of our own minds, entirely dependent upon us, while at other times we think of them as permanent public objects in a space we share with other people. So while we cannot help adhering to a common-sense view of ourselves as inhabiting such a space (and being confident of quite a lot about what is in it), philosophy can do nothing to underwrite that confidence. On the contrary, the path of wisdom is not even to think about it: faced with this inevitable contradiction in our world view 'carelessness and inattention can alone afford any remedy'.[5] We are always potentially at war with ourselves, inasmuch as our natural beliefs can never gain the approval of our reflective, self-conscious attempts to systematize them, understand them and make them consistent.

Kant was the first to complain that the problem lies at the very beginning, where Locke 'sensualizes the understanding'. For the more we think about it, the less plausible seems the idea of sensations as messengers at all. Perhaps sensations are just *dumb*. Talking of Locke's phrasing in the passage quoted, the nineteenth-century writer T. H. Green objects:

Phraseology of this kind, the standing heritage of the philosophy which seeks the origin of knowledge in sensation, assumes that the individual sensation is from the first consciously representative; that it is more than what it is simply in itself – fleeting, momentary, unnameable (because while we name it, it has become another) and for the same reason unknowable, the very negation of knowability; that it shows the presence of something, whether this be a 'body' to which it is referred as a quality, or a mind of which it is a modification . . . This assumption for the present has merely to be pointed out; its legitimacy need not be discussed. Nor need we now discuss the attempts that have been made since Locke to show that mere sensations, dumb to begin with, may yet become articulate upon repetition and combination; which in fact endow them with a faculty of inference, and suppose that though primarily they report nothing beyond themselves, yet somehow come to do so as an explanation of their own recurrence.[6]

In his exposition of the same theme, Richard Rorty quotes Green describing

the fundamental confusion, on which all empirical psychology rests, between two essentially distinct questions – one metaphysical, what is the simplest element of knowledge? the other physiological, what are the conditions in the individual human organism in virtue of which it becomes a vehicle of knowledge?[7]

William James shared Green's thought and put it in his usual vivid way:

A sensation is rather like a client who has given his case to a lawyer and then has passively to listen in the court-room to whatever account of his affairs, pleasant or unpleasant, the lawyer finds it most expedient to give.[8]

It is only the speech of the lawyer (the rational, thinking self) that can enter into thought and reasoning, that can determine expectations or give us views about what to do.

Finally, in probably the most influential work on the foundations of knowledge in the last generation, Wilfrid Sellars argued that the classical conception of an 'impression' or a 'sense datum' confounded together two entirely distinct things.

The idea that there are certain inner episodes – e.g. sensations of red or of C# which can occur to human beings (and brutes) without any prior process of learning or concept formation; and without which it would *in some sense* be impossible to see, for example, that the facing surface of a physical object is red and triangular, or *hear* that a certain physical sound is C#.

And:

The idea that there are certain inner episodes which are the non-inferential knowings that certain items are, for example, red or C#; and that these episodes are the necessary conditions of empirical knowledge as providing the evidence for all other empirical propositions.[9]

Sellars called this conflation the 'Myth of the Given'. It imposed on knowledge a certain foundational structure, in which beliefs would be chased down to their 'basis' in empirical experience, a basis which, being not itself a belief but a sensation, could stand on its own feet, confirming the things that rested on it. Arguing that this picture is impossible, Sellars introduced the distinction between 'the space of causes', in which molecules and photons bounce around and brains respond to them, and the 'space of reasons', in which things get accepted, inferences are made and reasons given. In this metaphor there is a complete dissociation between the 'space of reasons' where beliefs and thoughts have their place, and the 'space of causes' where things impact on other things.[10]

This initially reasonable and influential complaint of Sellars is surprisingly explosive. It cocks a gun and points it at the heart of any project of epistemology, and many philosophers have been happy to pull the corresponding trigger. Indeed a century earlier, in Green and other 'absolute idealists' this kind of criticism inaugurated a drift away from the idea of knowledge as having any kind of footing at all in sense-experience. Instead, attention shifted to the whole system, the entire corpus of a person's beliefs, whether formed by interactions with the world, or by habit or by reasoning. This is holism, which we now pause to look at.

3. Holism

Holism refuses to take our beliefs one at a time. It insists that any indicative sentence, such as might express a proposition or belief, is embedded in a context which itself plays an essential role in creating and shaping and giving identity to the proposition expressed. Individual sentences are like limbs on a body: they mean what they do only so long as they are not severed from the context, the whole which alone forms a determinate unity of significance. We can sympathize with holism when we think of learning something, such as a new science. We do not understand things one at a time. Rather, as Wittgenstein put it,

When we first begin to believe anything, what we believe is not a single proposition, it is a whole system of propositions. (Light dawns gradually over the whole.)[11]

Holism is now as much a commonplace of the philosophy of mind and meaning as is the idea that 'the given' is a myth.

Yet holism, together with the disappearance of solid footing in experience, puts us firmly on the journey out of paradise. We no longer have a rational hierarchy in which observations, as foot-soldiers, bear information up to the staff who, using experience and reason, organize it and then, with the cooperation of values, generate plans for using it. We have a disorderly muddle, in which everything has a say in everything else. Values and theories, memories and expectations, determine even how the observations speak. There will be different patterns of organization, so that while in one mind a perturbation of one part of the 'web of belief' will excite certain changes in another part of it, in a different mind it might not. We get 'incommensurability' or the sense that there is no identity between differently organized theorists (and we will each be differently organized in one way or another). Firmness of meaning totters, since meaning is now only a role within a whole system, and systems are mobile and fluid, so that even ones that seem to be shaped alike may be poised to differ in unpredictable ways. There is no firm footing, and there are no hard partitions preventing the denizens of one department from interfering with the business of another.

There will be as many systems as there are persons to whom the light shines differently. Just as there are probably as many webs as there are spiders, so there are as many whole systems of belief, differing in large or small ways in their contents and their patterns of inference, as there are people. And any notion of control by individual facts absconds. For individual facts have no place in this picture: they could only make themselves known to us, only be singled out, by individual beliefs and announcements. But nothing is single: any change makes the whole jelly quiver.

Now, even the holism would be all right if reason (*logos*) could hold the ring, determining which observations are good, which interpretations are reasonable, which memories and theories and beliefs are sound, and which should not get their voice heard. It would be all right if we had a determinate sense of who or what gets listened to about what. But we do not. To the modern ear, that sounds too much as though reason has a place outside the ordinary hurly-burly of influencing belief, doing science, arguing about religion, persuading other people. It would be *logos* claiming an authority over how those interactions should be transacted, and by now we know how any such claim is apt to be regarded.

Here it is appropriate to dig a little into the background of modern empiricism, and its old problems with human reasoning. Once more Hume provides us with the pivotal moment. Hume was preoccupied not so much with the nature of the world as with our thinking about the world. And when he considered this thinking, he convinced himself that almost nothing about it is explained by reason. Instead there are mechanisms of 'natural belief': the subjective inevitability that a human nature like ours, giving rise to minds like ours, will end up thinking about the world in the ways we do. We will turn our strings of impressions into objects, and convert the patterns in our experience into causal laws, but although this is natural, and useful, it has no other basis in reason. But it is worse than that. Not only does reason not generate our thinking, there is also no standpoint from which reason can reassure us that in thinking as we are bound to do, we get things right. Nature may or may not conform to the ways we think, but there is nothing we can do to reassure ourselves that she is likely to do so. In fact, as already sketched, when it comes to the external world reason actually insists that what we do is inconsistent.

This would not do for Kant at all. Kant wanted not subjective inevitability, but objective validity. He wanted a guarantee or a 'deduction' (a legal term meaning a proof of title) that in thinking as we do, we indeed get things right. He even thought he could provide it, but only at a cost. For Kant, like Hume, finds that he cannot prove that an independent, real world must conform to our habits of thought. Locke's transcendental realism remains untenable. But Kant thinks he can show that the 'world as it is for us' must conform to our ways of thinking. So he concludes that the things we think about and perceive 'are in all their configurations and alterations nothing but mere appearances, that is, representations in us, of the reality of which we are immediately conscious'.[12] The harmony between thought and world is certified only because the world about which we think is somehow 'constituted' by the conditions of our thought and experience of it.

We might well think that Kant gives us a dreadful alternative to Hume (with a hideous title: transcendental idealism). And both Hume and Kant together began to look worse when the optimistic Enlightenment belief in a fairly universal human nature came under suspicion. Given this suspicion, then as history unfolds, there will be not one subjective inevitability, let alone one valid or accurate way of thinking, but simply a procession of differently minded people each equally entrapped in their different world views. Once more, it would be all right if there was something called reason or *logos*, accessible to us and enthroned above the fray, and able to judge the competitors. But this is what Hume denied.

In analytical philosophy Hume was updated in Quine's famous paper 'Two Dogmas of Empiricism'. Quine had several fish to fry, one being the Sellarsian mistrust of the idea that observation answers to nothing but the world. But here it is reasoning that concerns us. Like the British Idealists, with whom he had a considerable affinity, Quine substituted a massive holism: the unit of empirical significance, he proclaimed, is the whole of science. But Quine introduced a connection between holism and the breakdown of the 'a priori', which here includes any putative rules of right reason, playing the role of a judge who determines, from a position beyond empirical experience, how that experience should be interpreted and how it should be used. Just because of the jelly-like nature of the whole system, Quine argued that meaning itself is unstable. And if meaning is unstable, so are logical relations between individual things we say: inference itself, far from following a priori, rigid norms or rules, becomes just part of the whole, and is capable of being jettisoned or changed whenever it may be expedient to do so. (Quine was undoubtedly influenced here by the breakdown of apparently a priori certainties about the structure of space and time in modern physics.)

The remaining image is of the whole jelly of belief quivering in reaction to 'recalcitrant' or surprising experience. But there is no one right way for the jelly to tremble after such a prod. There could be an indefinite variety of ways, none able to claim the blessing of *logos* any more than another. It will only be time that eventually, and then only provisionally, anoints one reaction as having proved more useful than another.

This is bad, but it gets worse.

4. Davidson's Mantle

Probably the most influential heir to Sellars and Quine was the late Donald Davidson. Building on Quine's metaphor of the web of belief, and following Sellars on the Myth of the Given, Davidson reaffirms the hermetically sealed, self-contained nature of the web: 'Nothing can count as a reason for holding a belief except another belief.'[13] Davidson also quotes Rorty:

Nothing counts as justification unless by reference to what we already accept and there is no way to get outside our beliefs and our language so as to find some test other than coherence.[14]

Observation itself, since it is now to be thought of in terms of the perceptual beliefs that come into our head when we open our eyes or move around our world, becomes just a generator of beliefs, and the only things our thought can occupy itself with are the beliefs thus generated. The result, as John McDowell phrased it, is an image of thought 'spinning frictionlessly in the void'.[15] The thinking person becomes not so different from a blind solipsist, hearing only voices in his head. The voices give him beliefs, perhaps, but 'checking' a set of beliefs would simply be a matter of bringing more beliefs up into juxtaposition with the originals, and letting the chips fall where they may.

It is not difficult to think that something has gone wildly wrong by this point. (I feel like echoing something Thomas Nagel felt compelled to add, discussing Rorty: 'I'm not making this up.')[16] Yet few modern philosophers have managed to escape from the trap that has been sprung. The problem, obviously, is going to be that of retaining any conception of the *authority* of either observation, or theory, given this much downgrading of the role of experience. If sensory occurrences are dumb then they do not justify one speech or another by the Jamesian lawyer. And if they have no intrinsic authority themselves, it is equally difficult to retain any sense of intrinsic authority in any particular way of thinking about them.

It is not just observation and theory that become subtly downgraded, however. The loss of authority, the loss of *logos*, of our ways of *getting at* the truth, quickly transposes to loss of authority in the notion of *truth itself*. If there is nothing so special about any particular method of coming at sayings, what can be special about the sayings themselves?

Davidson himself managed a kind of substitute for contact with the world. The substitute was to cast a snow-white mantle of truth over any system of beliefs, purporting to show that even in the absence of any such rational connection with experience, most of them have to be true. His argument for this was as follows. Davidson invites us to consider our position when we interpret someone else. We find someone saying various words, in circumstances where we ourselves believe one thing or another. We want to interpret him, to know what the words mean. Davidson argues that our only strategy has to be to invoke a 'principle of charity', seeing the target as more or less right (by our lights) about things. The idea is that if he says 'Lo! a tiger', pointing to an animal which we judge to be a tiger, it is a better bet that he means 'tiger' by what he is saying than, for instance, 'cockroach'. We have to assume that he shares a good deal of our take on things to progress at all in interpreting what he says and thinks. Indeed we can get to the point of attributing mistakes to him at all only against a background of supposing him to share most of his conception of the world with us.

How does this get us to most of our beliefs being true? It gets us as far as 'most of the beliefs of anybody we can interpret must be ones we share', but that seems a long way away. Perhaps we are seriously out of line with the way things are, and then, obeying the principle of charity, take our poor target to be just as seriously out of line – whether he is so or not. We would be rather like Christians who like to think that everyone, however strenuous their apparent denials, is really a Christian as well, since in their minds that is so obviously the way to be that anybody failing to be that way would simply make no sense. We get to the inevitability of our substantially imposing our take on things on anyone we set out to interpret, but we don't, unless we are very complacent, get a sense that we must thereby be interpreting our target rightly (the Christians would be wrong, about me for example). And we don't, unless we are even more complacent, get an enlarged sense of we ourselves being right about things (the point so far scarcely looks like a promising defence of Christianity).

Davidson tried to close the circle. He did this by invoking the idea of an omniscient interpreter: a God who knows how things stand. Such a being *would* have mostly true beliefs, and then, because he has to exercise the principle of charity in order to come to understand us, he would have to interpret *us* as having mostly true beliefs. And since he *would* be right if he did this – presto! – we do have mostly true beliefs.

It is easier to feel astonished by this splendidly, gloriously devious argument than it is to put a finger on exactly what is wrong with it. But one deficiency stands out plainly enough. From a sceptical standpoint, the problem is that we do not know what beliefs the omniscient being would suppose us to have. We know he interprets us as having true beliefs, but we do not know what those are. Reverting to the religious model, it is as if we know that he takes our words, whichever words we say, to refer to the One True Deity (himself!). But we don't thereby learn which is the one true deity: that of Christians, Muslims, pantheists, pagans or something else altogether. It as if having thought yourself a good Christian, you might ascend to heaven and not only find the panoply of Greek gods, but (perhaps fortunately) find that unbeknownst to yourself, you had actually been worshipping them all your life.[17]

Davidson was trying to throw a blanket mantle over beliefs, not of course trying to show that we are right about everything, but that we are right about most things. But that is a poor substitute for what we really want. We don't want to be told that we are mostly right, overall, especially if we are left unsure what we are mostly right about. Rather we want specific certainties in specific contexts. I want to be sure about the here and now, my surroundings, my contact with the world, my observations, in short. But we are expelled from paradise: it was this everyday security that got lost in the holistic picture, once observation and inference were demoted to just being more of the whole.

It took the flamboyant French philosopher Jacques Derrida to come up with the defining motto of postmodernism – 'Il n'y a pas de hors-texte' ('There is nothing outside text') – but it begins to look as if allegedly sober Anglo-Americans were right behind him.

5. Rorty's Talking World

It would be nice if there were a way of undercutting the whole problem, pointing the gun at some concept that everyone in these salt mines unwittingly shares. Perhaps something went wrong as soon as we listened to Hume's scepticism, or clutched at Kant's idealism as a response to it. Perhaps Davidson's attempt to throw a mantle of truth over our naked contingencies was itself an attempt to grapple with a problem on which we would do better to turn our back.

Once this suggestion is made, a candidate leaps to the eye. Everyone in these debates is bothered about our capacity to describe truly, or represent the world. So each shares an ideal of representation. But suppose that this very idea is itself a delusion – suppose the mind is not even in the business of representing the world? This is Richard Rorty's proposal. We must scrap the idea that language and mind are there to enable us to represent the world, either truly or not.

Instead Rorty takes from Darwin the idea that language is an adaptation and words are tools. Like William James and John Dewey, the American pragmatists of the early twentieth century, Rorty thinks the essence of language is what we do with it. Language is about knowing how, not knowing what or knowing that. Or, as Rorty likes to say, it is for coping not copying. So he can write:

There is no way in which tools can take one out of touch with reality. No matter whether the tool is a hammer or a gun or a belief or a statement, tool using is part of the interaction of the organism with its environment. To see the employment of words as the use of tools to deal with the environment, rather than as an attempt to represent the intrinsic nature of that environment, is to repudiate the question of whether human minds are in touch with reality – the question asked by the epistemological sceptic. No organism, human or non-human, is ever more or less in touch with reality than any other organism.[18]

This may be a little bit over the top (the last sentence alone is enough to annoy many of us, since some people seem to be much less in touch with reality than others). But the attractive idea is that linguistic tools have their purpose, and so can be retired when that purpose is done, while other projects and other tools rise to supersede them. Rorty calls this a change of vocabularies, echoing Thomas Kuhn's famous description of scientific change in terms of paradigm shifts, and echoing as well Carnap's own view that questions about the overall adequacy of any particular conceptual scheme represent choices rather than discoveries.

Rorty can then walk away from the traditional problems, and better still he can walk away with his head held high. He does not have to accept the labels of relativism or scepticism that the old dialectic forced upon us. Those labels apply if we think that representation is 'just us' (relativism) or that it really tells us nothing of the real nature of what we represent (scepticism). But Rorty's idea is that he is now free of representation altogether, and so he refuses the labels. Only people who have not got the message that we should not be talking of representation at all use them.

We are to replace, Rorty advocates, a vocabulary of 'objectivity' or 'representation' with a vocabulary of 'justification' and 'solidarity'. The idea is that

we understand knowledge best when we understand the social justification of belief, and thus have no need to view it as accuracy of representations. Instead of seeking 'vertical' relationships between language, or ourselves as language users, and the world, we must concentrate upon 'horizontal' or inferential processes, whereby we advance and accept reasons from each other. Justification becomes a 'social phenomenon' rather than a transaction between a 'knowing subject' and 'reality'.[19]

Note the inverted commas over the knowing subject and reality. This substitution of course coincides with realizing that, contingently and historically situated as we are, the norms that govern the activity of gaining solidarity with our peers are *our* norms. They are not norms provided by the world itself, or 'nature's own norms'. This is the line of thought that issued in the pronouncement that Putnam turned his recoil argument against, in chapter 2, that 'truth is what your contemporaries let you get away with'. Put just like that it looks ridiculous, and is surely untenable. But we can now see it more charitably, as the perhaps misleading summary of a very powerful line of thought, and one followed by many philosophers.

To many of us, however, the solution looks worse than the problem: language is not there to represent how things stand – how ridiculous! It is as if Rorty has inferred from there being no innocent eye that there is no eye at all. For after all, a wiring diagram represents how things stand inside our electric bell, our fuel gauge represents the amount of petrol left in the tank, and our physics or history tells how things stand physically or historically. Rorty thinks this kind of protest shows a naive attachment to the old vocabulary, which he wants us to abandon. And the way to get people to change vocabularies is not by argument but by persuasion. So he wants to persuade us of the benefits of his preferred pragmatist alternative. He has many techniques of persuasion, but two stand out.

One is familiar to us by this point in our journey. Rorty argues that any ambition to anchor our beliefs, to really find that they deserve the cherished labels of truth and falsehood, will require standing outside our own skins, or standing on an Archimedean point free from all theory or preconceptions, hoping vainly for a 'view from nowhere'.

We have seen this thought often enough. The second diagnosis, however, is much more interesting. It associates the idea of representation with the idea of a world that *demands* to be talked of one way or another. Representing the world correctly then becomes representing the world in the way it demands to be talked about. Rorty often presents his realist opponent as supposing that there is 'one privileged discourse' or a preferred vocabulary: the vocabulary of the Book of Nature. The enemy is the idea that 'the final vocabulary of physics will somehow be Nature's own',[20] or that there is a vocabulary that is 'somehow already out there in the world, waiting for us to discover it'.[21]

This may sound cheap, a caricature of anything that people who think of us as representing the world want to hold. Indeed, the French analytical philosopher Jacques Bouveresse has said, discussing these passages, that the target seems to be absurd, and taking this absurdity to imply the defeat of realism is 'to hold over realism a victory that is frankly much too easy not to be held suspect'.[22]

But we are now in a position to make at least some sense of Rorty's thought, in terms of the Sellarsian separation of the space of causes from the space of reasons. This gave us, in Davidson, that only beliefs justify beliefs. It is supposed to follow from this that there is no *rational* relationship between anything outside the sphere of language – as the world might seem to be – and mental states expressible by means of language. There could at best be *causal* relationships between anything 'outside the sphere of thought' and our thoughts themselves. Our interactions with the world are just the boundary crossings as one buzzing hive of particles and energies (outside) interacts with another buzzing hive of particles and energies (ourselves). And then how we react to the buzz will be a matter of utility and adaptation: our words are only the current survivors in a Darwinian jungle. Others will undoubtedly supplant them in time.

Rorty, like Derrida, is in fact updating Berkeley's complaint against Locke that an idea can only resemble another idea. In the updated idiom this becomes that a piece of language can only represent another piece of language. The ambition of representing the world explodes, since the world does not speak – it only causes. Rorty compares Sellars's insight to the realization that it is not God who provides moral laws. The human race attained one stage of maturity when it realized there is no alien, external giver of laws, as God was supposed to be. It attains a further stage of maturity when it realizes that the world is silent about how it is to be described. Rorty's fundamental thought is that there is no such 'alien authority'. His hostility to the notion of 'representation' is that for him it goes along with the idea of an objective reality that has replaced God in people's minds, as constituting this authority.

Rorty likes the comparison between the notions of truth and representation, and God. Asked of any inquirer, the question 'Does he love truth?' is, Rorty claims, no more verifiable than 'Is he saved?' or 'Does he love the Lord his God with all his heart and soul and mind?' In the secular West we have lost interest in the last two questions. We have got bored with the theological vocabulary. It is time we got bored with the first, the vocabulary of accurate representation or truth. Once we really absorb Sellars's metaphor of the two spaces, Rorty reasons, we see that any reaction to the causal flux is as 'reasonable' as any other, although some may stand us in better stead. But words are tools, and beliefs are habits of action: pick up any you like, and the Darwinian jungle, not reason, will determine which comes out on top.

A useful example of what is going on comes from literary criticism, which Rorty likes to display as a paradigm intellectual endeavour. So consider the 'reader response' view of what goes on in this activity. According to this there is never one right reading of a text. There are only the different meanings different readers find bubbling up as they read it. The text here functions merely as a stimulus, and what any particular reader makes of it is not a matter of being justified or not, but simply a matter of being nudged or blown one way or another. So in older times a grandee of literary criticism, a Lionel Trilling or an F. R. Leavis, could assert a hard-won right to determine how a text was to be read. They could proclaim truth and real authority for their knowledgeable, cultivated, educated reading, but now there is only a plurality of voices vying to establish their own view as the view that is to be preferred by fellow interpreters. The notion of discovery is then not one of uncovering something that was there already, but rather the notion of fertile invention, such as discovering a new way to play King Lear. It is what Rorty calls inventing a new vocabulary. In the *après*-truth literary world, the aim of voicing opinion is not to arrive at the truth, but to bring the others to your opinion, thereby gaining their solidarity with you. There is no difference between inventing something new and discovering what was there anyway.

This sounds a bit like the danger with which William James flirted, in chapter 1, of abolishing the distinction between wishful thinking and accuracy, and actually that's fine by Rorty. Writing of feminist accounts of the difference between men and women, he says:

The question of whether these differences were there (huddled together deep down within the entity, waiting to be brought to light by deconstructing excavators), or are only there in the entity after the feminist has finished reshaping the entity into a social construct nearer her heart's desire, seems to me of no interest whatever.[23]

You can make it up as you go along: discourse is a social activity, with a social purpose. If a Trilling or a Leavis looks down his nose and proclaims reason and truth for his own interpretations, it is just one more power move in the democratic conversation. It is what conservatives say when they see King Lear played a new way, and it is not an exercise of right authority, but (unsurprisingly) an exercise of conservatism. If we agree with the conservatives, well and good, but if we do not agree, well and good too. Or at least, well and good unless our innovations fail to gain an audience, and it turns out that we do not cope very well as a result.

The best way to understand Rorty is simply to see him as generalizing this view of humanity and its literatures across the board. In science or history, law or psychology, politics or ethics the same model applies. There is the community of interpreters, and the aim of getting them to be of one mind. There is invention and innovation. But just as a text allows for multiple readings, so does the world. Truth, and reason as the anointed method of sifting it, disappears.

It is obvious that this stance will find a sympathetic ear among social constructivists, multiculturalists and pluralists, and conversely it is tailor-made to infuriate anyone inclined to claim right reason and earned authority for themselves. People who pride themselves on their accuracy are insulted by being described as inscribing their wishes on the world.

6. Keeping our Feet on the Ground

Many of us may think in terms of one world. God only had to make a piece of terrain once with all its abundance of features. But he did not thereby bring it about that there could only be one proper *take* on the piece of terrain. You can map it how you like: map the geology, topography, population, rivers, crops, and you can map all these in different ways for different purposes. A unique world is one thing, but it does not demand just one description.

So perhaps Rorty has failed to notice that his question of authority is ambiguous. Does a landscape tell us how it is to be mapped? In one sense, clearly not. Your purposes may dictate that you map on any of many scales, depicting topography, population, rainfall, geology, or a multitude of other things. Here you can choose whatever turns out useful. You can stress what you like and be as vague or precise as you like, and leave out what you like. Sometimes a brief sketch is enough, and sometimes only an admiralty chart will do. Pragmatism and Darwin and multiple perspectives are all in order. There is no competition between a geological map and a rainfall map.

In another sense, however, the landscape indeed dictates something. It dictates how it is to be mapped, *given* a set of conventions determining the meanings of the signs and shapes on the map, and the meanings of their presence or absence. That is why, once a set of conventions has been put in place, a map can be correct or incorrect. In other words, it can represent the landscape as it is, or represent the landscape as it is not. The map can show that there is a church in Little Gidding, when there is, or show that there is a church there, when there is not. It can show cliffs where there are none, and fail to show cliffs where they lurk.

These harmless platitudes should be sharply distinguished from the ludicrous idea that the only true map would map the landscape 'in itself', somehow embodying a 'final vocabulary' or 'nature's own vocabulary' dictating just how it is to be mapped, as if human selections, purposes and interests had nothing to do with it.

Maps may be made in many different ways, but they do not encourage an attitude that places all authority about what they mean in the diverse subjectivities of their various readers. Certainly, a maverick may decide to 'interpret' the Ordnance Survey map of Cambridge as the blueprint of the Great Pyramid (if this seems outlandish, we might remember that in order to capture some of the prestige of Greece, ancient historians have actually interpreted the geography of the

Odyssey as pertaining not to the Mediterranean, but, for instance, to the Caspian sea). He might have fun doing so, clambering in and out of burial chambers intently following the course of the Great Ouse on his map, but he is ignoring something that the rest of us have learned: the cartographic conventions, and the stability of the expectations and interests of map-makers and map-readers. Apart from anything else, these explain the production of the map in the first place. And those of us who have learned the conventions and know how to use them have acquired a technique or a skill, map-reading, which others may lack. Our projects of going to church or walking the hills go better as a result. If we are to read complex maps properly, we do well to defer to the equivalent of a Trilling or a Leavis after all.

That much cannot be denied by the pragmatist, but now we can hear Rorty declaiming the mantra of coping not copying, trying to drive a wedge between pragmatic success, which he admits and likes, and representation, which he does not. And all we have pointed out, he may say, is the success of the map, its utility to the churchgoer or the walker. Similarly the one undeniable measure of science's authority is the fact that its productions work.

At this point the unconverted ought to complain – loudly, very loudly – that the opposition between coping and copying totters and falls. The map enables us to cope, indeed, but we also know why. It enables us to cope precisely because it represents the landscape correctly; it enables us to anticipate what we shall find. Similarly, if Rorty is to catch a plane, he will doubtless look up the time of departure in a timetable. That enables him to cope better, but it does so just because the times written in the timetable represent the intended times of departure. It is not a miracle that the timetable helps Rorty cope. It would indeed be a miracle if there were no stable way of reading the figures on the page. But there is, and timetables beat tea leaves and crystal balls as a result. As we are about to see in the next chapter, science too offers us its own explanation of why it works, and there is none better. It works because it identifies the powers of things and the physical forces that make stuff happen. That enables us to harness those forces and adjust them, and make different stuff happen. That is how we cope.

If this disarms one part of Rorty's thought, we can similarly under-mine the idea that in talking of truth and representation we are vainly attempting to stand outside our own skins, measuring a correspon-dence between what we say and how the world is. A map can bear hallmarks of curiosity, accuracy, care and labour in the making. These are not hidden or mythical virtues, but ones on display. Great makers of maps and charts are revered because they display them. They are virtues you have to exercise if you care about truth, and we can be aware of them, or be aware of productions that lack them. We can also be aware of improvements in them, or fearful of decline. The maps of some countries are shoddier than those of others. Certainly, no map gives us the whole truth, entire, complete and final. There are new things to map, as new interests grip us. But many maps give us some truths, and some more than others. Good ones do not contain misinformation similar to 'Belgium invaded Germany'.

Newton famously compared himself to a 'small boy playing on the sea shore and diverting himself by now and then finding a smoother pebble or a prettier shell than ordinary, whilst the great ocean of truth lay all undiscovered before me'.[24] He could not have got the same effect by saying that the great ocean of vocabulary change lay all undiscovered before him.

When we came across minimalism about truth, in chapter 3, we may not have realized its full implication for these debates, but now we can see that just by being so small and modest, truth is not a candidate for retirement. And when we see this, we see that Rorty's position cannot be sustained either.

Consider this question for Rorty's own alternative to talk of truth and the rest. What exactly goes on in the *après*-truth salons where the conversation of mankind murmurs on? The problem is that it seems integral to the self-conception of mapmakers and timetable producers, as well as scientists, historians and perhaps even literary critics, that there is a kind of success that goes beyond common agreement. We do not make a map by sitting and talking it through until we are all agreed, but by measuring and checking. There is such a thing as get-ting it right, and agreement with others is a very imperfect signal of having got things right, being neither necessary nor sufficient. We cannot find truth by sitting around in the coffee-house, chatting until we seem to be all of one mind.

If they are denied any concept of a bull's-eye of truth, the target or goal of their activities, what do the *après*-truth mapmakers, historians and scientists actually do? Do they any longer make measurements, burrow in archives or build laboratories? The dilemma is that if they don't, then they have stopped being surveyors, historians and scientists altogether, like a child who draws what he calls maps but without checking what he does against any features of the landscape. But if the cartographers measure, the historians consult archives and the scientists carry out experiments, then they need some concept of discovery to make what they are doing intelligible. They are uncovering how things stand, uncovering the truth. Minimalism gives them this, with a conspicuous lack of fuss. The issue is the issue: once we know what they are looking to find out, we also know what its truth would be.

Thus, it is one thing to wonder whether some particular thing is true. And it is a quite different thing to wonder whether in asserting it we will be 'gaining the assent of our peers'. Asking that question is already looking at things with a squint. For normally our gaze is fixed not on the assent of our peers but on whatever is the issue at hand.*
Thus minimalism showed us that any sentence comes with its own 'norm' of truth. If the issue is whether pigs fly, the truth would consist in pigs flying, and that is what we must investigate. If the issue is

* Here I can't help recalling an anecdote I also told in *Ruling Passions* (Oxford: Oxford University Press, 1998), about a relativist historian and philosopher of science I once heard at a conference, who took himself to have learned the lesson of displacing the norm of truth by the norm of assent of our peers. The problem he then posed for his own view was that Michael Faraday, long celebrated as one of the greatest experimentalists, seemed to have designed instruments only for registering such things as electrostatic charge and never ones designed to detect the approval of his peers. The idea was that Faraday should have been more concerned to invent something like a Gallup poll, or perhaps an internet chat room, since consensus was his aim, and these provide ways of measuring whether we are getting towards it.

What seemed left out was that one of the things Faraday's instruments were excellent at doing was not *registering* the assent of his peers, but precisely *creating* such a consensus. When, hitherto, people did not have a view or share views on electrostatic charge, after Faraday they came to do so.

whether Cambridge is north of London, it is a different investigation, but equally directed at truth, that is, at whether Cambridge is north of London. So the very *content* of a sentence – the issue it introduces – directs where the serious inquirer should look and how to evaluate it. And only some very small subset of contents concern the assent of our peers.

Rorty has attempted to answer such queries. He insists that his view allows for the distinction between the serious and the frivolous, and he wants to insist that serious inquiry survives his reinterpretation of it. 'What, I still want to ask, is so "mere" about getting together with fellow inquirers and agreeing on what to say and believe?'[25] This is by way of resisting one critic's comparison between aiming at solidarity and aiming at unison in 'some perhaps purely decorative activity on a level with a kind of dancing'.[26] Rorty falls back on insisting that he fails to see 'how anything can be relevant to deciding whether a sentence *is* true except the outcome of actual or possible practices of justification to our fellows'.[27]

It is worth thinking about this a little more carefully. At first sight there seem to be two very different 'norms': one of answerability to the facts, and the different one of gaining unison or solidarity with our fellows. Rorty replies that he sees only one norm, rather than two. He does however admit some content to the cautionary or 'fallibilist' thought that current practice might tell us to affirm that X happened, although the facts may be otherwise. But he glosses the distinction as that between two answers to the question 'To whom are we trying to justify ourselves?' namely 'current practitioners' on the one hand, or 'some other, better informed or more enlightened practitioners' on the other.

This is fairly astonishing: how can Rorty deny and debunk truth, but keep notions such as 'better informed' or 'more enlightened' which are obviously inextricably entangled with it? We can see the cul-de-sac that lies this way, by looking at a dispute of a similar kind.

7. Interlude: Law, Tennis and the Coffee-house

Stanley Fish, a counterpart to Rorty, has conducted a long-standing dispute with Ronald Dworkin, who is nearer to being a realist, and is particularly concerned to establish concepts of objectivity and truth in areas such as law and morality.[28] Fish objects to Dworkin's elaboration of the idea of 'law as integrity'. Dworkin presents this conception of legal practice as a satisfying alternative lying between two different poles. One is 'positivism' or the view that legal practice is entirely dictated by pre-existent facts, such as the black letter statutes and decisions that are, as it were, on the page, or 'just there anyway'. The other, confusingly called 'realism' in the philosophy of law, is the subjective or purely pragmatic view, according to which what judges and lawyers do is answerable to nothing except their own perceptions of society's needs of the moment (or even just the judge's own needs of the moment).

Faced with these unappetizing alternatives, Dworkin's idea is that of a suitably serious, intelligently hermeneutic approach, according to which practitioners endeavour to fit their judgements into the pattern that, in their view, is best exemplified by previous decisions and statutes. This can all sound like good, cautious and professional common sense, and indeed in one way it is. The trouble, Fish complains, is that it is such good, cautious professional common sense that it is, in fact, entirely vacuous. It represents no peculiar or admirable or contestable ideal at all, yet it is as such that Dworkin presents it.

The reason, Fish argues, is that neither of the two 'poles' between which Dworkin is carefully steering represents a landmark. The positivist fantasy is one of constraint by precedent in a way that is *uncontaminated* by interpretation, revisitation, rethinking or active engagement with the meanings of what lies on the page or in the record. The positivist forgets that those meanings, being meanings *for us*, do not lie on the page or in the record. Here 'the record' plays the role of the buzzing causal flux, which comes into consciousness only when interpreted or understood in one way or another. The positivist forgets that you cannot read a case or a statute without, well, *reading* it, which means taking it into your mind in the form of judgements. The positivist is trapped in a version of the Myth of the Given, the fantasy of a self-interpreting, self-extracting text which is immune to the diversity of subjectivities, which does not even need a mind to take it up. He wants an *Odyssey* that simply *cannot* be read as referring to the Caspian.

On the other hand, the subjectivist, or in the philosophy of law sense 'realist', fantasy is one of 'judgement' that does not answer to the norms that in fact dictate what judgement *can be* in this area. A 'judge' who does not look at statute and precedent is, in legal practice, no judge at all, but perhaps someone who has gone off his head, or a maverick who is deliberately or cynically making a mockery of the whole institution. Avoiding *that* is a condition of playing the game, just as avoiding carrying a cricket bat is a condition of playing tennis.

In Fish's view this means an entire convergence of 'trying to judge according to the legal facts' and 'trying to judge so as to gain acceptance of your peers'. Judicial activity can be described as either. For to be accepted as peers a group must *submit themselves to the very discipline* that is known as 'trying to judge according to the legal facts'. There is no standpoint of proclaiming oneself or anyone else to be a competent judge, but unconcerned about legal truth, any more than there is one of proclaiming oneself or another as a competent scientist or historian, but unconcerned about the scientific or historical facts.

Fish describes the community within which assent is generated in terms of Gerald Postema: 'An interpretive community takes the form of a shared discipline and a thick continuity of experience of the common world of the practice.'[29] (This may sound optimistic in the life and times of doubtful legal exercises such as that of the Hutton Inquiry in Britain, or perhaps the activities of the Rehnquist Supreme Court in the United States, but even malfunctioning legal bodies maintain backhanded conformity to norms, to the extent of trying to disguise their misfires.)

If we look at Rorty's response to critics in this light, certain things fall into place. Firstly the whole issue becomes slightly deflated. What presents itself as a wholesale revolution now looks like a damp squib. For now we can imagine a Rorty who *accepts* a 'sane' conception of answerability to the facts: as we have seen, attempting to get the facts straight is just what anybody who is a paid-up member of the relevant community of inquirers must be described as doing. At a given time and for a given subject matter these inquirers – the serious scientists or historians or lawyers who have mastered the methods of the discipline – constitute the relevant normative community. And this sane conception can coexist peacefully with recognition of the amount of history, culture, learning, or immersion in a shared discipline that it takes in order to create a capacity to conduct inquiry, and so learn to confront the facts.

When Rorty first substituted the goal of consensus for the goal of truth, we shuddered at the outrageous image of someone valuing *après*-truth chitchat in the coffee-house above serious work in the library or the laboratory. It is this that was so shocking. But now it turns out that there is a qualification for membership of the coffee-house. The talkers in the coffee-house are to be masters of the library or the laboratory, just as the legal interpretive community includes only masters of the constitution and of precedent. It also turns out that we cannot achieve the consummation of consensus with them simply by mutual narcissism, each fixing our gaze on the other and chiming in with their sayings. For, in order to achieve consensus, both our gaze and that of our peers must be fixed on the point in hand. If the issue is whether Lee Harvey Oswald acted alone, the conversation must take place amid archives and news footage. If it is whether genetically modified foods are dangerous, it must take place in the biology lab. This is what is involved in being honest and curious – indeed, it is what is involved in understanding the issue in the first place. But having got this far, we can also describe ourselves as people who want to know what happened, or as people who want to find the truth, and a good thing too.

We can see Rorty struggling to avoid this upshot when he tries to rebut the charge that he offers comfort and solace to the relativistic postmodernists and their ilk, the 'bullshitters' of the academy:

I have no wish to cast doubt on the distinction between the frivolous and the serious. This is a serious and important distinction. It is well exemplified in the contrast between the silliest, least literate, members of academic departments of literature and honest, hard-working, intellectually curious, laboratory scientists – just as the distinction between self-righteous priggery and tolerant conversability is well exemplified by the contrast between the sulkiest, least literate, members of academic philosophy departments and honest, hard-working, intellectually curious, literary critics.

Neither of these distinctions, however, has any connection with the difference of philosophical opinion between those who do and those who do not believe that truth consists in accurate representation of the intrinsic nature of reality.[30]

Rorty then fires his favourite comparison: 'Does he love truth?' is, he claims, no more verifiable than 'Is he saved?' or 'Does he love the Lord his God with all his heart and soul and mind?' So how are bullshitters to be detected? They are distinguished not by their goal (not being bothered to get things right). Rather, they are 'unconversable, incurious and self-absorbed'. Others are 'serious, decent and trustworthy'.

The question must be pressed: if Rorty is entitled to say as much as he does, why will he not say more? There are virtues he does evidently regard as detectable, such as curiosity, seriousness and trustworthiness. So we have to postulate an interpretive community that has the ability to winnow out those who are not really curious whether p or who are not serious in their inquiry whether p or not trustworthy in reporting whether p. Perhaps, as it were, these impostors get their opinions from the newspapers or show alarming tendencies to wishful thinking, or to parroting fashionable jargon. Rorty describes such people as being 'unconversable', but the word is inadequate for, of course, they are only unconversable if the conversation is of a particular type. Bullshitters can be voluble, and to some audiences readable. The postmodernists whom Sokal exhibited as having no understanding whatsoever of the science they loved to use in their writings had big enough audiences. The failure they really show is better located by the word 'incurious', but incurious means just not curious whether *p*. And if we can detect those in that state and separate them from those who are curious whether *p*, why not apply the T word? The former don't care about the truth (on this issue) and the latter do.

Once more, then, we find that with sufficient beef put into the notion of an inquiry, and a community of inquirers, the promised contrast between radical pragmatism and sane realism threatens to evaporate. Piece by piece, it looks as though the conventional building blocks of Western thought – representation, truth, objectivity, reason, knowledge – can and must survive Rorty's battering. Getting things right is not a transcendental dream, but a detectable, and laudable, achievement.

8. A Political Message

Justifying something to your peers is not necessarily the same thing as getting it right. It is a *political* achievement to make sure that wherever it matters – in science, history, law, politics or ethics – the people to whom you need to justify yourself have their gaze pointed in the right direction, and so will accept something only when it is likely to be true. Like any political achievement, it needs careful protection.

Sometimes Rorty seems to recognize this, though it appears to clash with his ambition to demolish the honorific notions with which we would describe this achievement: words such as truth, reason or objectivity. Rorty remains fond of saying that if we look after freedom, truth will look after itself. In a free world, he seems to think, only the people with the library tickets and the microscopes, masters of precedents and archives, eventually get into the coffee-house. But without the honorific words, it seems romantically optimistic to expect the achievement to sustain itself. Rorty has this optimism. He has a soft spot for uplifting visions of the psalm of the people, as muscular workers stride shoulder-to-shoulder down limitless vistas into ever more glorious sunrises, which they greet with ever more creative vocabularies.

Lost in this Whitmanesque glow, it is easy to forget that there is no reason whatever to believe that by itself freedom makes for truth, any more than there is to suppose that labour makes one free. Freedom includes the freedom to blur history and fiction, or the freedom to spiral into a climate of myth, carelessness, incompetence or active corruption. It includes the freedom to sentimentalize the past, or to demonize the others, or to bury the bodies and manipulate the record. It is not only totalitarian societies that find truth slipping away from them: the emotionalists of contemporary populism, or the moguls of the media and the entertainment industries, can make it happen just as effectively. That is why Plato felt that he had to forge the vocabulary of reason and truth in opposition to democratic politics; and it is why it remains vandalism to denigrate the honorific words. Orwell thought this, and anybody worried about such things as the ideology of those who own the press, or the Disneyfication of history, should think it, too.[31]

Rorty does hold political views, and he thinks that there is a definite if subtle relation between his pragmatism and his political views. He is celebrated for recommending 'liberal irony' as the proper standpoint on life, the liberalism being the doctrine that 'cruelty is the worst thing we do', and the irony arising from the knowledge that our vocabularies are transitory and contingent and always on the verge of obsolescence. Critics have been infuriated by the aestheticism or the weightlessness that Rortyan irony seems to suggest; but the more important point is that irony appears philosophically out of place in the philosophical situation that Rorty recommends.

Irony, in Rorty's teaching, is supposed to follow on the realization that your vocabulary is always provisional, that better ways of saying things – more useful ways, at least to our descendants – might come along one day. But why on earth should this beget irony? Unless you are the victim of an *après*-truth cartographer, you do very well to take the map seriously when it says there are cliffs, even if you foresee future maps that do not bother about them. The hill-walker who finds this thought destabilizing, and takes an ironic detachment towards his map, is likely to do worse. It is hard to imagine, of course, how any future maps that do not indicate cliffs could be useful to walkers, but then it is hard to see how a successor vocabulary – say, one which does not talk in terms of suffering, or equality, or freedom, or power or justice – could be of much use in politics. So I think that we can safely set the irony aside. It has nothing like the credentials of Greek suspension of belief, for that arose from finding balanced arguments on two sides of a question. But the fantasy about later maps does not provide a balancing argument against there being cliffs where my map places them.

And irony aside, it is a little difficult to know what to make of the liberalism. A political philosophy that simply reminds us that cruelty is the worst thing that we do has not really got very far; and there is nothing especially liberal about it. Conservatives are not in favour of cruelty.

So we should not follow Rorty. But should we have followed the route that led to him? In my view an air of unreality entered the enterprise long before his particular reaction to it. In particular, the combination of accepting the Myth of the Given, of imposing a dualism between the space of reasons and the space of causes, and finally celebrating a formless holism, together did the damage. And lying behind all of them there is a philosophy of mind that needs to be supplanted: the dualistic separation of mind and body that beset Locke and Hume.

So, let us revisit Davidson's slogan that 'Nothing can count as a reason for holding a belief except another belief' – the overture to the hermetically sealed, self-contained picture of the mind. The slogan is untrue on the face of it. Sights, sounds, glimpses, smells and touches all provide reasons for beliefs. If John comes in and gets a good doggy whiff, he acquires a reason for believing that Rover is in the house. If Mary looks in the fridge and sees the butter, she acquires a reason for believing that there is butter in the fridge. If John tries and tries but cannot clear the bar, he learns that he cannot jump six feet. In other words, it is the whole *person*'s interaction with the whole *surround* that gives birth to reasons. John and Mary, interacting with the environment as they should, are doing well. If they acquired the same beliefs but in the way that they might hear voices in the head, telling them out of a vacuum that the dog is in the house or the butter in the fridge, or that the bar can or cannot be jumped, they would not be reasonable in the same way; they would be deluded, and perhaps dangerous. They might make immaculate inferences on the basis of these new beliefs, but they are still defective. Beliefs need a parentage in what surrounds us. They should not be virgin births.

Are we backtracking into the Myth of the Given (see above, p. 143)? Not at all. The sights and smells and feels arising from our interaction with the environment can strike us in various ways, and they can themselves be subject to variation depending on what history and experience we bring to them. There are still potential variations of subjectivity: the same piece of music can sound like an exquisite development of a theme to one listener, and a meaningless set of noises to another. One person may not recognize the whiff as a doggy smell at all, and another may not associate it with Rover. All that we are insisting on is the Giving: the causal interaction with the world that brings about belief and is the basic determination of whether we are doing well or badly in forming it. In effect, we are criticizing Davidson and Rorty for confusing the Myth of the Given, about which they can follow Sellars, with what we could call the Myth of the Giving, the false belief that we can peel away the importance of environmental input in the way we think about belief and truth. The result is disaster.

The roots of this disaster lie in thinking of the mind in spatial terms, as a kind of glassy blob that extends so far and no further. Its occupants are beliefs. But the way beliefs entered into it lies for ever beyond its purview (it may have beliefs about that, but they stay within the blob). Some writers have kept the image, but tried to restore contact with the world by placing the boundaries of the mind further out, beyond the boundaries of the body, into the world itself, hoping that this 'direct realism' restores a satisfactory relationship to the world. This is a wrong turning, however: it invites us to take seriously the comical question of whether an American mind can stretch as far as Europe, or a twenty-first-century mind can embrace the Renaissance. And it makes false perceptions and apprehendings very hard to understand: there remains nothing in common between a mind that 'embraces' a fact, and one that believes falsely that the same fact obtains. The spatial image just tells us that one has something in it, like an egg in a nest, and the other does not.[32]

What we must learn to do instead is to uproot the whole spatial metaphor, which is itself a legacy of a Cartesian separation of mind and body. My mind is not inside me, or partly outside me. Talk about my mind is talk about how I am, mentally. My mind is nowhere except where I am, at a particular place and time, the here and now. My causal connection with things near and far puts me in an explanatory context, and it is the things that explain my words that are their reference, and give them their truth.

Davidson went wrong by wondering what justifies a belief, in the abstract. We ask the question of justification largely in order to apply norms to persons: the question is what justifies John in his belief, and the answer is not confined to mentioning John's other beliefs. John's explorations and investigations, his situation, his observations, experiences, what he has seen and heard, smelled, touched and felt, are all potentially part of the answer. An answer that abstracts away from all that is no answer at all: it leaves it open that John is malfunctioning as crazily as may be.

So we are not going to agree with the great postmodernist slogan made famous by Jacques Derrida: 'Il n'y a pas de hors-texte' ('There is nothing outside the text'). Perhaps this has whatever appeal it does mainly to urban intellectuals, people sufficiently immersed in words and images, and sufficiently divorced from the activities of life (at least at the times when they are writing about life) to really begin to imagine themselves in a virtual reality, the sealed world of their own beliefs and sayings. The cure, as Wittgenstein saw very clearly, is to remember, and perhaps to practise, the practical techniques and skills of doing things in the real world (there are amusing episodes of radical postmodernists who suddenly forgot all about the death of the author and the indefinite plasticity of meaning when it came to fighting about copyright and the accuracy of translations of their own works). As it bears down on you, it is not possible to hold that the oncoming bus is a piece of text. A bomb may be an image or a piece of text to a French social theorist such as Jean Baudrillard, watching the Gulf war on television, but it is not an image or piece of text to the person whom it kills or maims, or who has lost a child or parent to it.[33]

It is unintelligent, however, to get too worked up about the more flamboyant epigrams of postmodernism. Baudrillard had a serious enough point, which is that images and scenarios can dominate our perceptions although they do not represent reality, and of course they can also create, for good or ill, the patterns and points of reference, the scripts in terms of which we interpret what we suppose to have happened. If a theorist says that Scotland is a social construction, he is unlikely to be thinking that a bunch of people with picks and shovels built Ben Nevis or the Cairngorms. He is more likely to be thinking, rightly, that a deal of myth and invention lies behind the way people read Scottishness. After all, the kilt was the invention of an eighteenth-century Englishman, and there never were distinctive clan tartans.[34]

To end this chapter we can connect what we have been saying with issues in the philosophy of science. When we make maps, or use them, we have a 'folk theory', a proto-scientific theory, connecting beliefs and causation. When we write that there is a church on the corner, we take our writing to have been caused by the church, and we take it that it will cause other people who may want to approach or avoid the church to pay attention to the corner. What we talk about is intimately involved in our doings. Now this 'folk theory' of our own success does not take us outside the everyday. We are not 'stepping outside our own skins' as we say these things; we are staying firmly inside them, but secure in our own explanations of our own doings. If Baudrillard's contemporaries saw the bombs as real, this is not because they were getting above themselves, but because they were prepared to think about where their beliefs came from, and if anyone averts their gaze from such a question this means that they do not acknowledge their embodiment in the world at all.

In the next chapter we expand this point in connection with the nature of natural sciences.

7

Realism as Science; Realism about Science

*And in general every student of nature must hold in suspicion
whatever most captures and holds his understanding; and this
warning needs to be all the more applied in issues of this kind,
to keep the understanding clear and balanced.*

Francis Bacon, *The New Organon*, LVIII, p. 48

1. No Miracles

The last chapters have been dominated by the niggling idea that the issue of whether theory matches the real world can be judged only from outside theory. But if theory includes all of our best empirical and scientific understanding of the world, then the outside position is necessarily 'transcendental': we could never occupy it, or even get nearer to occupying it, whatever the length and success of our empirical and theoretical inquiries. In chapter 5 this was the principal motive for preferring the quietism of the south-east to the strenuous realism of the north-east. And while plenty of scientists and philosophers of science want to sign up to being called realists, the transcendental nature of the position has often bothered them – we quoted Thomas Kuhn on just this issue in chapter 3, but perhaps the physicist Niels Bohr summed up the attitude best when he said that 'It is wrong to think that the task of physics is to find out how nature *is*. Physics concerns what we can say about nature.' Yet this too is not entirely satisfactory. It may remind one of the boxer who said in his pre-match interview, 'I can only see it going one way. My way. Of course, how it will actually go I can't say.' There is something wrong about this; is there similarly something wrong about taking realism to be so dispensable?

A reasonable realism needs some kind of reinterpretation, and philosophers have tried to provide it. One attractive modern view treats realism not as involving any transcendental comparisons, but as itself an explanatory hypothesis, on all fours with other theoretical explanations already common in science. Realism becomes, as it were, science's own theory about itself, and with all science's credentials. This refiguring of realism (intended as *real* realism) is largely due to two philosophers, Hilary Putnam and Richard Boyd, and I shall call it the Putnam–Boyd transformation.

The idea is that science is treated as an object of study, and we have certain data about it. These data are best explained by realism. The data include first and foremost the overwhelming success science gives us in predicting and controlling events. In order not to beg any questions, success must not here mean 'success as a realist (alone) conceives it', that is, some kind of success in corresponding with an independent world of fact. Success means success in the empirical, or practical, or observational domain: the kind of success that even devotees of strange cults recognize when they use their mobile phones and emails, aeroplanes and tide-tables. It is a datum that has to be recognized by all parties in these debates. It has a second aspect, which is the convergence of informed opinion upon one view, or the gradual shrinkage of questions left open to serious debate. Relativists may mutter about dark forces privileging Western science or male science, but over huge areas there are no real alternatives and no conflicting lines of inquiry. People who are 'open minded' about, say, whether the Grand Canyon was formed quite recently by a single flood, are simply ignorant about the way the dating of things is done, and has to be done, and ignorant as well about the certitude of the results that geology and allied sciences bring in.

Such thoughts open the way to the 'no miracles' argument for realism. Realism is the only philosophy of science that makes this abundant and continuing success anything other than a *miracle*.[1] This is a hugely intuitive argument. How come that the aeroplanes stay up, the probes land where they should, the reactions follow their predicted path, and the cures work, unless we are getting something *right* about nature? If our maps don't represent the land properly, it will be a miracle that we end up where we want to go. Conversely, the fact that we do end up so often where we want to go is best explained by the simple truth that our maps do represent the land properly. So do tide-tables and timetables, and this in turn is all that explains why we use them. They turn what would otherwise be the miracle of success into a humdrum pattern.

The plan, then, is to transform what seemed like a transcendental doctrine of doubtful meaning into a piece of natural explanation, assessable as other scientific explanations are. In this, the Putnam–Boyd transformation resembles other similar strategies in philosophy. For example, one route to general scepticism starts by thinking of us as acquainted only with our own ideas, and then the world outside becomes an unknowable object whose resemblance to our ideas is at best an idle hope. A plausible response is to think of the external world simply as a respectable causal explanation of our pattern of experience. It deserves our confidence because it is the best explanation we have of why the continued order and predictability of experience is anything other than a miracle.

Do we manage to refer to the theoretical entities of science, the atoms, photons, neutrons, forces, fields of energy, whose magnitudes explain things? Certainly. Reference to theoretical entities follows on nicely. For once gravity, viruses or electrons occupy an explanatory role in our thoughts about nature, they will also occupy that role in explaining why we and our predecessors talk as we do about nature, even if our predecessors got bits of it wrong. For that is just one more complex natural phenomenon. Talk is a consequence of sophisticated human beings learning to detect electrons and the rest. And to see our theoretical entities as playing this explanatory role is in effect to see them as the reference of our remarks and our predecessors' remarks. The electromagnetic force that deflected his galvanometer also made Faraday say what he did about it, and makes us in turn see him as having referred to it. It would not matter to this that he had some false or superseded views about the nature of the force. And this, incidentally, solves the problem that bedevilled Cratylus or Nietzsche about the 'adequacy' of words to things. Our words are adequate to things when they represent them as they are, and centrally that requires that what we say best explains our sayings, just as the actual voltage explains the result of a good measurement of the voltage, or a real cliff explains the symbol for a cliff appearing on the map.

So is it as simple as that? What happens if we debate on the ground set by the Putnam–Boyd transformation?

2. *Science Red in Tooth and Claw*

One doubt about the 'no miracles' argument is due to the distinguished philosopher of science Bas van Fraassen, who points out that 'Any scientific theory is born into a life of fierce competition, a jungle red in tooth and claw. Only the successful theories survive.'[2] In other words, without its empirical and practical success we would not be talking about *that* theory: it would have gone the way of its rivals. If this is all that needs to be said by way of explaining success, there is no need to invoke any kind of 'adequacy to reality' as an element in the story of science.

Van Fraassen's idea is also intuitive enough. Think of scientific theories as denizens in a jungle. Success comes to ones that work; others get discarded. If science has been supported long enough, so that we are no longer in an era of pure speculation and repeated failure, then theories will have been selected because they make predictions that turn out as we expect, or enable us to control things in ways that we want. This kind of 'empirical' success is a sieve, and only theories that get through the sieve survive. The success of science is then not a miracle, any more than the fact that birds see the berries they need, or that primates are innately afraid of snakes.

However, in advancing this explanation we were silent about science as 'adequacy to the facts'. All we relied upon was the superior practical and empirical activities of those who rely upon the theories that then survive the Darwinian winnowing process.

This response to the 'no miracles' argument does not explain the continuation of success of once successful science. Once a theory has beaten off its competitors in the jungle it may be selected, but why is that an indicator that it will continue to be successful? This is the problem of induction: the problem of understanding why regularities that have held in our observed portion of space and time may be expected to go on holding in further regions yet to be encountered. The problem of induction invites us to marvel at the cosmic coincidence of events falling out as they do, time after time, in their fixed, apparently unalterable patterns. Realism (*real* realism) adds another regularity: the cosmic coincidence of reality continuing as it is, time after time. But this is just one more example of induction at work. So when the problem is that of understanding why the patterns of nature have no discernible limit to their shelf-lives, it scarcely adds to be told that they are the outcome of things and laws that themselves have no discernible limit to their shelf-lives. Realism is no solution to inductive vertigo, as David Hume himself very clearly saw.[3]

Another question van Fraassen's response does not address is why nature is such that any competitor emerges as more successful than its fellows: in other words, why it is such as to permit of successful theory, by creatures using our methods in our time spans. It does not tell us why we are so clever or so well attuned to things that any theory at all gets through the Darwinian sieve. Indeed, perhaps in some areas, such as fundamental particle physics or cosmology, we may reach a point of final bafflement, where nothing much further will ever get through the sieve. All our attempts at understanding might eventually grind to a halt. But once more, that issue proves neutral. If it is surprising, or lucky, that the patterns of events are simple enough for us to catch on to them and predict and control other events by their discovery, then it is also surprising or lucky that whatever reality is responsible for them is itself such as to issue in this simplicity.

The phenomena, then, might seem not to need the kind of explanation that realism proffers. And if this is so the natural thing to say is that the Putnam–Boyd transformation fails. Realism would have to slink back into a transcendental darkness, for normal explanatory practices do not suggest any need for it.

But is there something wrongheaded about the opposition between the Darwinian explanation of success and the explanation that the Putnam–Boyd transformation set out to provide? Consider the examples of success we cited earlier. We do well by consulting timetables and maps, because they represent correctly times of departure on the one hand and the spatial layout of things on the other. Suppose someone challenges this, saying instead that we do well by consulting timetables and maps, because the only versions of those things that have survived for us to hold in our hands are precisely ones that have enabled us to do well. That seems right as well – but isn't there something fishy about supposing that we have to *choose* between these two explanations? Surely we can have both together, without in the least feeling driven to admit that the existence of the one renders the other superfluous. We should want to say *both* that the timetable or map I hold may have won, or would have won, in competition with other less useful competitors, *and* that it is useful because it represents times or places as they are, which no doubt the less useful competitors would not have done so well. We don't have to choose between 'copying' and 'coping'. We cope because our best theories get things right, or nearly right or right enough.

Actually, with timetables and maps, we are more certain of their representative credentials than we are that they have come through any Darwinian winnowing process. It is not as if there are spates of timetables and maps flooding off the presses at any time, of which only the good ones get into our hands. Although, of course, we are confident that if inaccurate ones were to get manufactured alongside accurate ones, they would be of less use and their production would soon cease.

Furthermore, in saying this we do not step outside science and common sense. Here we come across a peculiar feature that these share, and one which is not shared by every 'discourse' such as ethics or aesthetics or pure mathematics. Science and common sense offer *their own* explanation of why we do well using them. It is not the privilege of some second-order, philosophical, subtle and elusive theory called realism to explain that success. Science and common sense do it all by themselves. In terms of chapter 5, we are staying within the north-east corner of the discourses themselves. We are not mounting a second-order commentary on them. Science explains why science is successful, wherever it is so. No philosophical commentary is required. If this is so, then by following Boyd and Putnam we are not led anywhere beyond quietism.

3. Explaining from Within

Suppose my practice is successful: my space rockets land where and when they should. What is the best explanation of this success? I design my rockets on the assumption that the solar system has the sun at its centre, *and it does*. Why is our medicine successful? Because we predicted that the viruses would respond in such-and-such a way, *and they do*. In saying these things we are not at all stepping outside our own skins and essaying the mythical transcendental comparison. We are simply repeating science's own explanation of events. There is no better one – unless there is a better scientific rival. Once we believe that the best explanation of geographical and optical data is that the world is round, we also believe that the best explanation of our successes as we proceed upon this hypothesis is that the world is round. It is not that there was a *further* set of data about science (its success) that required something like an independent, sideways explanation. It is just that the very regularities in the phenomena that required the theory in the first place should now be looked on as including any success we have in using the theory. Shadows fall at night because of the revolution of the earth, and success awaits those who expect shadows to fall at night because of the revolution of the earth. Science explains the success of science.

Think of human belief as a phenomenon in nature, and human practice and its successes and failures as its expression. The nature in which these phenomena are situated is the one we describe in the best way we can: it has, for instance, a solar system with a sun at its centre. It once contained living things called trilobites. The sun warms us, and rewards those who plan on being warmed by it. The past existence of trilobites explains the fact that when they died they left fossil remains, and those in turn explain why we believe there were once trilobites, and why we are sometimes successful as we hunt for their fossils in deposits from places and times when they lived.

It is the same with any science. Gases are made up of mobile molecules whose energies are described by the kinetic theory of gases, which explains the empirical gas laws telling of the variation of pressure with temperature and volume. If the kinetic theory is the best explanation of the gas laws, then it is also the best explanation of our success in relying on the gas laws, and hence of our belief in the gas laws. In other words, there is no difference between explaining the gas laws in terms of the kinetic theory of gases, and explaining why we do well relying on the gas laws, which has to be done in the same terms. There is no getting *behind* the explanation.

There is nothing here that is either vicious or virtuous. A scientist certainly ought to suppose that the nature of the electromagnetic field explained Faraday's results – and therefore explains the things he said in his papers. Equally, unfortunately, a theologian (or at any rate an onto-theologian) ought to believe that she accepts Christ because Christ acted on her mind, and her acceptance is neither worse nor better grounded because she so claims. It is just inevitable that her explanation will proceed from within her own best theory. Insofar as she believes her theory, this is what she is bound to say. Her own best theory about why she says the things she does may be very bad indeed, but it is not bad *because* it gives her an explanation of why she is saying them. We are fallible, but no less and no more when we explain how we come to be where we are, than when we explain anything else.

Now there is, in thinking about science (or other 'theoretical' enterprises), a way of doing without these explanations. We could consider our evidence and our responses to it without drawing on any theory we then made up to account for the evidence. We can preserve a theoretically uncontaminated picture of what went on: such and such observations were made, and in response to them such and such a theory was adopted. The enterprise of theorizing can be discussed while 'bracketing' the truth of the theory itself.

In some contexts this is a good thing to do: we might indeed want to discuss the acceptance of scientific commitments in a somewhat anthropological spirit, the same spirit as that in which we discuss the acceptance of Protestantism or voodoo. For some purposes, such as investigating why, given some experiment, some theory did or did not strike significant numbers of people as the right way to go, this bracketing is needed. If I ask why Galileo did trust his telescope, whereas (allegedly) Cardinal Bellarmine did not, the fact that Galileo turned out to be *right* to have trusted it is disallowed. To answer this historical question, we need to bracket that fact, and look only at the situation as it must have appeared to the contemporary actors.

It is easy, but a mistake, to get lured into thinking that the bracketing is mandatory.* Richard Rorty, for example claims outright that:

A pragmatist in the philosophy of science cannot use the truth of Galileo's views as an explanation either of his success at prediction or of his gradually increasing fame.[4]

But so much the worse for Rorty's pragmatism. Galileo would not have been so famous had he not got something right. And it is the same across science. Faraday's fame arose partly because he measured accurately (that is, found true or near true values for) electromagnetically induced currents. That is, when a current existed, he said that one existed; when one was that much stronger than another, this is what he reported, and so on. If these things had not been so, he would not have been so famous; he would have been forgotten as incompetent. There is nothing at all wrong in saying this. If a theory is *our* theory we only 'bracket' its truth by ignoring something which we in fact accept: our own explanation of the phenomena that led to the theory in the first place. And that explanation is exactly the one provided by the theory itself.

The point is obvious applied to common sense. Suppose I come into the room, open the fridge and see the butter, and thereby come to believe that there is butter there. Suppose someone sets out to explain why I believe that there is butter there. He *could* proceed by resolutely 'bracketing' the question of what there is in the fridge. He might start, for instance, behind my eyeballs, and put down only talk of the energies hitting my retina. And for some purposes, in cognitive science, say, this may have a point. If he is interested only in the pathways from retinal excitation to belief, it is indifferent to him how the retinal excitation was caused.

* I believe that ignoring the context and purpose of explanations is responsible for much of the confusion and the heat in debates in the philosophy of science. In my view it is right both to say that we believe Jupiter has four moons because it has, and right to avoid the issue of how many it has if we are explaining why Galileo did and others did not take the telescope to be a reliable device for registering that number of moons. An excellent case history of scientific controversy illustrating these issues is given in Keith M. Parsons, *Drawing Out Leviathan*, Bloomington: Indiana University Press, 2001.

A different investigator in a different context might bracket the question of what was there as well. Suppose I have been prepared for this occasion by being carefully briefed that the fridge frequently contains butter look-alikes: packets or tubs of stuff that is not butter but looks like it. If in spite of this I happily jump to the conclusion that it is butter, my overconfidence seems odd and might require explanation, even on an occasion when I am in fact right. But this is an unusual context, although it can have parallels in science. There could be occasions when an investigator knows that there are other equally likely explanations of his evidence, but suppresses them, and this would require explanation, even if he turned out, luckily, to have been right.

For other purposes and in most contexts of explanation, however, truth makes all the difference. If our investigator is not a cognitive scientist but a psychiatrist, puzzling over me as a patient, then there is all the difference in the world between my tendency to believe that there is butter in the fridge when there is and I have seen it, and a tendency to believe it when there is nothing that even looks like butter. In the first case I am normal, and in the second prone to delusions. In the first case there is nothing out of the ordinary to say, whereas in the second more unusual remedies may be required.

The shocking thing about Rorty's remark is that it seems to want to put Galileo, and the scientific civilization that followed him, into something like the second category, whereas in fact they are in the first. Jupiter's four moons explained Galileo's sighting and his belief, just as the butter explains my more everyday belief. And just as we do not have to draw upon sinister dark forces to explain my status as an announcer of butter, so we do not have to resort to dark forces swaying Galileo and his posterity in that case either. This point is independent of debates over the nature of explanation. All that is required is that perfectly good explanations can be given by *descriptions* of the world, as when we say that there is a chair in the room, or the world once contained living trilobites, or that molecules make up gases. These are things that explain things. And only what is true explains what happens.

4. Animation and Belief Again

So why should we believe our sciences? Some philosophers have held that we should not. Popperians hold that all our sciences give us is hypotheses that have survived attempts to falsify them so far. But as has often been pointed out, this hyper-intellectual take on science leaves out the practical *trust* we put in its results. We do not design things in accordance with theory just because theory has survived so far, but because, since it has survived thus far, we expect it to continue to do so.

Science's credibility derives from its credentials as a provider of explanations. Suppose we call inference to the best explanation of some phenomenon, abduction (the term was coined by C. S. Peirce). Then van Fraassen's position is not just that realism is a poor abduction, because it is trumped by his Darwinian explanation of scientific success, but that abduction itself is never a sufficient ground for *belief* in scientific theory. Van Fraassen insists on a distinction between belief in a theory and its acceptance as merely empirically adequate. According to his approach, realism is the view that science aims to give us in its theories, a literally true story of what the world is like, and for the realist acceptance of a theory involves the belief that it is true (this is a variant of the Story + Meta Story account of realism in chapter 5).[5] Van Fraassen's south-westerly alternative, which he calls constructive empiricism, settles for less: science aims to give us theories that are empirically adequate, and acceptance of a theory involves only the belief that it is empirically adequate.[6] What we have then is an endorsement of one particular epistemic attitude to any explanatory theory that takes us beyond the empirical. The attitude is not one of full-fledged belief, but only acceptance in this distinct and lesser sense.

This counsel opens a rather different front, analogous to that opened by the Wittgensteinian theologians of chapter 1. The Putnam–Boyd transformation was initially attractive not because it invoked anything about belief. The image behind it was not that something special about the nature of scientists' psychological states explained what would otherwise be a miracle, but something special about science's relation to nature, namely that it seems to have got it right.

The constructive empiricist is entirely in favour of scientific theorizing. It is the essential method of reducing phenomena to order, producing fertile models of how things stand, bringing about methods of control, and doing all the things that science does. So van Fraassen wants us to *immerse* ourselves in successful theory. We should learn to speak it like a native, but the distinctive plan is that we immerse ourselves in our best theory of an area (at least provided that our best theory seems to be working well) while 'bracketing its ontological implications', or in other words, without believing it to be true.[7] We might say that the theoretical part gives us only an *instrument* for generating predictions. Or we might say that it gives us a *model* of the way things might be, rather than a description of the way they are. Some people like to say that science gives us *constructions*, perhaps implying the most forthright thing to say, which is that it gives us useful *fictions*, which are to be accepted only as such.

These are fighting words, and calculated to make scientific realists huff and puff. They certainly sound like departures from realism, or at least from *real* realism in the sense of chapter 5 – the realism that accepted both Story and Meta Story. But the contrast with realism as we have seen it in this chapter is actually not so great. In the Putnam–Boyd view, realism is produced as a good explanation of a set of data, such as the ongoing success of science. So it would be open to anybody who approved of the explanation to *accept* realism, however strong or weak acceptance turns out to be. After all, philosophers calling themselves realists would be delighted to find that their theory deserves the same status as, say, the heliocentric account of the shape of the solar system, even if there are voices saying that we should not believe that, but accept it only in an instrumental or empiricist spirit.

The concern here is how far evidence reaches. Most people think it reaches far enough to enable us to believe the kinetic theory of gases or the heliocentric theory of the solar system; the constructive empiricist thinks that it gives us good grounds for the empirical adequacy of those theories, but no more. So we are told to accept, but not to believe:

Like a pubescent child receiving parental advice, we are admonished not to go all the way (although, provided we save appearances, virtually anything less will do!) But this behaviour will neither preserve innocence, nor avoid sin – and sensible parents know better.[8]

At least parents know what they are counselling against. Are we sure we know what belief is, as opposed to mere acceptance as empirically adequate? Did we know the difference between saying 'I have a redeemer' as an onto-theologian, and saying it as a poetry lover? What is the difference between getting nature right, and erecting a scaffolding of fictions that bring us simplicity and predictability, and so enable us to cope?

We must be careful to put properly the two alleged competitors. On the one hand we have whatever the constructive empiricist allows. This includes not only belief that a theory is empirically adequate, but also 'immersion' in the theory. Immersion will include acceptance as empirically adequate, but it includes other things as well. In particular it includes having one's dispositions and strategies of exploration, one's space of what it is easy to foresee and what difficult, all shaped by the concepts of the theory. It is learning to speak the theory as a native language, and using it to structure one's perceptions and expectations. To be immersed in a theory is to have distinct habits of *entry* into the theoretical vocabulary, taking various pieces of evidence to bear positively upon it, habits of *manipulation* of its sentences in making inferences, and habits of *exiting* to empirical prediction and the use of it to control events. Van Fraassen is quite explicit that all of this is absolutely legitimate, and indeed that the enormous empirical adequacy of science is an excellent argument for learning its language like a native.[9] Immersion, then, is belief in empirical adequacy plus what we can call being 'functionally organized' in terms of a theory. This means being at home in its inference patterns and models. We are really talking of someone who has, perhaps tacitly, internalized the conceptual organization a theory involves. We could better call this *living* a theory, or to use the term I introduced in chapter 1, being *animated* by a theory. It is all of *this* that is still to be contrasted with belief. But is there a real distinction? What is the difference between being animated by a theory, and believing it? This is the very question that occurred in chapter 1, when we wondered what told us whether the Wittgensteinian interpretation, or that of the onto-theologian, best fitted religious practice.

We can certainly contrast empirical adequacy *so far* with overall, final empirical adequacy. We can believe that a hypothesis accounts for the data so far, but remain agnostic about whether it will accord with data yet to come. This is a typical scientific position, where we suspend belief because we have no confidence that something surprising will not turn up. We want to wait and see. We may accept a hypothesis in an instrumental spirit, to work out tide-tables or predict or control events, while this is still our attitude. But this is not the relevant contrast. What we are to deal with is the contrast between confidence (real belief) that a theory is *totally* empirically adequate, not just now but for ever, on the one hand, and real belief on the other. When we remain tentative, it does not just affect belief, it equally affects belief that the theory is totally empirically adequate. So it does not make the contrast.

Another caveat. Total empirical adequacy could itself be read in a small, human way, or in a larger way in which the brakes on human awareness are taken off. Thus a theory might be empirically adequate only because we do not look in the right place: constraints of time or space may prevent us from making observations that show that the theory is not, in the wider sense, adequate to the phenomena. This is the contrast between 'empirically adequate as far as we shall tell' and 'empirically adequate as far as ideal investigation could tell it, or as far as it could ever be told'. Total empirical adequacy means only the latter.

Another spurious support for an acceptance/belief distinction comes if we surreptitiously think of the amount of confidence we should ever have in science. 'Belief' has an all-or-nothing, close-the-inquiry ring to it: the more tentative 'acceptance' seems a better-mannered substitute, making room for revolutions of theory and polite open-mindedness. But it must be objected to this that van Fraassen's acceptance is itself a kind of belief – belief in empirical adequacy – and hence is capable of being just as dogmatic or ill-mannered as belief in truth.

Confidence in scientific theory is sometimes dented by the so-called 'pessimistic meta-induction', premised on the continuous history of scientific revolution. We should not believe theories, it is suggested, because it is a very good bet that any current theory will be superseded in its turn, just as it will have superseded its predecessors. The induction does not help constructive empiricism. Previous theories will have been superseded, rather than incorporated in new theory, because they turned out not to be empirically adequate by comparison with their new competitors. So if the induction from the history of false theories is supposed to undermine *belief*, it must also undermine *belief in empirical adequacy*, that is, acceptance. We get no contrast between the two out of the pessimistic induction. We get only a more vivid sense of the tentative spirit in which we might believe things, or equally in which we might accept them.

Of course, one can become very humble contemplating the vastness of scientific claims: can the small, earthbound animal really claim true belief about the vast, extended cosmos? Perhaps not, but then he ought not to claim total empirical adequacy either: God alone knows how things would turn out at other regions or times.

So dogmatism is not the issue. We should not be contrasting dogmatic, closed-minded insistence on the truth of a theory with something more open-minded. Belief in empirical adequacy can be just as dogmatic and inimical to imaginative attempts at falsification. If I conceive myself as knowing that a theory is totally empirically adequate, I might look on attempts to investigate further as a waste of time. On the other hand, belief in a theory can itself be scaled: it can include belief that falls short of certainty, and co-exist with the flexibility of mind that encourages further investigation. So it is wrong to make the issue into one of good scientific manners. We are talking about *considerate*, *well-mannered* belief. We can similarly talk of a considerate way of being animated by a theory: a functional organization in some shape that coincides with awareness of a potential for change and improvement.[10]

A third invitation to make the contrast is that we may accept a theory in an instrumentalist frame of mind, but withhold belief if the theory, while empirically adequate, is inadequate in other ways. It may violate norms of logic, or of method, to which, rightly or wrongly, we are deeply wedded. Quantum physics may be an example: we may have every confidence that it gives correct results, but nevertheless find it deeply unsatisfactory, since we gain empirical adequacy only by treating particles one way in some contexts and a different way in others, but with no surrounding theory enabling us to understand the difference. It can feel as if we had to treat them one way on some days of the week, and a different way on other days. We might refuse to believe such a theory in spite of its empirical adequacy. Our discomfort would show: we would keep working or hoping for a better framework or unifying set of principles.

Again, however, this situation is not to the point. The constructive empiricist is not telling us to suspend belief when a theory generates great discomfort, violating norms of intelligibility. He wants to counsel the contrast even when no norms of acceptance are violated.

Suppose then we are dealing with a theory we believe to be *totally* empirically adequate, which contains no *uncomfortable* internal ruptures and patchworks, and where *well-mannered animation* (immersion) is surely permissible: the common view of the geological past, for example, or the molecular theory of gases, or the heliocentric view of the universe. What then of the contrast between our position and belief? Now we have the issue square, what is it that the children are being told not to do?[11]

5. Underdetermination

Among philosophers there is one common reaction to this question. People acknowledge its force, but suppose that there simply *has to be* a difference, since otherwise we end up in verificationism: the view that the entire content of a theory is exhausted by the evidence for it. The idea is this. We have to face the possibility that many different and even inconsistent theories are all of them totally empirically adequate. If there were nothing more to belief than acceptance as empirically adequate, then we would have to believe each of them. But we do not do this, and if the theories are mutually inconsistent we should not do so.

The only way past this, holding on to the idea that belief is accept-ance, is to deny the underdetermination of theory by data, or in other words to reduce the content of theories to the content of their total empirical consequences. This is the distinctive position of verifica-tionism or positivism. But nobody believes them any longer. To have a theory is not just the same thing as to have the empirical data.

This argument for distinguishing belief from acceptance does not work. It underestimates what can properly be involved in *animation*. We have seen how van Fraassen makes it plain that his acceptance involves immersion in a theory and its world picture. But by itself this enables us to preserve the needed distance from positivism. For to live in this way in one theory is not to live in the same way in another, and still less to live without any theory at all, but simply exposed to the totality of the empirical data. The constructive empiricist is not claim-ing that theories are *dispensable*, even in principle. He obviously could not do so while continuing to advertise the theory as a kind of *instrumentalism*. Theories are indeed instruments, and to have one will be to organize one's conceptual repertoire for prediction and control in a different way from those having another – and in an even more different way from those having none at all.

It is not at all easy to say how two theories might each be totally empirically adequate, yet properly be identified as more than nota-tional variants, but we can allow, for the sake of the argument, that it can happen. If so, it happens only because the inner structures of one theory are different from those of the other; the network has a differ-ent shape. Being animated by it will not issue in different empirical predictions, but it will give a different set of procedures, arguments, behaviours and conceptual routes to those predictions. In Quine's account of this issue, the distinction between two such theories will depend on the difficulty or impossibility of finding translations from one to the other.[12]

We met another diagnostic for the difference between animation and belief in chapter 1. Intuitively if we believe some theory, we can-not believe an inconsistent rival; we have to believe that the propon-ents of the rival are wrong on the points on which they differ from us. But perhaps animation by theory does not have this consequence.

We might structure our thoughts in terms of one theory, which we believe to be totally empirically adequate, and simply pass by people structuring their thoughts in terms of the other, even if we believe it inconsistent with ours. There is no reason to see them as in competition. So perhaps real belief differs from animation in just this way. It does so because there can be just one way the world is, and hence it can accord at most with one of a proposition and its negation. A belief is given its identity by what it excludes.

A fiction is not. We can happily read one story about a fictional character, and then a different story, without finding it necessary to reconcile them. True, aficionados can get very shirty if in one story it is said that the hero has fair hair and in the next story he is said to have black hair, but that is because they are trying to join the two stories together, which they don't have to do. Whereas if the stories were histories of one actual man, they would have to be reconciled. We would expect science to resemble the second more than the first.

It is not all that easy, however, to test van Fraassen's preference for acceptance over belief by applying this test. The scientific predicament is usually that of trying to find one totally empirically adequate theory, not taking up attitudes to several rivals. Furthermore the methodology of determining inconsistency is not at all evident. Remember that the notion of immersion or animation required a stress on different functional organization to show how we might properly talk of *different* yet totally empirically adequate theories. This very difference, however, undermines any sense of how we would recognize them as flatly inconsistent with each other (remember, they are not issuing in different predictions).

So what we are likely to do, if we have a prima facie case of a theory in which we are immersed, and a rival whose inconsistency with ours we acknowledge, but whose total empirical adequacy is also apparent? Our first reaction would be to mistrust the appearance. Either the inconsistency is only apparent, or the rival has comparative defects. If it is really empirically adequate, then perhaps it violates those other norms of acceptance. But suppose none of this applies (as if Berkeley can convince us that his idealism has no internal flaw, no hidden misunderstanding about the nature of mind, for example, and is as simple and empirically adequate as common-sense realism, but inconsistent with it). Is it right that the believer remains *against* the rival, while the merely animated can simply pass it by as a curiosity?

Surely not. Suppose the rival proposes his inconsistent commitment (for example, 'There are just two minds, mine and that of God'). I cannot do anything with this – incorporated in my view it makes something unusable. I have no alternative but to reject it from my standpoint. What seems demanded is at most an increase in consideration. Contemplating that a genuinely equally good way of looking at things exists that is just as adequate, violating no norms, and that is genuinely inconsistent with mine, gives me pause whatever my philosophy of science. The natural reaction is either to find the hidden flaw, or remove the appearance of inconsistency, or increase the degree of open-mindedness in one's acceptance, by backing away from thinking that one's theory is uniquely virtuous. But *everyone* has to do that: there is no reason why these reactions are differently compatible with belief and mere animation.

To put it another way, when I say that these are the natural re-actions, we might remember that another, less admirable reaction is just to shrug and turn one's back on the inconsistent rival. I may be not just animated by my theory but genuinely immersed in it, sunk to the point of shrugging away alleged rivals. It may be that I pass Berkeley's theory by, as we all do most of the time, just by waving it away. But this is hardly, as the present suggestion would have it, a sign of merely instrumental acceptance! Surely the masses who ignore Berkeley believe in an external world. Dr Johnson believed that there was a stone there when he purported to refute Berkeley by kicking it. Indeed his unwillingness or inability to engage Berkeley seriously is often taken as a symptom of blind belief, and certainly not of something less than belief.

Here is a positive way of thinking about it. Both belief and animation are states postulated by a psychological theory, explaining people's expectations and their inferences. Both will be 'multi-track', capable of issuing in a variety of reactions in different circumstances. This means that there will be scope for individual differences. Some

believers, such as Johnson, will find it easy to ignore contrary theories; some will not. Some will be more dogmatic than others. Some
are conservative, tetchy and dismissive of alternatives; others are
open-minded, considerate and exploratory. Someone may work with
a theory happily enough, but work also with other terms that contradict it.

The terms on either side of the belief/animation divide are terms of
art, terms used in our best explanation of ourselves and others. So
what is the method of discovering whether a person is best described
by the one or by the other? The problem is that there is very little
difference indeed between, for example, on the one hand being
animated by the kinetic theory of gases, confidently expecting events
to fall out in the light of its predictions, using it as a point of reference in predicting and controlling the future, and on the other hand
believing that gases are composed of moving molecules. There is no
difference between being animated by a theory according to which
there once existed living trilobites and believing that there once
existed living trilobites.

To resurrect the realism/instrumentalism divide, given all this, we
would need to isolate a dispositional difference that also sustains a
normative discussion, enabling us to *criticize* people who fall on the
wrong side of the divide. For the constructive empiricist it is important that we do not *cross* from acceptance to belief. And if we turn to
the rationale for this cognitive norm, things become even more
perplexing. For if we lose a clear view of what the children are being
told not to do, it is even worse when we then ask why they are
being told not to do it. Even if some yet more subtle diagnostic test
came up, the normative question would demand answering: what is
the authority of a norm specifically against belief?

Van Fraassen himself comes closest to tackling this question when
he expresses disdain for the 'appearance of greater courage' involved
in embracing additional beliefs 'which will *ex hypothesi* never brave
a more severe test than belief in empirical adequacy'.[13] But the disdain cuts both ways: if no pitfalls surround the subject who, *ex
hypothesi* only appearing more courageous, advances across the great
divide from animation to belief, what possible objection can there be

to doing so? What possible extra caution is being shown by refusing to cross the gulf? What can we do but disdain the fake modesty: 'I don't really believe in trilobites; it is just that I structure all my thoughts about the fossil record by accepting that they existed'?

So what is the upshot? If science has no firmer basis than science itself, as Quine put it, perhaps the result is a kind of draw.[14] Applied to the issue of science, the absolutists of our first chapters wanted a kind of 'external' or foundationalist guarantee that by following scientific method, we get things right. Following the twists and turns of the last two chapters, we have failed to give them this much. Nevertheless, by following scientific method, we get things that work: theories that deliver results, technologies that enable us to do things. No other method does as much, and this gives us every reason to pursue it and admire it. We thus become what I called animated by the science, and when we do we go round saying things such as 'electrons have negative charge'. We also hold – for this is what science tells us – that it is the negative charge on electrons that explains our saying the things we do, and hence we can properly hold, for just the same reason, that we are describing, and describing truly (remember minimalism), the nature of the electron.

Is anything missing? Did *real* realists want more? Perhaps they wanted *logos* again, here meaning a proof of unique rationality, a deduction in Kant's sense that would underwrite scientific reasoning for more than the (grubby, worldly) reason that it works. They wanted what is often called a 'first philosophy', a proof transparent to all rational minds of the inevitable success of our methods. Or perhaps they wanted a thoroughgoing exorcism of all the positions in the south-west: the ones that flirt with those dangerous words instrumentalism, constructivism, fictionalism. And this too we have not given them. Indeed, as we have seen in this chapter, it is very difficult indeed to distinguish animation that amounts to real belief, and animation that amounts to immersion in a story that we are prepared to use to predict things and explain things. Our beliefs on the one hand, and the models, fictions, dreams, approximations or metaphors that we employ on the other, may be closer than they seem.

In a way, though, this is only a problem for philosophers. The problem for the culture in general is to maintain confidence, without worrying too much about any subtle differences between animation and belief, or realism and constructivism. And of course, in one sense we do maintain confidence. Our words may sound insecure, but our practice is as robust as may be. There may be rhetoric about the socially constructed nature of Western science, but wherever it matters, there is no alternative. There are no specifically Hindu or Taoist designs for mobile phones, faxes or televisions. There are no satellites based on feminist alternatives to quantum theory. Even that great public sceptic about the value of science, Prince Charles, never flies a helicopter burning homeopathically diluted petrol, that is, water with only a memory of benzine molecules, maintained by a schedule derived from reading tea leaves, and navigated by a crystal ball.

8

Historians and Others

Such then are the illusions that we call idols of the tribe, *which have their origin either in the regularity of the substance of the human spirit; or in its prejudices; or in its limitations; or in its restless movement; or in the influence of the emotions; or in the limited powers of the senses; or in the mode of impression.*
Francis Bacon, *The New Organon*, LII, p. 46

1. Conceptual Schemes

In this final chapter we confront the idea of the Other: the person or persons whose minds are shaped so differently – by language, experience, culture or beliefs – that interpretation and understanding are baffled by them. Their entire way of thinking is different. The same stimuli provoke entirely different reactions. The world as they apprehend it is different from the world as we apprehend it. Here the 'diversity of subjectivities' that we met at the very beginning of the inquiry engulfs so much that mutual understanding is impossible. Their whole 'conceptual scheme' is different. Pessimists see this as bedevilling everyone, as in the Yorkshire saying, 'All the world's queer except thee and me. And even thee's a little queer.' Attempts to understand others, they say, are exercises of power: We impose upon Them. By interpreting them our way, we annex them, colonize them, trample on their difference, and force them into our own mould. Not so, reply optimists. We can join hands, find ourselves in them, obtain a 'fusion of horizons', partake of a common humanity.[1]

Here, very clearly, a political edge creeps into our reflections. If we are pessimistic about mutual understanding, then divisions are inevitable, and we must contour our politics around them. Perhaps men cannot understand women, the East cannot understand the West, and our period cannot understand any previous period. Perhaps classes can only fight, and we are left with a divisive, uncomprehending politics of identity. Nowhere is the immediate political and moral impact of ideas more obvious, or potentially more depressing.

Some help is to hand. In one of the most discussed papers in recent philosophy, a head-on attack on the relativist tradition from Protagoras to Kant and Nietzsche, Donald Davidson argued influentially that the kind of difference that is imagined here should not trouble us. The others are supposed not to share our 'conceptual scheme', but, Davidson argued, the role allocated to conceptual schemes in these pessimistic scenarios is incoherent.

Conceptual relativism is a heady and exotic doctrine, or would be if we could make good sense of it. The trouble is, as so often in philosophy, it is hard to improve intelligibility while retaining the excitement.[2]

Davidson points out that examples designed to soften us up to accept the idea of massive diversity are not all that compelling. The issue is one of translation, for, Davidson argues, the enterprise of understanding the thoughts of another is the same as the enterprise of finding our own words for those thoughts, or in other words translating the others' words into our own. But typically this goes well enough, for in spite of whatever differences we find, it turns out that we can say in our own terms what the others think. And, Davidson claims, this is not an accident for, when it comes to interpretation, 'We cannot make sense of total failure.' This brings him to the first statement of the argument:

It is tempting to take a very short line indeed: nothing, it may be said, could count as evidence that some form of activity could not be interpreted in our language that was not at the same time evidence that that form of activity was not speech behaviour.[3]

This sounds shockingly complacent, and Davidson himself draws back a little: 'as fiat the thesis lacks the appeal of self-evidence.' It certainly does. It sounds like the imposition of a kind of linguistic imperialism, whereby anything that cannot be said in late twentieth-century American terms doesn't make sense at all. More precisely, we might worry about the implicit verificationism – the philosophically unpopular idea that possibilities that we cannot verify as obtaining cannot be real possibilities at all. And we might worry even more about the kind of verification that is demanded, namely translation back into our own language. For this to seem wholly arbitrary, we have only to consider the enterprise of learning to understand something or someone by expanding and changing our own conceptual repertoires. When someone joins a university physics department, he verifies that his teachers make sense not by translating what they say back into terms he brings with him, but by discovering new vocabularies, new theories and new ways of understanding the new phenomena to which he is also introduced.

Nevertheless, Davidson promises us an argument for his conclusion, and the subsequent pages of his paper are dense with points that build up to one. He supposes that when we talk of conceptual schemes, we picture a division between 'scheme and content'. The empirical content of a thought is explained by reference to 'the facts, the world, experience, sensation, the totality of sensory stimuli, or something similar'. And the 'scheme' is presented as the 'categories, the organizing structure of language, and so on'.

I want to urge that this second dualism of scheme and content, of organizing system and something waiting to be organized, cannot be made intelligible and defensible. It is itself a dogma of empiricism . . . perhaps the last, for if we give it up it is not clear that there is anything distinctive left to call empiricism.[4]

Davidson's distance from empiricism was commented upon in chapter 6, and does not concern us for now. He continues his assault on the idea of a conceptual scheme by showing that in the writings of many conceptual schemers the dominant metaphors fall into two distinct groups:

conceptual schemes (languages) either *organize* something, or they *fit* it . . . the first group contains also *systematize, divide up* (the stream of experience); further examples of the second group are *predict, account for, face* (the tribunal of experience). As for the entities that get organized, or which the scheme must fit, I think again we may detect two main ideas: either it is reality (the universe, the world, nature) or it is experience (the passing show, surface irritations, sensory promptings, sense data, the given).[5]

Davidson's plan is to undermine each metaphor. His first argument therefore is against the idea of a scheme 'organizing' experience. He reasonably points out that only pluralities (like the shoes in a closet) get organized: 'If you were told not to organize the shoes and shirts, but the closet itself, you would be bewildered.'[6] He concedes that a language may contain predicates (terms that apply to different things, such as common adjectives) that are not matched by those in another language, but points out that this possibility itself depends on there being enough in common between the two languages to make it clear that they are talking about the same things (they share an ontology, in philosophical jargon). You and I might organize the same closet differently, but we are each alike dealing with shoes and shirts.

If we turn to the idea of language organizing experience, the same point applies.

Whatever plurality we take experience to consist in – events like losing a button or stubbing a toe, having a sensation of warmth, or hearing an oboe – we will have to individuate according to familiar principles. A language that organizes *such* entities must be a language very like our own.[7]

He also drily points out that language cannot be supposed *only* to organize experience (sensations, sense data, and so on). 'Surely knives and forks, railroads and mountains, cabbages and kingdoms also need organizing.'

Before evaluating this attack on the 'organizing' metaphor, we will briefly turn to the other prong, where Davidson attacks the idea of sentences of language 'fitting' things, or 'facing the tribunal of experience'. He urges, again reasonably, that what the metaphors in this group come down to is the idea of the sentences of a language being *true*. And then

Nothing, however, no *thing*, makes sentences and theories true: not experience, not surface irritations, not the world, can make a sentence true. *That* experience takes a certain course, that our skin is warmed or punctured, that the universe is finite, these facts, if we like to talk that way, make sentences and theories true. But this point is put better without mention of facts. The sentence 'My skin is warm' is true if and only if my skin is warm. Here there is no reference to a fact, a world, an experience, or a piece of evidence.[8]

As far as this point goes, Davidson is at one with the minimalism about truth that we met in chapter 3. There is nothing general or abstract to say about truth. You give me a sentence, and provided it locates a definite issue, I will say what makes it true, but only in the very terms that the sentence provides, or more accurately, using a translation of them into my own language. There is no general answer to the question: what makes French sentences true? But if we are given an intelligible candidate, there will be an answer, only not one that refers to any of the grandiose notions whose use Davidson is attacking. What makes the French sentence 'La neige est blanche' true? It is true if, and only if, snow is white.

Davidson claims that this much minimalism undermines any attempt to 'divorce' the notion of truth from the notion of trans-lation.[*] It prevents us, he thinks, from making use of any notion of 'true but untranslatable'. Of course, in a particular context I may suppose some foreign sentence to be true although I cannot myself translate it. But I can envisage a translation, and only that would enable me to identify the content of the sentence, and thereby to tell what would count as its truth.

The scope and ambition of Davidson's paper are breathtaking, but is the attack on conceptual scheming actually as strong as it appears? There are several reasons for doubt. Perhaps the most obvious is that by attacking the utility of notions such as 'fitting experience' Davidson seems to detach language too far from the detailed, piece-meal procedures of verification that are part and parcel of our lives. As we saw in chapter 6, he is eventually left only with the uncon-vincing substitute of covering our beliefs with a snowy mantle of truth, leaving their particular and individual footing in experience of no importance (hence the claim to have destroyed any final allure of empiricism).

---

[*] I say 'this much minimalism' because officially Davidson denied that he was a min-imalist. He shared a great deal with the idea, however, and at this point it is the over-lap that matters.

And each side of the argument seems to have holes in it. First, conceptual schemers who emphasize the contingent factors that shape our minds need not by any means be wedded to the 'organize' metaphor. In fact, it is a particularly crude parody of their position; it indeed implies an underlying commonality, possession of the same experience, waiting like the same shoes in the closet, ready to be organized one way or another. But that is appropriate only for the Humean or Lockean theory, stuck with the Myth of the Given. Post-Kantian conceptual schemers are far more likely to use the different metaphor of our conceptual repertoire *shaping* or *moulding* our experience, or in other words playing a role in determining the form it takes. Consider, for instance, the change that occurs when one begins to recognize patterns of speech in the hitherto chaotic noise of foreign talk, or begins to hear the melody in what was previously a welter of noise produced by a jazz musician. We should agree with Davidson that it is not appropriate to talk as if the experience before the change, and the experience after it, contain the same ingredients differently organized. But we should agree with conceptual schemers that there has been a change going right down to experience itself. Things sound different after the change. In these cases the change, it is true, is not really effected by shifts of language or theory. Fundamentally, it is experience that shapes experience. But that affords no argument that we must all have ended up in the same place, or even all ended up in some place from which we can, by ordinary processes of understanding, get to any other place. We can certainly hope to do so, but we may fail, just as some of us will never understand physics, or for that matter, jazz.

The other prong of Davidson's argument attempts to undermine conceptual scheming with thoughts drawn from minimalism about truth. But it is hard to see it as doing any better. We can accept the minimalist premise that no 'thing' makes sentences true, or perhaps more cautiously that it is philosophically useless to say that any 'thing' does, just as it may be harmless, but philosophically useless, to think of truth in terms of correspondence with the facts. It is also true, of course, that I cannot say what makes an alien sentence true unless I can say what it means. But neither of those points gets us near to denying the possibility of a massive dissociation between two minds, each of which has locked on to different versions of the world. To the conceptual schemer it is no objection that we cannot 'verify' what the alien is saying or which truths he may have cottoned on to; it is simply part of the position that this may be so.[*]

However, we can concede this much to Davidson: even if the bare possibility of untranslatable difference is left, there is not very much that we can actually do with it. Faced with more-or-less incomprehensible aliens, our only possible approach is to soldier on, doing what we can to share their perspective and to understand the world as they see it. If we seem unable to do so, it may be sad to reflect that we may never know whether it was their failure to manage any kind of thinking, or our failure to get on all fours with them, that was the problem. But we should not cheer ourselves up by a blithe certainty that it must have been the former.

2. Mind Reading

When a hive of bees loses its queen, a beekeeper needs to introduce a new one, but if a new queen is simply introduced into the hive, the workers will detect her as an alien, and kill her. The solution is to wrap her in something that provides a temporary barrier, such as a ball of sugar or candy, and then by the time the workers do reach her, she will have assimilated the scent of the hive, will no longer appear alien, and will not be killed.

This story illustrates the problem for disciplines such as history or anthropology. Here the aim is to interpret a particular swathe of human actions, and there is a stark interplay between what we bring with us to the enterprise, and what was there anyway, before we conducted it. The fear is that we are not so much reading the minds of others, as reading our own minds into theirs, investing them with

[*] In *Spreading the Word* (Oxford: Oxford University Press, 1984, chapter 7), I urge that Davidson may have misled himself here by a mistaken reading of Tarski. Since the argument is somewhat technical, and subsidiary to the main theme of this chapter, I shall not repeat it here.

versions of our beliefs, our desires, our priorities and values. Perhaps as we investigate the people of other places or times, we bleach out their alien colours, just as the bees working to get at the alien queen thereby turn her into one of their own hive.

And then an almost irresistible Protagorean or Nietzschean current starts to flow. If all we can do is to interpret the others from our particular standpoint in history, we must be aware that earlier historians – whom we no doubt regard as quaintly mistaken and biased by their own concerns and their own times – did just the same. And historians yet to come will do it as well, and in so doing they will consign our own contingent, situated, partial or biased descriptions to the very same rubbish tip on to which we pile the work of previous writers.

A related despair is wonderfully voiced by Claude Lévi-Strauss, speaking not as a historian but as an anthropologist, lamenting the way in which the modern world has penetrated and changed everything that he wants to know:

Then, insidiously, illusion began to lay its snares. I wished I had lived in the days of *real* journey, when it was still possible to see the full splendour of a spectacle that had not yet been blighted, polluted and spoilt . . . for every five years I move back in time I am able to save a custom, gain a ceremony or share in another belief. But I know the texts too well not to realize that by going back a century, I am at the same time forgoing data and lines of inquiry . . . And so I am caught within a circle from which there is no escape: the less human societies were able to communicate with each other and therefore to corrupt each other through contact, the less their respective emissaries were able to perceive the wealth and significance of their diversity. In short I have only two possibilities: either I can be like some traveller of the olden days, who was faced with a stupendous spectacle, all, or almost all, of which eluded him, or worse still, filled him with scorn and disgust; or I can be a modern traveller, chasing after the vestiges of a vanished reality. I lose on both counts, and more seriously than may at first appear, for, while I complain of being able to glimpse no more than the shadow of the past, I may be insensitive to the reality as it is taking shape at this very moment, since I have not reached the stage of development at which I would be capable of perceiving it. A few hundred years hence, in this same place, another traveller, as despairing as myself, will mourn the disappearance of what I might have seen, but failed to see. I am subject to a double infirmity: all that I perceive offends me, and I constantly reproach myself for not seeing as much as I should.[9]

Lévi-Strauss is here talking about the literal impact of the modern world, but also the metaphorical impact of the anthropologist's own understanding: the sensibility that both fantasizes what it might have seen in the past and fears what other sensibilities might follow in the future, and be amazed at our present blindness. The whole passage may remind us of Nietzsche's remark about history, quoted above on p. 96.

Lévi-Strauss is talking about a permanent aspect of the human condition, but historians are not often so kind to themselves, or at any rate to their colleagues. In the rest of this chapter I shall follow out the particular case of the philosopher and historian David Hume who is commonly charged with having a simplistic and, in particular, a completely unhistorical view of human nature. It may seem strange to approach a highly politicized issue by reflecting on the practice of an Edinburgh gentleman of the eighteenth century. But I concentrate upon the charge as it is raised against Hume, firstly for its own interest, secondly because it so nicely illustrates general philosophical concerns, and thirdly because it illustrates our own difficulties with the Enlightenment, a central contemporary flashpoint for the truth wars.

By Victorian times the downgrading of Hume as a historian and philosopher of history was well under way, spearheaded by John Stuart Mill's slanderous attack on his veracity.[10] But it was not only Hume's accuracy and integrity that became questioned. The critic Leslie Stephen said that history was to Hume an undecipherable hieroglyphic. In the twentieth century the great philosopher and Roman historian R. G. Collingwood said that

Hume never shows the slightest suspicion that the human nature he is analysing in his philosophical work is the nature of a western European in the early eighteenth century and that the very same enterprise if undertaken at a widely different time or place might have yielded widely different results.[11]

Hume is here billed as deserving the suffix '-centric', with all its pejorative charge: phallocentric, bourgeois-centric, West-centric, Scotocentric, and indeed Edinburgh-centric. Bernard Williams more recently made the same charge and justified downplaying Hume in his own work on ethics by claiming that Hume is insufficiently modern. He is too *provincial* in his assumptions about human nature to get to grips with the problems that are important for Williams, including centrally those of multiculturalism and relativism.[12] Hume, the charge goes, blithely ignores diversity. In Hume's world there are eighteenth-century Scottish gentlemen, and then there are the rest: barbarians, fanatics, the superstitious, manifestations of a perverted and unnatural side of human nature that we either gently mock or try not to notice.

The central text for this view occurs in the section 'Of Liberty and Necessity' in the first *Enquiry*:

It is universally acknowledged that there is a great uniformity among the actions of men, in all nations and ages, and that human nature remains still the same in its principles and operations. The same motives always produce the same actions: The same events follow from the same causes. Ambition, avarice, self-love, vanity, friendship, generosity, public spirit: these passions, mixed in various degrees, and distributed through society, have been, from the beginning of the world, and still are, the source of all the actions and enterprises, which have ever been observed among mankind. Would you know the sentiments, inclinations, and course of life of the Greeks and Romans? Study well the temper and actions of the French and English: You cannot be much mistaken in transferring to the former *most* of the observations which you have made with regard to the latter. Mankind are so much the same, in all times and places, that history informs us of nothing new or strange in this particular.[13]

At first blush this well supports the charge of provinciality, but further acquaintance with Hume redresses the balance, and opens up profound problems about the nature of historical method.

To begin with, Hume's writings display not only awareness of divergence in human nature, but something of a preoccupation with it. We need look no further than the 'Dialogue' from *An Enquiry*

Concerning the Principles of Morals, the work that Hume himself said was incomparably his finest. Here he first describes an apparently bizarre, almost unintelligible people, 'The Fourli', whose barbarous and savage manners seem 'scarcely compatible with human nature'. A man of merit among them, it turns out, might be 'such a one as with us would pass for incestuous, a parricide, an assassin, an ungrateful, perjured traitor, and something else too abominable to be named.' But then there is a similar description of a very different people among whom adultery, the prostitution of wives, pride in abjection and slavery, a quick propensity to murder and so on count as their 'maxims of honour'. These monsters turn out to be, respectively, the ancient Athenians and the modern French. The man of honour in each would be, to the other, 'an object of the highest contempt and ridicule, and even hatred'.

Hume's reconciliation comes in a famous image on the immediately succeeding page:

The Rhine flows north, the Rhone south; yet both spring from the *same* mountain, and are also actuated, in their opposite directions, by the *same* principle of gravity. The different inclinations of the ground, on which they run, cause all the difference of their courses.[14]

What we need to do, to understand the Athenians and the French, is to account for their differences by deploying the 'most universal, established principles of morals'. His procedure is to come to understand the influence of political necessity, culture and other social causes in generating differences of custom and morality. The picture is that while we are to recognize the *material* on which these causes operate as universal, the upshot, as with the Rhone and the Rhine, may be differences as great as you please. The common material is still there: the Athenian and the Frenchman share an enormous amount: each values 'good sense, knowledge, wit, eloquence, humanity, fidelity, truth, justice, courage, temperance, constancy, dignity of mind'. But the local expression of the common material in the common life of the community is superficially entirely different.

We understand the differences, when we do, only by understanding the causes that give rise to them. But these are particular kinds of causes. Elsewhere, Hume calls the causes he has in mind 'moral causes', and he distinguishes them sharply from 'physical causes', such as the influence of climate (part of the point of his essay is to rebut Montesquieu's theory that divergence of culture is due to such a physical cause).[15] Moral causes are 'all circumstances, which are fitted to work on the mind as motives or reasons, and which render a peculiar set of manners habitual to us'. What Hume then offers is an account enabling us to 'see' how circumstances would affect agents' conception of themselves and their circumstances, in order to give rise to whichever differences interest us. In modern terms, he wants to give a narrative or history of the society that renders the manners intelligible: an upshot of the same human nature that we can feel ourselves to share with its members.

This 'seeing' is of the first importance. It is effected by imagination and sympathy, which together enable us to reconstruct the influence of the circumstances that act on the mind as motives or reasons. We can do this only because the 'minds of men are mirrors to one another:'[16] insofar as we are not given something that we can mirror we cannot gain a distinctively historical understanding of an epoch or a people. But when we succeed we can be said to have 'lived through' the history we recount: 'A man acquainted with history, may, in some respect, be said to have lived from the beginning of the world, and to have been making continual additions to his stock of knowledge in every century.'[17]

3. Mirroring

Hume famously conceived of himself as doing for the workings of the mind what Newton had done for the workings of the physical world, teasing out the reliable patterns in which events follow one another. But is he mimicking the method of the natural sciences here: understand events 'from the outside' simply by finding the most general patterns into which they fall as the Newtonian self-image would lead us to expect? The mirror analogy suggests something else. Hume is certainly close to what has become known as the re-enactment or *ver-*

stehen account of historical understanding, associated with Wilhelm Dilthey or R. G. Collingwood. The historian is presented as starting 'from within' and proceeding by 'a wholly different foundation and structure than the natural sciences'.[18] Ordinary scientific processes of observation, generalization and theory-building are wholly inappropriate. As an aside, as Donald Livingston remarks, it is a nice irony that Hume, holding a doctrine so similar to that of *verstehen* or re-enactment, is criticized by Collingwood precisely for lacking it, the criticism itself being a failure on Collingwood's part properly to re-enact Hume's own historical thinking.

On this account the historian does not observe the doings of others in the way that the scientist observes the evolutions of a physical system, or the biologist observes the behaviour of butterflies or ants. Rather, he 'throws himself into' the situation of others, thinking (as best he can) how it must have appeared to them, and what projects or dangers must have beset them, and on this basis he reconstructs their reasonings, eventually seeing what their actions meant, or in other words why they acted as they did. Hume's talk of the minds of men mirroring one another fits beautifully into this account of the historian's method. But although there is a substantial overlap, there is also an important difference between Hume and the later expressions of the doctrine.

This arises because the later expressions tend to concentrate entirely upon the *reasonings* of historical agents. The thesis is that we understand them by re-enacting their reasonings for ourselves, in what is sometimes called a replication or an 'off-line simulation' of the situation in which they found themselves, and the thoughts they were able to deploy in answer to it. But although the application of Hume's 'moral causes' to a situation clearly includes replicating an individual agent's reasonings and motivations, it includes other things as well.

A nice and typically droll example of what else it includes is given by his account of some of the features that characterize soldiers and priests – the first example he gives of 'moral causes' in action. Soldiers, Hume believes, are lavish and generous as well as brave. Priests are seldom virtuous. Why? Well, the soldier's life is uncertain, and often dangerous, but also full of leisure and changes of company.

By imagining ourselves in such a life, we can feel why this makes for careless displays of lavishness and generosity. As we imagine, or enact in our own minds, the life of change and uncertainty, we feel our bourgeois prudence dropping away. Meanwhile priests, being human, will find moments when they need to feign more devotion than they are, at the time, possessed of. They must learn to 'set a guard over their looks' and promote the spirit of superstition by a 'continual grimace and hypocrisy'. This destroys any candour or innocence they start with, and 'makes an irreparable breach in their character'. Hence, you may expect to find priests, in this respect at least, less virtuous than the rest of mankind.[19] And again, if we imagine or enact in our own minds such a life, we can almost feel ourselves shrinking into a posture of concealment and evasion, wrapping our arms around our chests and looking slightly aslant at our fellows, or alternatively adopting the whine of persuasion, or the bright hectoring parade of conviction of the salesman or politician.

Now, what needs to be highlighted about these explanations is not whether they accurately pinpoint soldiers and priests. The point here is that Hume does not give us what Collingwood calls the 'inside' of events: the internal deliberations of the priest or the soldier. Rather, he presents their external circumstances in such a way that we, imagining ourselves in those circumstances, can 'mirror' the emergence of generosity or hypocrisy. But we do this not by thinking, only 'off-line' or in a part of our mind dissociated from actual motivation and practice, 'I had better become generous (or a hypocrite).' Rather, we recognize the operation of these circumstances as the very kind of thing that would, or could, *make* us become generous or hypocrites. In other words, we do not re-enact the reasonings, but as it were feel the tendency within ourselves, mimicking the evolution of the different characters. Here 'we are guided by a kind of *presentation*; which tells what will operate on others by what we feel immediately in ourselves'.[20] We can trace an operation to 'springs and principles, of which everyone has within himself, or from observation, the strongest assurance and conviction'.[21] Once we have arrived at such springs and principles we have rendered the historical fact intelligible – as intelligible as anything of this kind ever can be.

This understanding of the way of the social world derives from self-knowledge. The fact that we feel in ourselves the working of this causality, as we re-enact the circumstances of the agent, is just that: a fact like any other. Hume, however, holds that it renders the unfamiliar familiar; it brings it home to us, and renders the historical situation intelligible. I also think there is no doubt that Hume's wider category of moral causes enriches his historical armoury, actually rendering it superior to the *verstehen* tradition. The reason is that the *verstehen* tradition falters when it comes to reasonings we cannot consciously re-enact. One kind of case arises where the agent's reasonings were too bad for us to make them our own – Collingwood himself goes so far as to believe that we can obtain a historical understanding only of successes, never of failures. The losing general or admiral reasoned in ways that we cannot re-enact. Our charity cannot extend so far. The loser thought only what was *not* to be thought, whereas we understand an agent by simulating what *was* to be thought.

4. Infirmities

Hume is, rightly, more generous. For we are all familiar with infirmity from the inside. We can feel ourselves the victims of whatever flaws and failures brought about the disaster. So the fact that something is *irrational* does not, for Hume, mean that it is historically inexplicable.

Probably the most famous and influential application of these ideas comes in the great essay 'Of Miracles', which forms Section X of the *Enquiry Concerning the Principles of Human Understanding*. The first part of that essay sets out a logic of testimony, culminating in the crowning principle

'That no testimony is sufficient to establish a miracle, unless the testimony be of such a kind, that its falsehood would be more miraculous, than the fact, which it endeavours to establish: And even in that case there is a mutual destruction of arguments, and the superior only gives us an assurance suitable to that degree of force, which remains, after deducting the inferior.' When any one tells me, that he saw a dead man restored to life, I immediately consider with myself, whether it be more probable, that this person should either deceive or be deceived, or that the fact, which he relates, should really have happened. I weigh the one miracle against the other; and according to the superiority, which I discover, I pronounce my decision, and always reject the greater miracle. If the falsehood of his testimony would be more miraculous, than the event which he relates; then, and not till then, can he pretend to command my belief or opinion.[22]

This sets a hurdle which it is (almost) impossible for human testimony to surmount, for as Hume goes on to detail, falsity in human testimony is not so very unusual, whereas the 'prodigies' that people love to believe in because they have been told about them are by their very nature entirely outside the normal run of things.

The point here is not to assess Hume's argument.* The point is that while this principle ends part I of his essay, in part II Hume recognizes that he has set himself a problem of *understanding* those millions across the ages who have preferred to believe in miracles, on the basis of endlessly dodgy testimony, rather than to believe in the way of the world as it lies before their senses. Alongside Francis Bacon, whose aphorisms about Idols of the Mind I have used as epigraphs to these chapters, his investigation is one of the founding texts of that branch of inquiry that investigates cognitive dysfunction. The investigation is timely, in a world of spin, PR, or the personal convictions of a Blair or a Bush:

With what greediness are the miraculous accounts of travellers received, their descriptions of sea and land monsters, their relations of wonderful adventures, strange men, and uncouth manners? But if the spirit of religion join itself to the love of wonder, there is an end of common sense; and human testimony, in these circumstances, loses all pretensions to authority. A religionist may be an enthusiast, and imagine he sees what has no reality: He may know his narrative to be false, and yet persevere in it, with the best intentions in the world, for the sake of promoting so holy a cause: Or even where this delusion has not place, vanity, excited by so strong a temptation,

* I do so in more detail in *Think* (Oxford: Oxford University Press, 1998), chapter 5, pp. 176–85.

operates on him more powerfully than on the rest of mankind in any other circumstances; and self-interest with equal force. His auditors may not have, and commonly have not, sufficient judgment to canvass his evidence: What judgment they have, they renounce by principle, in these sublime and mysterious subjects: Or if they were ever so willing to employ it, passion and a heated imagination disturb the regularity of its operations. Their credulity increases his impudence: And his impudence overpowers their credulity.[23]

But we understand the gullible not by thinking (as it were): 'Only someone who loves to indulge passions of surprise or wonder would believe that – so let me believe it!' We understand them by feeling for ourselves how the passions of surprise and wonder are agreeable enough to sway judgement, and then recognizing that this is what happened in their case. We recall ourselves being charmed and seduced by stories which we should have known from the outset to be untrue. But then, we are often not as reasonable as we like to think. *Logos* plays a smaller role in these matters than we like to suppose. So Hume's hostility to *rationalism* is here transmuted into a *generosity* of explanatory technique. Similarly, we may not ourselves be able to re-enact the reasonings of those who are fanatical or superstitious, but we can feel in ourselves the way in which those qualities of mind would grow, given the right circumstances. Thus the historian can make contact with even the minds of those whose nature he appraises as flawed and regrettable.

If we now recall Collingwood's and Williams's complaint against Hume, we can see that not only is it unjustified, but that Hume's answer to it is the only answer that can be given. (Here as so often, the Humean predicament is the human predicament, as W. V. Quine memorably remarked.) The complaint, remember, is that Hume is too provincial and the answer is not only that Hume explicitly tries to accommodate the largest possible variety of human diversity, but that he does so by carefully balancing diversity with uniformity. To repeat, it is only when we can find ourselves mirroring the others that we understand them. So indeed our understanding reaches no further than our sympathy and the uniformity of the springs and principles governing human behaviour. The difference from Davidson is that for Hume it is contingent that we are sufficiently alike, whereas Davidson attempts to show a priori that it could not be otherwise. If uniformity fails, then indeed we remain trapped within our own provinciality, or to use the more common modern idiom, within the incommensurable discourses of our particular time and place. History is then impossible. But over huge tracts of human affairs, uniformity does not fail, and history is possible. History (which here includes any discipline of interpretation) is inevitably, but trivially, written from one vantage point or another. And the historian will naturally find it easier to understand men and manners whose resemblance to those with which he is familiar is the greatest. If that were all there is to it, then *all* history would be condemned to being provincial. We would be like the workers turning the queen into one of themselves as they reach towards her, being endlessly condemned to reading only ourselves back into the past. The only reason that this is not our predicament is that there is sufficient uniformity of human nature to ensure that what we read back was really there. Furthermore, by uncovering the uniform operation of moral causes the historian can actually enlarge his understanding: flowing north himself, he can nevertheless come to see how people might flow south, as it were. Then, as we have seen, he can in a manner be said to live again the epochs he uncovers.

How do Hume's critics fare when confronting the problem of Otherness? None too well, it has to be said. It was, after all, Collingwood who wrote that the historian 'must be, in fact, a microcosm of all the history he can know'.[24] So how does he attempt to deal with the problem of understanding real diversity and difference? He recognizes that simply postulating abstract 'thoughts', available to be shared by different people at different historical periods, merely labels the problem but offers no reliable guide to knowledge of whether or not we are replicating the thoughts of historical agents. On the other hand his hostility to importing the methods of natural science into history forbids him from countenancing any empirical method of generalization or trial and error. This leaves him, in effect, waffling.

In other words Collingwood very much wanted to distance himself from Croce's claim that all history is contemporary history, but arguably he disallowed himself the materials for doing it. A rather touching example is his discussion of Admiral Lord Nelson's refusal to take off his medals at Trafalgar (thereby leaving himself more conspicuous to enemy riflemen), with the words 'in honour I won them, in honour I will die with them'. Collingwood says that

Nelson's thought, as Nelson thought it and as I re-think it, is certainly one and the same thought; and yet in some way there is not one thought, there are two different thoughts. What was the difference? No question in my study of historical method ever gave me so much trouble.[25]

As well it might, especially when we reflect how much Collingwood, the proud child of a naval family stretching back to one of Nelson's admirals, must have had invested in the claim that he thoroughly understood Nelson.

Again, then, we find that Hume turns the tables on his accusers. It is now not he who stands convicted of provinciality, but those who retreat into exaggerated worries of incommensurability and relativism. It is the provincial who finds the ways of the rest of the world too baffling to understand, or who gratuitously reads only the minds of his own narrow circle back into the wider past. But it is Hume, himself far from an enthusiast, neither superstitious nor fanatical, who sets about understanding those who are. And in turn this has a political message. Both Hume and Collingwood hold that it is only when we can find enough in the others that mirrors things in ourselves that we can treat the others as 'conversible', that is, thinking beings susceptible to the considerations we advance, partners in cooperative and political enterprises. Otherwise they remain alien, and our only reaction is that of managing them with whatever force we need to muster to stop them from being an obstacle or danger to ourselves. Hume's own confidence in uniformity underlying diversity gives him confidence that nothing human is alien to him. (He would have been familiar with the saying from Terentius, or Terence: 'Homo sum, humanum nil a me alienum puto': I am a man; nothing human is alien from me. Terentius also conceives the mirroring as a two-way process.) And it leads politically to his trying to bring everyone into the fold. He succeeds notably with women, not to mention the Athenians and the French, and fails only where the historical record fails.

The 'mirroring' of which Hume speaks does not have to be one-way traffic. Our minds should be thought of not as rigid mirrors, but as potentially flexible. If we come across diversity, we can bend to understand it, until in the end we share the routes of feeling and thought that initially may have seemed quite alien. We grow into being like-minded with others – the process that Davidson seemed to ignore with his emphasis on *translation* as the only device for generating understanding. Collingwood himself is excellent on this:

The child's discovery of itself as a person is also its discovery of itself as a member of a world of persons . . . The discovery of myself as a person is the discovery that I can speak, and am thus a persona or speaker; in speaking I am both speaker and hearer; and since the discovery of myself as a person is also the discovery of other persons around me, it is the discovery of speakers and hearers other than myself.[26]

Here, there is no distinction between the discovery of others and the discovery of oneself.

Some celebrants of diversity dislike Hume's Enlightenment attitudes on more specific grounds. Bernard Williams cites some of the quaint categories Hume uses as fairly derogatory assessments of people and cultures: fanatical, enthusiastic, superstitious or barbarous. But these words do not represent off-hand verdicts, but rather stand as the summaries of much longer and more careful discussions. In fact, Hume put immense effort into understanding the first three of them.[27] Superstition, enthusiasm and fanaticism mark particular aspects of what Kant called human tutelage, the childhood of the human race. Kant was unfortunately wrong about that, for unlike childhood they are recurrent phenomena. They naturally arise in particular circumstances where combinations of fears, beliefs and needs are found, just as illnesses arise naturally when particular physical causes are found.

Barbarism deserves treating separately. For Hume it is a term that functions largely to mark the boundary of historical understanding.

Barbarian times, such as those of the Saxons, baffle historical understanding because too little has come down to us to enable us to find
a mirror in the barbarian mind. The eighteenth century knew some
names, perhaps some events, some rude traces, but too little to give
significance to those events or to bring them within the scope of a
historical narrative. (To be fair I should add that Collingwood at one
point seems to admit that his complaint against eighteenth-century
historians is partly that they just knew too little.)*

5. Collectives and their Histories

We can close this discussion of Hume with one final example, but one
of enormous importance to him, and to us. Hume seeks an understanding not only of individuals, but of collectives, such as civil society.
Consider the emergence of convention in society, a problem often
approached through the fiction of a 'social contract' in which previously warring parties sat down, as it were, to agree to honour treaties,
keep promises and abstain from aggression. Hume is an implacable
opponent of using the idea of a social contract as any kind of historical tool in explaining the emergence of the institutions of civil society.
He sees, again rightly, that we cannot envisage people reasoning themselves out of a 'state of nature', any more than we can envisage them
reasoning themselves into respect for promises, or for that matter into
language ('Let's all use the word "cows" to mean cows') or government. But this does not block the search for 'moral causes', here meaning an account of the pressures that would lead people like us into
evolving the institutions of language, or money or property and contract, and evolving as well the moral motivations they command. The
evolution of convention, for Hume, is sharply distinct from the *design*
of convention. But this does not mean that institutions have no history,

* 'No one in his time had done enough work on the history of thought to know that
both the science and the experience of an eighteenth-century European were highly
peculiar historical facts, very different from those of other peoples and other times.'
R. G. Collingwood, *The Idea of History*, Oxford: Oxford University Press, 1946,
p. 224.

only that the history is written in terms of moral causes, rather than the individual or collective intentions of agents. We can see how, given the 'circumstances of justice', which mean the limited extent to which we care for others as opposed to ourselves, and the limited supply of goods that nature provides for us, unbridled self-interest would lead to a war of all against all. But we can also see how we could each feel a pressure to self-restraint, and then there is at least the possibility of collective action to better our situation. And we can thus re-enact or feel how contagion and emulation could weld a divergent group of individuals into a coherent social collective.*

6. Peace Breaks Out

I have tried to take the reader through a long corridor. At the end of the journey, can we find a stable place to stand? We have seen few great victories: Clifford and James, Plato and Protagoras, Davidson and Hume, van Fraassen and Putnam, Gadamer and Derrida, still glower at each other and rattle their armour. We have had to visit areas where even the best philosophers have lost their way in the fog. Fictionalists, expressivists, constructivists and instrumentalists still trouble *real* realists, while quietists gently sleep and eliminativists fly to their desert hermitages.

On the other hand we also found reason for hope. We found that once we have an issue to decide, it comes with its own norms. Once the issue is the issue, relativism becomes a distraction. In natural science we have found no reason to qualify Clifford's optimism about the method of harnessing observation to theory, producing well-mannered animation by whatever is shown to work. Indeed, we found no reason to differentiate that from believing whatever our best theories tell us to believe. In the human sciences we have learned to respect difference of perspective without identifying it with illusion and error.

Perhaps we never found *logos* or a 'first philosophy', an underlying

---

* The first treatment is in *Treatise*, III, ii, 1–6, pp. 477–534.

foundational story telling us, from somewhere outside our own world view, just why that world view is the right one. But perhaps we have learned to do without that, just as we learn to retain our hard-won confidences, without closing our minds to any further illuminations that the future may bring. Above all, I hope we have become confident in using our well-tried and tested vocabulary of explanation and assessment. We can take the postmodernist inverted commas off things that ought to matter to us: truth, reason, objectivity and confidence. They are no less, if no more, than the virtues that we should all cherish as we try to understand the bewildering world about us.

Notes

Introduction

1. Bernard Williams, *Truth and Truthfulness*, Cambridge: Cambridge University Press, 2002.
2. William James, Lecture 1 in *Pragmatism*, New York: Longmans, Green and Co., 1907, p. 12.
3. Ibid., p. 67.
4. Ibid., p. 54.

1. Faith, Belief and Reason

1. Francis Bacon, *The New Organon*, ed. Lisa Jardine and Michael Silverthorne, Cambridge: Cambridge University Press, 2000, p. 44. All the aphorisms at the head of chapters are from this work, where Bacon, originally writing in 1620, is enumerating the 'idols' (illusions) of the mind. He was under no illusion himself about the infirmities of the mind, but he believes that by following the right (scientific) method we can overcome them.
2. Edward Gibbon, *The Decline and Fall of the Roman Empire*, London: Everyman, 1993, chapter II, p. 34.
3. Clifford's paper, James's response and commentaries are collected in *The Ethics of Belief Debate*, ed. Gerald D. McCarthy, Atlanta: Scholars Press, 1986. The quotes from Clifford are from pp. 19–36, and those from James from pp. 55–71.
4. '"The True," to put it very briefly, is only the expedient in the way of our thinking, just as "the right" is only the expedient in the way of*

our behaving. Expedient in almost any fashion; and expedient in the long run and on the whole of course; for what meets expediently all the experience in sight won't necessarily meet all farther experiences equally satisfactorily. Experience, as we know, has ways of *boiling over*, and making us correct our present formulas' (William James, *Pragmatism*, New York: Longmans, Green and Co., 1907, p. 222). Hilary Putnam defends James against equating truth and expediency in *Pragmatism*, Oxford: Blackwell, 1995, p. 8.

5. For a representative collection, see *Religion after Metaphysics*, ed. Mark Wrathall, Cambridge: Cambridge University Press, 2003.

6. Hans Vaihinger, *The Philosophy of As-If*, trans. C. K. Ogden, London: Routledge & Kegan Paul, 1935.

7. The best account of Bentham on fiction and reality is Ross Harrison's *Bentham*, London: Routledge, 1983, chapters 2–4.

8. Ludwig Wittgenstein, *Lectures and Conversations on Aesthetics, Psychology, and Religious Belief*, ed. Cyril Barrett, Oxford: Blackwell, 1966, p. 71.

9. Percy Bysshe Shelley, *Adonais*, §52.

10. Voltaire, *Candide*.

11. David Hume, *An Inquiry Concerning the Principles of Morals*, ed. Tom L. Beauchamp, Oxford: Oxford University Press, 1998, p. 95. I am told that he was wrong, or not entirely right, about official Catholic doctrine on this point.

2. Man the Measure

1. Plato, *Theaetetus*, 171a.

2. G. E. Moore, 'Proof of an External World', in *Philosophical Papers*, London: George Allen & Unwin, 1959, p. 146.

3. The modes have attracted an enormous weight of commentary. J. Annas and J. Barnes (eds.), *The Modes of Scepticism*, Cambridge: Cambridge University Press, 1985 is a classic collection. R. J. Hankinson, *The Sceptics*, London: Routledge, 1995 is a valuable overview for the non-specialist.

4. Michael Williams, *Problems of Knowledge*, Oxford: Oxford University Press, 2001, p. 62.

5. Plato worries about this at *Theaetetus*, 160d–e; Aristotle at *Metaphysics*, 4: 5, 1009b1–10.

6. Ludwig Wittgenstein, *Philosophical Investigations*, Oxford: Blackwell, 1953, §258.

7. In England in the spring of 2002 the celebrity artist Tracey Emin, famous for exhibiting her own rumpled and none-too-clean bed, had the misfortune to lose her cat, Docket. She put ordinary 'lost cat' notices around her London neighbourhood, which were promptly taken down and treasured as valuable works of genius. If she had added 'Please do not remove, this is not a work of art' that would have been read only as a different (and yet more amusing) work of art. The artistic bull's-eye is whatever Tracey does. The moving bull's-eye is a consequence of the culture of celebrity. Docket returned.

8. The idea of the relativist as constantly adding 'that's just us' is prominent in Thomas Nagel's argument against the position, part of which is discussed in the next chapter.

9. Quoted by Ralph Walker, 'Gassendi and Skepticism', in *The Skeptical Tradition*, ed. Miles Burnyeat, Berkeley: University of California Press, 1983, p. 322.

10. For readers not familiar with British politics: in 2003–4, the judge Lord Hutton presided over an inquiry into the suicide of a government scientist, which accumulated vast and to most people incontrovertible evidence of government manipulation and deceit, all of which he gave the impression of ignoring, and by seemingly following a theory of evidence and law of his own invention was able to declare the government innocent of everything.

11. I discussed this argument, the so-called Euthyphro dilemma, in *Being Good*, Oxford: Oxford University Press, 2001, chapter 1.1.

3. Ishmael's Problem and the Delights of Keeping Quiet

1. Thomas Nagel, *The Last Word*, New York: Oxford University Press, 1997, pp. 14–15.

2. William James, 'Humanism and Truth', in *The Meaning of Truth*, New York: Longmans, Green and Co., 1909, p. 74.

3. Bernard Williams, *Morality*, Cambridge: Cambridge University Press, 1993, p. 20.

4. Thomas Kuhn, *The Structure of Scientific Revolutions*, Chicago: University of Chicago Press, 1970, p. 206.

5. The best account of this view and of its strengths is Paul Horwich, *Truth*, Oxford: Blackwell, 1990. A good introduction to these themes is Pascal Engel, *Truth*, Chesham: Acumen, 2002.

6. Gottlob Frege, 'The Thought: A Logical Inquiry', in Simon Blackburn and Keith Simmons (eds.), *Truth*, Oxford: Oxford University Press, 1999, pp. 85–105. I discuss the argument at greater length in *Spreading the Word*, Oxford: Oxford University Press, 1984, pp. 226–9.

7. I have also discussed moral relativism, in a slightly different way, in *Being Good*, Oxford: Oxford University Press, 2001, chapter 1.2.

4. Nietzsche: the Arch Debunker

1. Friedrich Nietzsche, *The Will to Power*, ed. Walter Kaufmann, London: Weidenfeld & Nicolson, 1967, §481.

2. 'On Truth and Lies in a Nonmoral Sense' (1873), from *The Portable Nietzsche*, ed. Walter Kaufmann, New York: Viking Press, 1954, p. 45. Hereafter Kaufmann.

3. Friedrich Nietzsche, *The Antichrist*, §41, Kaufmann, p. 616.

4. Friedrich Nietzsche, *Beyond Good and Evil* §38, trans. Walter Kaufmann, New York: Random House, 1966, p. 49.

5. Ibid., §51, p. 65.

6. Friedrich Nietzsche, *Daybreak,* §175, trans. R. J. Hollingdale, Cambridge: Cambridge University Press, 1982, p. 106. His remark is certainly true about England, whenever, for instance, the civil service tries to express the value of education or universities.

7. Friedrich Nietzsche, *Human, All Too Human,* §634, trans. R. J. Hollingdale, Cambridge: Cambridge University Press, 1986, p. 201.

8. Martin Heidegger, *Nietzsche*, trans. David Krell, New York: Harper & Row, 1982.

9. These include: Sarah Kofman, *Nietzsche et la métaphore*, Paris: Payot, 1972; Alexander Nehamas, *Nietzsche: Life as Literature*, Cambridge, Mass.: Harvard University Press, 1985.

10. Jacques Derrida, *Spurs, Nietzsche's Style*, trans. Barbara Harlow, Chicago: University of Chicago Press, 1979.

11. Paul de Man, *Allegories of Reading*, New Haven: Yale University Press, 1979, quoted in Maudemarie Clark, *Nietzsche on Truth and Philosophy*, Cambridge: Cambridge University Press, 1990, p. 16.

12. There is a pleasant paradox in the idea of a sublime thumbnail sketch. Edmund Burke thought that the idea of the sublime originated in a terrifying 'greatness of dimension' which thumbnails, being small, contradict. But there is something great (and a little terrifying) about the scale of Nietzsche's vision, and the force with which he compresses it. Edmund Burke, *On the Sublime and Beautiful*, Part IV, section 9, in *The Works of Edmund Burke*, vol. 1, Oxford: Oxford University Press, p. 182.

13. The most influential interpretation holding that Nietzsche changed his mind, especially in his final works, is that of Maudemarie Clark, *Nietzsche on Truth and Philosophy*. Doubts are raised in R. Lanier Anderson, 'Overcoming Charity', *Nietzsche-Studien*, v. 25, 1996, 307–41.

14. Friedrich Nietzsche, *The Genealogy of Morals*, III, §12 trans. Walter Kaufmann and R. J. Hollingdale, New York: Random House, 1967, p. 119.

15. William James, *Pragmatism*, New York: Longmans, Green and Co., 1907, p. 248.

16. Iris Murdoch, *Metaphysics as a Guide to Morals*, London: Penguin Books, 1994.

17. Immanuel Kant, *The Critique of Pure Reason*, trans. Norman Kemp Smith, London: Macmillan, 1933, p. 71.

18. This point is well made in Adrian Moore, *Points of View*, Oxford: Oxford University Press, 1997, chapter 3.

19. Friedrich Nietzsche, *Twilight of the Idols*, §3, 5. Kaufmann, p. 482.

20. Nietzsche, *Genealogy of Morals*, III, §24.

21. Ibid., §34.

22. I have attempted to describe this side of Kant in *Think*, chapter 7, 'The World'.

23. Nietzsche, 'On Truth and Lies', Kaufmann, p. 46.

24. Ibid., p. 45.

25. Here I follow the magisterial account in David Sedley, *Cratylus*, Cambridge: Cambridge University Press, 2003.

26. Friedrich Nietzsche, *The Gay Science*, §112, trans. Walter Kaufmann, New York: Vintage Books, 1974, p. 172.

27. Ibid., §34, p. 104.

28. Nietzsche, *The Will to Power*, §55.

29. Charles Lyell, *The Principles of Geology*, I. 164 (1820).

30. Aristotle, *Metaphysics* Gamma, 1010a7–15.

31. Nietzsche, *The Gay Science*, ed. Bernard Williams, trans. Josefine Nauckhoff, Cambridge: Cambridge University Press, 2001, §112, p. 113.

32. Nietzsche, *Will to Power*, §493.

33. Nietzsche, *The Gay Science*, §111.

34. Again, Maudemarie Clark is the most influential exponent of this view.

35. Impressive papers bearing on this, by Ken Gemes, Maudemarie Clark and Peter Poellner, are collected in *Nietzsche*, ed. John Richardson and Brian Leiter, Oxford: Oxford University Press, 2001.

5. The Possibility of Philosophy

1. In his book *The Social Construction of What?* (Cambridge, Mass.: Harvard University Press, 1999) Ian Hacking amusingly lists actual book titles of the kind *The Social Construction of . . .* or *Constructing . . .*, ranging through every letter of the alphabet except 'X', from *Authorship* to *Zulu Nationalism*.

2. John Mackie, *Ethics: Inventing Right and Wrong*, Harmondsworth: Penguin, 1977.

3. Stephen Stich, *From Folk Psychology to Cognitive Science*, Cambridge Mass.: Bradford Books, 1983.

4. Michael Devitt, in *The Oxford Handbook of Contemporary Analytic Philosophy*, ed. Frank Jackson and Michael Smith, Oxford: Oxford University Press, forthcoming.

5. De Finetti thought, oddly, that this liberating doctrine had affinities with what he saw as the promised liberations offered by the then-growing Italian Fascist movement ('Il Probabilismo', ms, unpublished).

6. M. O'C. Drury, 'Conversations with Wittgenstein', in *Recollections of Wittgenstein*, ed. Rush Rhees, Oxford: Oxford University Press, 1981, p. 157.

7. Ludwig Wittgenstein, *Remarks on Philosophical Psychology*, Oxford: Blackwell, 1980, I, §48.

8. Ludwig Wittgenstein, 'Lecture on Ethics', *Philosophical Review*, 1965. Quotations are from pp. 5–12.

9. Rush Rhees, 'Some Developments in Wittgenstein's View of Ethics', *Philosophical Review*, 1965, p. 23. The two subsequent quotes are from the same passage.

10. Ludwig Wittgenstein, *Remarks on the Foundations of Mathematics*, Oxford: Blackwell, 1964, Pt II, 26, p. 77.

11. Ibid., Pt V, 6, p. 163.

12. Ibid., Pt V, 15, p. 173.

13. Ludwig Wittgenstein, *Zettel*, Oxford: Blackwell, 1967, §299.

14. Ludwig Wittgenstein, *On Certainty*, Oxford: Blackwell, 1969, §204, p. 28.

15. Ibid., §200, p. 27.

16. Wittgenstein, *Zettel*, §330.

17. Ludwig Wittgenstein, *Philosophical Investigations*, Oxford: Blackwell, 1953, p. 190.

18. Ibid.

6. Observation and Truth: from Locke to Rorty

1. Quoted in Francis Wheen, *How Mumbo Jumbo Conquered the World*, London: Fourth Estate, 2004, p. 88.

2. 'Perhaps', because contemporary historians of positivism, or logical empiricism, find much more complexity here than did a previous generation, which was more concerned to pillory it.

3. John Locke, *Essay Concerning Human Understanding*, ed. P. H. Nidditch, Oxford: Oxford University, Press, 1975, Book II, chap. xi, sec. 17, p. 163.

4. Rudolf Carnap, *Der Logische Aufbau der Welt*, Berlin: Weltkreis Verlag, 1928.

5. David Hume, *A Treatise of Human Nature*, ed. L. A. Selby-Bigge,

rev. ed. P. H. Nidditch, Oxford: Oxford: Oxford University Press, 1978, Book I, Part IV, sec. 2, p. 218.

6. T. H. Green, Introduction to David Hume, *A Treatise of Human Nature*, ed. T. H. Green and T. H. Grose, London: Longmans, Green and Co., 1874, p. 16.

7. Richard Rorty, *Philosophy and the Mirror of Nature*, Oxford: Blackwell, 1980, p. 140. The quotation is from p. 19 of Green and Grose, *A Treatise of Human Nature*.

8. William James, *Pragmatism*, New York: Longmans, Green and Co., 1908, p. 246.

9. Wilfrid Sellars, *Empiricism and the Philosophy of Mind*, Cambridge, Mass.: Harvard University Press, 1997, pp. 21–2.

10. Ibid., p. 76.

11. Ludwig Wittgenstein, *On Certainty*, Oxford: Blackwell, 1969, §141.

12. Immanuel Kant, *Critique of Pure Reason*, trans. Norman Kemp Smith, London: Macmillan, 1963, A 371–2, p. 347.

13. Donald Davidson, 'A Coherence Theory of Truth and Knowledge', in *Subjective, Intersubjective, Objective*, Oxford: Oxford University Press, 2001, p. 141. The essay was written in 1981.

14. Rorty, *Philosophy and the Mirror of Nature*, p. 178.

15. John McDowell, *Mind and World*, Cambridge, Mass.: Harvard University Press, 1994, p. 18.

16. Thomas Nagel, *The Last Word*, p. 29.

17. Edward Craig, 'Davidson and the Sceptic: The Thumbnail Version', *Analysis*, 1990, pp. 213–14.

18. Richard Rorty, *Philosophy and Social Hope*, London: Penguin Books, 1999, Introduction, p. xxiii.

19. Rorty, *Philosophy and the Mirror of Nature*, p. 9.

20. Richard Rorty, *Consequences of Pragmatism*, Minnesota: University of Minnesota Press, 1982, p. xxvi.

21. Richard Rorty, *Contingency, Irony, and Solidarity*, Cambridge: Cambridge University Press, 1989, p. 6.

22. Jacques Bouveresse, 'Reading Rorty, Pragmatism and its Consequences', in *Rorty and His Critics*, ed. Robert B. Brandom, Oxford: Blackwell, 2000.

23. Richard Rorty, 'Feminism, Ideology, and Deconstruction: A Pragmatic View', *Hypatia*, vol. 8 (spring 1993).

24. L. T. Moore, *Isaac Newton*, New York: Scribner, 1934, p. 664.

25. Richard Rorty, 'Response to John McDowell', in *Rorty and His Critics*, ed. Brandom, p. 125.

26. John McDowell, 'Towards Rehabilitating Objectivity', in *Rorty and His Critics*, ed. Brandom, p. 118.

27. Rorty, 'Response to John McDowell', p. 125.

28. Stanley Fish's contributions are well seen in his *Doing What Comes Naturally*, Oxford: Oxford University Press, 1989. Dworkin's relevant writings include *A Matter of Principle*, Cambridge, Mass.: Harvard University Press, 1985.

29. Fish, *Doing What Comes Naturally* p. 580, quoting Postema, 'Protestant Interpretation and Social Practices', *Law and Philosophy*, vol. 6, no. 3, December 1987.

30. Rorty in *Rorty and His Critics*, ed. Brandom, pp. 104–5.

31. I talk at some length of Rorty's attempt to interpret Orwell, making the same point that minimalism undercuts his criticism, in *Ruling Passions*, chapter 9.2.

32. This paragraph sums up a longer complaint against, for example, John McDowell's theory in *Mind and World* (Cambridge, Mass.: Harvard University Press, 1996), made in my 'Julius Caesar and George Berkeley Play Leapfrog', in *Reading McDowell*, ed. Cindy and Graham Macdonald, forthcoming.

33. Jean Baudrillard, *The Gulf War Did Not Take Place*, trans. Paul Patton, Bloomington: Indiana University Press, 1995.

34. See Hugh Trevor-Roper, 'The Invention of Tradition: The Highland Tradition of Scotland', in *The Invention of Tradition*, ed. Eric Hobsbawm and Terence Ranger, Cambridge: Cambridge University Press (Canto), 1983.

7. Realism as Science; Realism about Science

1. Hilary Putnam, 'What is Mathematical Truth?', in *Philosophical Papers*, vol. 1, *Mathematics, Matter and Method*, Cambridge: Cambridge University Press, 1975, p. 73.

2. Bas van Fraassen, *The Scientific Image*, Oxford: Oxford University Press, 1980, p. 40.

3. David Hume, *Treatise of Human Nature*, Oxford: Oxford University Press, I, iii, 6, p. 91. If this introduction to the problem of induction is a little brisk, readers may like to consult *Think* (Oxford: Oxford University Press, 1998), chapters 6 and 7.

4. Richard Rorty, 'Feminism, Ideology, and Deconstruction: A Pragmatic View', *Hypatia*, vol. 8 (spring 1993).

5. Van Fraassen, *The Scientific Image*, p. 8.

6. Ibid., p. 12.

7. Ibid., p. 81.

8. Arthur Fine, 'Unnatural Attitudes: Realist and Instrumentalist Attachments in Science', *Mind*, vol. 95, 1985, pp. 149–79.

9. Van Fraassen, *The Scientific Image*, p. 82.

10. 'It should go without saying that, even when acceptance is unqualified, it need not be dogmatic; fervent and total commitment still need not be blind or fanatical.' Bas van Fraassen, 'Empiricism in the Philosophy of Science', in *Images of Science*, eds. P. Churchland and C. Hooker, Chicago: University of Chicago Press, 1985, p. 281.

11. The difficulty of distinguishing animation from belief was highlighted by Paul Horwich in 'On the Nature and Norms of Theoretical Commitment', *Philosophy of Science*, vol. 58, 1991, pp. 1–14.

12. W. V. Quine, 'On Empirically Equivalent Systems of the World', *Erkenntnis*, vol. 9, 1975, pp. 313–28.

13. Van Fraassen, *The Scientific Image*, p. 255.

14. W. V. Quine, *From Stimulus to Science*, Cambridge, Mass.: Harvard University Press, 1995, p. 16.

8. Historians and Others

1. Optimists include Hans Georg Gadamer; pessimists look to Derrida or Foucault.

2. Donald Davidson, 'On the Very Idea of a Conceptual Scheme', in *Inquiries into Truth and Interpretation*, 2nd edn, Oxford: Oxford University Press, 2001, p. 183.

3. Ibid., p. 185.

4. Ibid., p. 189.

5. Ibid., p. 191.

6. Ibid., p. 192.

7. Ibid.

8. Ibid. p. 194.

9. Claude Lévi-Strauss, *Tristes Tropiques*, trans. John and Doreen Weightman, London: Peregrine Press, 1984, pp. 50–51. I owe thanks to Roger Huss for showing me the passage.

10. John Stuart Mill's intemperate essay 'Brodie's History of the British Empire' first appeared in the *Westminster Review* in 1824 (when Mill was eighteen). It is reprinted in *The Collected Works of John Stuart Mill*, Toronto: University of Toronto Press, 1982 (reprinted London: Routledge, 1996), vol. 6, pp. 3–58.

11. Both these are quoted in Donald Livingston's excellent *Hume's Philosophy of Common Life* (Chicago: University of Chicago Press, 1984). I am much indebted to this work in what follows, and my agreement with Livingston exceeds the divergence from him that I eventually describe.

12. Bernard Williams, 'Reply to Blackburn', *Philosophical Books*, vol. 2, no. 4, 1986.

13. David Hume, *An Enquiry Concerning Human Understanding*, ed. Tom L. Beauchamp, Oxford: Oxford University Press, 1999, p. 150.

14. David Hume, *An Enquiry Concerning the Principles of Morals*, ed. Tom L. Beauchamp, Oxford: Oxford University Press, 1998, p. 192.

15. David Hume, 'Of National Character', *Essays Moral, Political and Literary*, Oxford: Oxford University Press, 1963.

16. David Hume, *Treatise of Human Nature*, Oxford: Oxford University Press, 1978, II, ii, 5: 'In general we may remark, that the minds of men are mirrors to one another, not only because they reflect each other's emotions, but also because those rays of passions, sentiments, and opinions, may be often reverberated, and may decay away by insensible degrees' (p. 365).

17. David Hume, 'Of the Study of History', *Essays*. This essay was published in the 1741 edition of Hume's *Essays*, but later withdrawn, possibly because of the rather laboured raillery about 'the fair sex'.

18. Wilhelm Dilthey, *Introduction to the Human Sciences, Collected Works*, vol. 1, trans. Rudolph Makkreel and Frithjof Rodi, Princeton: Princeton University Press, 1989, p. 158.

19. A good pair of essays illustrating these themes is 'Of National Characters', already mentioned, and Essay X from the 1752 set of *Political Essays*, 'Of Some Remarkable Customs'.

20. Hume, *Treatise of Human Nature*, II, iii, 6, p. 332.

21. Hume, 'Of Some Remarkable Customs', *Essays*, Pt II. Both this and the previous passage are quoted by Livingston, who interprets them as the good reasons for which the agent acted as he did, and which the historian must be able to reconstruct in his own mind (*Hume's Philosophy of Common Life*, p. 195). It is this equation that I doubt.

22. Hume, *An Enquiry Concerning Human Understanding*, p. 174.

23. Ibid, p. 175.

24. R. G. Collingwood, *An Autobiography*, Oxford: Oxford University Press, 1939, p. 115.

25. Ibid., pp. 112–13.

26. R. G. Collingwood, *The Principles of Art*, Oxford: Oxford University Press, 1938, p. 248.

27. David Hume, *The Natural History of Religion*, 'Of Miracles', and the last three volumes of his *History of England*, dealing with the rise of Puritanism and its relation to Catholicism and the Church of England are three of the relevant large-scale texts.

Index

READ MORE IN PENGUIN

In every corner of the world, on every subject under the sun, Penguin represents quality and variety – the very best in publishing today.

For complete information about books available from Penguin – including Puffins, Penguin Classics and Arkana – and how to order them, write to us at the appropriate address below. Please note that for copyright reasons the selection of books varies from country to country.

In the United Kingdom: Please write to *Dept. EP, Penguin Books Ltd, Bath Road, Harmondsworth, West Drayton, Middlesex UB7 0DA*

In the United States: Please write to *Consumer Services, Penguin Putnam Inc., 405 Murray Hill Parkway, East Rutherford, New Jersey 07073-2136.* VISA and MasterCard holders call 1-800-631-8571 to order Penguin titles

In Canada: Please write to *Penguin Books Canada Ltd, 10 Alcorn Avenue, Suite 300, Toronto, Ontario M4V 3B2*

In Australia: Please write to *Penguin Books Australia Ltd, 487 Maroondah Highway, Ringwood, Victoria 3134*

In New Zealand: Please write to *Penguin Books (NZ) Ltd, Private Bag 102902, North Shore Mail Centre, Auckland 10*

In India: Please write to *Penguin Books India Pvt Ltd, 11 Community Centre, Panchsheel Park, New Delhi 110017*

In the Netherlands: Please write to *Penguin Books Netherlands bv, Postbus 3507, NL-1001 AH Amsterdam*

In Germany: Please write to *Penguin Books Deutschland GmbH, Metzlerstrasse 26, 60594 Frankfurt am Main*

In Spain: Please write to *Penguin Books S. A., Bravo Murillo 19, 1°B, 28015 Madrid*

In Italy: Please write to *Penguin Italia s.r.l., Via Vittorio Emanuele 45/a, 20094 Corsico, Milano*

In France: Please write to *Penguin France, 12, Rue Prosper Ferradou, 31700 Blagnac*

In Japan: Please write to *Penguin Books Japan Ltd, Iidabashi KM-Bldg, 2-23-9 Koraku, Bunkyo-Ku, Tokyo 112-0004*

In South Africa: Please write to *Penguin Books South Africa (Pty) Ltd, P.O. Box 751093, Gardenview, 2047 Johannesburg*

PENGUIN MODERN CLASSICS

THE PENGUIN FREUD READER
SIGMUND FREUD

Edited by Adam Phillips

'Freudian psychoanalysis changed the self-image of the western mind' Roy Porter

This major new collection brings together the key writings from every stage of Freud's career to offer the perfect introduction to his life and work. Here are the essential ideas of psychoanalytic theory, including Freud's explanations of such concepts as the Id, Ego and Super-Ego, the Death Instinct and Pleasure Principle, along with classic case studies like that of the Wolf Man.

Adam Phillips's marvellous selection provides an ideal overview of Freud's thought in all its extraordinary ambition and variety. Psychoanalysis may be known as the 'talking cure', yet it is also and profoundly a way of reading. Here we can see Freud's writings as readings and listenings, deciphering the secrets of the mind, finding words for desires that have never found expression. Much more than this, however, *The Penguin Freud Reader* presents a compelling reading of life as we experience it today, and a way in to the work of one of the most haunting writers of the modern age.

Penguin Politics

GLOBALIZATION AND ITS DISCONTENTS
JOSEPH STIGLITZ

'A massively important political as well as economic document … we should listen to him urgently' Will Hutton, *Guardian*

Our world is changing. Globalization is not working. It is hurting those it was meant to help. And now, the tide is turning …

Explosive and shocking, *Globalization and Its Discontents* is the bestselling exposé of the all-powerful organizations that control our lives – from the man who has seen them at work first hand.

As Chief Economist at the World Bank, Nobel Prize-winner Joseph Stiglitz had a unique insider's view into the management of globalization. Now he speaks out against it: how the IMF and WTO preach fair trade yet impose crippling economic policies on developing nations; how free market 'shock therapy' made millions in East Asia and Russia worse off than they were before; and how the West has driven the global agenda to further its own financial interests.

Globalization *can* still be a force for good, Stiglitz argues. But the balance of power has to change. Here he offers real, tough solutions for the future.

'Compelling … This book is everyone's guide to the misgovernment of globalization' J. K. Galbraith

'Stiglitz is a rare breed, an heretical economist who has ruffled the self-satisfied global establishment that once fed him. *Globalization and Its Discontents* declares war on the entire Washington financial and economic establishment' Ian Fraser, *Sunday Tribune*

'Gripping … this landmark book … shows him to be a worthy successor to Keynes' Robin Blackburn, *Independent*

PENGUIN POLITICS

**FREE WORLD: WHY A CRISIS OF THE WEST REVEALS THE
OPPORTUNITY OF OUR TIME**
TIMOTHY GARTON ASH

'A compelling manifesto for the enlargement of freedom and a new era of world
politics' Vaclav Havel

At the beginning of the twenty-first century, the world plunged into crisis. What
began as an attack on the West by Osama bin Laden soon became a dramatic
confrontation between Europe and America.

Britain has found itself painfully split, because it stands with one foot across the
Atlantic and the other across the Channel. The English, in particular, are divided
politically between a Right that argues our place is with America, not Europe, and
a Left that claims the opposite. This is today's English civil war. Both sides tell us
we must choose. In this powerful new work, Timothy Garton Ash, one of our
leading political writers, explains why we cannot, need not and must not choose
between Europe and America.

Drawing on an extraordinary range of sources, from unique conversations with
leaders such as Bush, Blair and Schröder, to encounters with farmers in Kansas
and soldiers in Aldershot, from history, memoir and opinion polls to personal
observations based on a quarter-century of travelling in Europe and the US, he
demolishes the popular claim that Americans are from Mars and Europeans are
from Venus. He shows why Washington can never rule the world on its own, why
the new, enlarged Europe can only realise its aspirations in a larger, transatlantic
community, and why the torments of the Middle East and the developing world
can only be addressed by working together. To remain true to itself, the West must
go beyond itself.

In fact, this crisis reveals a historic opportunity for free people everywhere to
advance together from the cold war West to a new international order of liberty.
Defying conventional wisdom and eschewing easy answers, this timely,
provocative book should be read not just by those who purport to lead and inform
us, but by anyone who wishes to be a citizen of a free world.

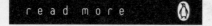

PENGUIN SCIENCE

MADNESS EXPLAINED
RICHARD BENTALL

Winner of the British Psychological Society Book Award 2004

'A radical new look at madness … This is a book to seduce a new generation into psychiatry and psychology' *Independent*

'Full of insight and humanity' *Sunday TImes*

'A monumental new study … brave, well-researched and accessible'
Scotland on Sunday

'Bentall demystifies psychosis and restores the patient to a proper place with the rest of humankind' Aaron T. Beck

SO SHALL WE REAP
COLIN TUDGE

'Dazzling … humane … important … this book is a wake-up call'
Felicity Lawrence, *Guardian*

'Anyone who understands that the politics of food production is at least as important for the future of the planet as the politics of war or of business will want to read this excellent book' Hugh Fearnley-Whittingstall

'Masterful … *Fast Food Nation* shed light on junk food. Tudge goes further, showing how junk politics have turned the adage "agriculture is just a business like any other" into a pernicious new global orthodoxy' *The Herald*

'Everyone concerned for the longer-term future of humanity should read this'
The Times Literary Supplement

PENGUIN ARCHITECTURE

THE EDIFICE COMPLEX:
HOW THE RICH AND POWERFUL SHAPE THE WORLD
DEYAN SUDJIC

Why have presidents, prime ministers, mayors, millionaires and despots come to share such a fascination with grand designs? What makes the rich and powerful want to leave their mark on the world?

In *The Edifice Complex* renowned writer and critic Deyan Sudjic explores the intimate relationship between buildings, power, money and politics in society. Architecture, he shows, has a unique place in the wielding of authority. It can be used to impress, glorify or intimidate; as an instrument of nation-building and statecraft, an expression of ego or a bid for immortality. From Blair to Mitterrand, from Hitler to Stalin to Saddam Hussein, architecture has become an end in itself, as well as a means to an end.

Drawing on twenty years' thinking about and looking at buildings, on constant travels around the globe, and an unsurpassed knowledge of the major figures in contemporary architecture, Sudjic examines the greatest and most disastrous edifices that humankind has produced, and why they were built: from Winston Churchill's theatrical reconstruction of the House of Commons to the new structure on the twin towers' site, from Mussolini's marble-floored gym to the Mother of All Battles Mosque in Baghdad, from the telling contents of US presidential libraries to Tony Blair's championing of the doomed Millennium Dome. And he looks at the architects themselves – among others Albert Speer, Le Corbusier, Norman Foster and Leon Krier – and their role in the political arena.

This is a book of genuine vision and timeliness, throwing new light on the motivations of those who govern us, and on our profound relationship with the contemporary man made world. It is essential reading for anyone interested in the power of architecture – or the architecture of power.

PENGUIN LANGUAGE

THE STORIES OF ENGLISH
DAVID CRYSTAL

How did a language originally spoken by a few thousand Anglo-Saxons become one used by more than 1,500 million people? How have all the different versions of English evolved and changed? In this compelling global tour, David Crystal turns the traditional view of the history of the language on its head and tells the *real* stories of English that have never before been fully told.

'A spirited celebration . . . Crystal gives the story of English a new plot' *Guardian*

'Rejoices in dialects, argots and cants . . . enlightening – in a word, excellent' *Sunday Times*

'An exhilarating read . . . Crystal is a sort of latter-day Johnson' *The Times Higher Education Supplement*

'*The Stories of English* reads like an adventure story. Which, of course, it is' Roger McGough

'A marvellous book . . . for anyone who loves the English language(s) it will be a treasure-house' Philip Pullman

STEVEN JOHNSON

MIND WIDE OPEN
WHY YOU ARE WHAT YOU THINK

'Refreshingly personal ... endlessly fascinating' *Guardian*

In *Mind Wide Open* Steven Johnson takes us on a journey to the frontiers of brain science and reveals exactly how we're hard-wired to think and feel. Experimenting with the latest technology he discovers (among other things) that everything we do – from falling in love to forming a sentence – is caused by neurons firing and chemicals swirling around our heads; that there are gadgets which can enable us to control our own brainwaves; that everyone's mind, like their fingerprint, is unique; and that this can help us understand our own mental foibles - and see ourselves in a totally new way.

'Steven Johnson has an eye for the most interesting new ideas in this exploding field, and he explains them with insight and gusto' Steven Pinker

'As Steven Johnson explores his inner world ... we have a new sense of what it means to be human' *The New York Times*